Virgil's Garden

Virgil's Garden

The Nature of Bucolic Space

Frederick Jones

B L O O M S B U R Y

LONDON · NEW DELHI · NEW YORK · SYDNEY

Bloomsbury Academic

An imprint of Bloomsbury Publishing Plc

50 Bedford Square	175 Fifth Avenue
London	New York
WC1B 3DP	NY 10010
UK	USA

www.bloomsbury.com

First published by Bristol Classical Press 2011
Paperback edition first published 2013

British Library Cataloguing-in-Publication Data
A catalogue record for this book is available from the British Library.

ISBN: HB: 978-0-7156-3867-5
PB: 978-1-4725-0445-6

Library of Congress Cataloging-in-Publication Data
A catalog record for this book is available from the Library of Congress

Contents

Contents

Where was 'elsewhere'? Paris probably. But they didn't quite know, and wherever it was it seemed like a distant, forbidding place, some remote and sacred region where that unknown deity squatted on its throne deep in the inner recesses of its temple. They would never ever set eyes on this god, they just sensed it, as a force weighing from afar on the ten thousand colliers of Montsou.

Zola, Germinal, Part IV chapter 2

Fig. 1. Wall painting of garden in the 'Villa of Livia', Primaporta,
9 miles north of Rome, built and painted c. 20 BC.

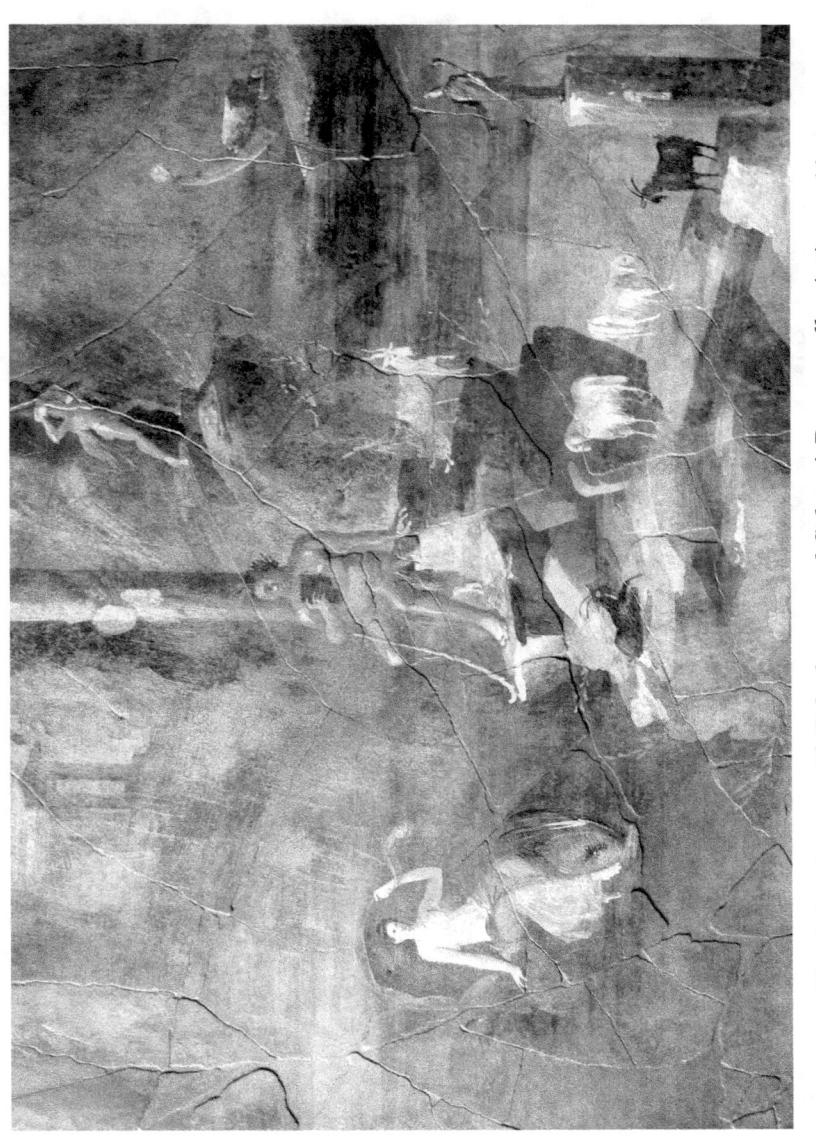

Fig. 2. 'Landscape with Polyphemus and Galatea'; Roman wall-painting, c. 11 BC; 'Villa of Agrippa Postumus', Boscotrecase, the Mythological Room (19).

Fig. 3. Sacral-idyllic landscape; central portico of east wall,
Black Room, 'Villa of Agrippa Postumus', Boscotrecase.

Preface

When we think of Augustan poetry, we tend to think of it as occupying the literary field in a compartmentalised grid. The poet-candidate selected a square from the generic grid and wrote accordingly epic, satire, elegy, didactic, bucolic, or lyric. However, this picture is a rather tendentious one. The generic system was not an eternal verity which the Augustans inherited fully fledged, nor did it come about all at once, nor at some point reach a perfect state and remain static, nor are the different and variously evolving genres autonomous of each other. Nevertheless, we have this impression largely because the Augustan poets sought to convey very much this kind of impression, defining their work apparently obsessively, and placing themselves repeatedly in relation both to each other and to their predecessors in generic terms. On the one hand, there is the simplicity of the image of the generic grid, and on the other there is the reality of the far more complex set of changing interrelations. However, the two levels are not simply a matter of image and a different reality, for the individual author in the course of writing negotiates between the quasi-timeless idea of a typical epic or book of elegies (or whatever) and his own agendas. 'Image' and 'reality' influence each other.

Virgil's Eclogue-book was, when it appeared (c. 39 BC),[1] something new in the Latin literary field, but when it pictures itself as bucolic it is to some extent suggesting that bucolic poetry is just one kind of poetry among other kinds – as though they were all timeless. Indeed, the Eclogue-book defines itself as bucolic very emphatically. It does this *inter alia* by repeated allusions to Theocritus[2] and by the weaving of numbers of programmatic symbols into its texture. Many of the names of the characters, moreover, come from Theocritus, and their typical occupations – a rather perfunctory herding, occasional basket-making, and sitting in the shade, piping, singing, and especially taking part in song exchanges – all recall Theocritus too. The plants and animals referred to also contrive cumulatively to reinforce this insistence that the book is bucolic. The songs to which the herdsmen devote such time are, moreover, bucolic song; those 'recorded' by Virgil (as in song exchanges in *Ecl.* 3, 5, 7, 8, 9) resemble the *Eclogues* themselves, and deal, like the *Eclogues*, with the singing, piping, and herding of the inhabitants. One of the herdsmen, indeed, quotes the openings of *Eclogues* 2 and 3 as part of his repertoire (*Ecl.* 5.86-7). In this way, there is a degree

11

of self-referentiality in the insistence of the Eclogue-book that it contains bucolic poetry.

This self-referentiality generates an ambivalence. Lines, passages, words, and images in the Eclogue-book draw attention to the book as bucolic, but neither 'bucolic' nor the book itself is identical with those lines, passages, words, and images. In this sense there is a doubleness about the collection, a doubleness which asks us to consider what 'bucolic' is, what the *Eclogues* are, and how the two are related to each other. The book is, on the one hand, a collection of ten poems which occupies a space (labelled bucolic) in the Roman literary field; on the other hand, it also contains its own bucolic space – that area filled with singing herdsmen, certain kinds of plant and animal life, named and described places and so forth. In this way, the collection points both inwards and outwards. This ambivalence imposes a reading which looks in two ways at the relationship between the world of the bucolic natives and the various literary, artistic, cultural, geographical, and contemporary contexts towards which its contents point, and in which the tension between the two may not, in the end, be fully reconciled.

This tension between inner and outer reinforces itself at various levels. Inside the Eclogue-book patterns are built up which create an impression of a core bucolicscape beyond which everything is remote, dangerous, and inhospitable, like the various places to which Meliboeus and some of his fellow Arcadians are expelled (*Ecl.* 1.64-6). In the literary space which surrounds and contains the *Eclogues*, there are generic patterns in which there are significant and defining differences between the various genres; when the *Eclogues* allude to other genres they draw attention to their place in, and their difference from, this larger literary field. Beyond this again, there is the division between what happens within a literary work and what happens in the real outer world. Neither between nor within these levels, however, do all the patterns stack up neatly with congruent features. There are tensions and imperfect crossings. On one level, Rome is both the real entity in which the *Eclogues* were produced and performed, and also a representation – of something potentially disruptive – inside the Eclogue-book; on another level, dangers that lie beyond the bucolic world are often marked in the *Eclogues* with remote geographical place names – but these are also the very kind of names which mark a potentially hostile 'outside' in the real Roman world too.

Roman art has also been adduced as part of the background to the *Eclogues*.[3] Mythologico-pastoral scenes, sacral-idyllic scenes, and paintings both of and in gardens are variously important here. There remains, however, more to be said about the boundaries between reality and representation, and about the conceptualisations of inner and outer and of nature in the visual arts. In addition, Roman art's deeply entrenched interest in a range of *trompe l'oeil* effects independent of content supplies analogues to important aspects of the *Eclogues*.

Since the Eclogue-book seems to contain a sort of artificial landscape, there is yet another context which asks to be considered, for it is not only artistic representations of landscape that are relevant to the culture of the *Eclogues'* audience, but those other artificial landscapes, gardens,[4] and the ways in which they too are represented. We need to look at the aesthetics, the semiotic and social functioning of gardens and related phenomena such as parks and villa-estates in literate Roman society. Here again we find the permeable boundaries between inner and outer to have significance. To take courtyard gardens as an example; they are both outside the house (they are in the open air) and also – architecturally and socially speaking – inside it and surrounded by its walls. The boundaries between inside and outside are further complicated by the portals that are windows and garden paintings (the latter of which are themselves found both inside the house and – in the garden – 'outside'). The garden, moreover, is a setting for social activity and seeks to give an impression to those allowed in to see it. It expresses something about its owner's self image or external persona – and about the society in which he lives – and provides a theatrical setting for him to impersonate himself in. It is adorned with paintings, sculptures, and fountains which allow the penetration of literature into its space. Guests may be invited into this artifical-natural space in a way analogous to that in which some Romans are allowed into the *Eclogues*, and in which any Roman in the audience can imagine himself into the bucolic setting. In fact, the garden can be seen as replicating the larger world in small form, and underpins the ways in which that larger world is perceived, constructed, and represented.

Given the ways in which the secludedness of the bucolic landscape calls the walled seclusion of gardens to mind, there is another garden feature which may be of significance, viz synchronicity. Of course gardens are dynamic, fluid, evolving things, subject to change and alteration, and subject to the passage of time in the form of the seasons as well; nevertheless, at any given moment, all the parts of the garden coexist, creating an extended present time within which the owner or guest walks around from part to part. A garden is not a direct through route from one part of the house to another and may have paths or walkways laid down imposing a patterned set of possible directions, and obstacles to other directions in the form of formal planted areas, all of which prevent a linear progress from point to point. As regards the Eclogue-book, either a performance of the poems or an individual reader's act of reading takes the words in the order in which they come. However, there are senses in which the complete book has a detemporised or synchronous existence. It all co-exists with itself as an assemblage of words which are found in physical copies; it exists also as the subjective concept of a verbal artefact in the mind of the individual who has read or heard it, a concept which can be brought out of storage by that individual for any number of reasons. This way of looking at the Eclogue-book treats it as a space which resembles that of a garden in that one may roam with a degree of freedom within its bounds, thus continually finding new angles, vistas, and prospects. The reader builds up a mental model of the book, just as the human entity in a space builds up a mental model of that space. This is to some extent true for readers of all kinds of text and not of the *Eclogues* alone, but to the extent that the Eclogue-book makes us think of a garden, it is arguable that there is a more than coincidental connection between the book as a metaphorical space and the metaphor of the garden in its case. The sense of the book as space rather than as simply a linear sequence of words is, moreover, reinforced by internal self-allusions and repetitions (such as the recollection of the beginnings of the second and third *Eclogues* at 5.86-7).

The underlying methodology of this study is that, from the starting assumption that a book is both a structure in itself and also part of the larger structure of the literary field, the *Eclogues* are investigated for combinations of internal features that draw attention to themselves and establish patterns and textures; these are then held up against the larger contexts. Combinations of features in these larger contexts which seem to make a point of contact with a pattern within the book are then investigated. The method is analogous to Differential Diagnosis as applied in the medical field, the method whereby a condition or circumstance which presents itself in a patient is examined in terms of its underlying causal factors and concurrent phenomena, and in the light of appropriate disciplinary perspectives and according to several theoretical paradigms, and then compared to known categories of pathology.

Differential Diagnosis depends on the elimination of candidate conditions from a shortlist of already known categories (which are defined in terms of clusters of identifying features – i.e. syndromes) by means of hypothetical anomalies. The method relies on an intuitive use of a variety of frameworks in order to combine speed and accuracy. However, patients and books are not exactly the same. In the case of the patient, the treatment is more likely to be successful if the diagnosis is correct, but in the case of a book the element of subjectivity is never tested by human mortality. Nevertheless, the intuitive application of various frameworks to generate the recognition of clusters of features is particularly appropriate as a way of replicating the real-life experience of reading. Moreover, in the case of books, there is indeed a positive value in the half way stages – in the similarities sensed but ultimately disregarded or seen as something else. That is to say, there can be an interpretive value in realising that a book might have been a book of category x but for the presence (or absence) in either the book or the category of some particular feature or set of features, and the reader may within limits legitimately toy with alternative readings.

*

I am grateful to Professor K.M. Coleman, Professor D.F. Kennedy, Dr G. Oliver, Dr L. Houghton, Dr P.M. Freeman, Dr M.P. FitzJohn, Professor H.M. Hine, Professor S. Harrison, Professor B.J. Gibson, and Professor N. Rudd for comments on earlier drafts of this book.

1

The Generic Landscape and Bucolic Space

'Bucolic Space' is a title which points in two directions.[1] There is, on the one hand, the space which the collection of ten poems occupies in the literary field, and, on the other, the space that this same collection contains within it. The collection points both inwards and outwards. The space within contains its own flora, fauna, geographical features, typical inhabitants and so forth. At another level, it is packed with programmatic indicators, symbols, and professions: the density of self-referential elements splits the text into two aspects, that of the text which refers and that of what is referred to. The elements in the text that refer to 'itself' are local: references to various kinds of pipe and to various animals and plants are sprinkled (as we shall see) throughout the collection and make programmatic references to bucolic poetry. 'Bucolic poetry' – that which is referred to –, however, is not found in particular lines, images, or passages, but is everywhere: it is both what the herdsmen who figure in the poems do for most of their time, and it is also what the Eclogue-book as a whole is an incarnation of.

This self-reflexiveness involves a degree of circularity. Bucolic poetry creates a landscape which can be labelled bucolic because it is the landscape of bucolic poetry; it is also a landscape which is different from landscape which is not bucolic. The content and insistent self-reflexiveness of the *Eclogues* encourage us to look at the world of the poems as a landscape sealed within itself and separate from an outside. This distinction between in- and outside, however, is far from straightforward. Within the collection itself, the bucolic landscape – the landscape about which the bucolic natives sing, and the landscape which Virgil marks as bucolic with a host of generic indicators – is in part defined as bucolic in terms drawn from inside and outside by the use of place-names, some of which are 'traditionally'[2] bucolic, and some which are more or less self-evidently *not* bucolic. The latter may have associations deriving from other genres, or from the audience's knowledge of the world.[3] Thus the 'outside' – that which is not bucolic – actually appears *inside* this collection of bucolic poems in the form of allusions to extra-bucolic genres, and in references to remote or other non-bucolic places and persons in the real world of Virgil's audience. Indeed, this outside does not just appear within the Eclogue-book at the fringes of the world

17

of the bucolic inhabitants, but sometimes reaches right into, and has effects in the heart of, this bucolic space. Some of the very place-names, moreover, that mark off what is outside the homeland of the bucolic inhabitants are typical of those places which construct an outside in the real Roman world too – places, that is to say, that are not Rome or Italy.

This inner-outer division is built into the poems at a number of levels, and obliges the reader to look at the book from multiple perspectives. Bucolic song is what the inhabitants of the poems make when they meet, but it is also what Virgil puts in their mouths;[4] in another sense, bucolic song is what the Eclogue-book as a whole is. The reader needs to see Rome (for example) through the eyes of both Tityrus and Meliboeus, but also through the eyes of the composer of the *Eclogues*, and through his own eyes as a Roman citizen. The reader needs also to see the contents of the Eclogue-book through various generic lenses, for the bucolic lens has a different colour and focal length from, say, elegiac and epic lenses, both of which feature in the collection as contrasts or foils to the bucolic vision.

The inner-outer division is also built into the concept of the generic grid. We think of the literary field in the Augustan period as a grid divided into squares[5] labelled epic, elegy, bucolic, lyric and so forth,[6] and this is partly because one after another the poets of the time build up an impression that the literary field is divided into genres with neither space left out, nor items left unassigned. Horace, for example, reviews contemporary verse production in generic categories (Hor. *Sat.* 1.10.40ff.) as part of his explanation of why he writes satire.[7] Ovid canonises the four elegists, Gallus, Tibullus, Propertius, and himself (Ov. *Tr.* 4.10.54). Horace writes of transferring lyric and iambic from Greek into Latin (*Epp.* 1.19.21-34). The picture we get from the preceding period is rather different. It is true that we have clear cases of satire, didactic, and epic, and it is also true that Catullus demonstrates quite distinct generic preconceptions of iambic, hendecasyllables, and lyric metres,[8] but the pre-Augustan concern with genre does not seem to be as intense and self-conscious as that of the Augustans. The Augustans begin the tendency towards an almost obsessive generic self-definition. It did not start fully fledged and all at once, of course. However, that is rather the impression the poets seem to want to give,[9] and among them Virgil in the *Eclogues* is prominent and early.[10] We should not forget other ways of looking at the generic picture, however. We could think of the *Eclogues* as a member of the genre of 'new imports into Latin from the Greek', and we could see 'bucolic' as Virgil's retrospective invention.[11]

If then, with due qualification, we consider the Augustan literary field so divided, we can consider the bucolic square as a space which the bucolic poet fills more or less appropriately. That is to say, the poet signs up for the space and fills it with bucolic material. There is, of course, no pre-existing, definitive list of elements that constitute 'bucolic material'; rather the candidate-poet selects and presents material in a way which colours its reception as bucolic. There is an element of self-referentiality and self-definition in bucolic, as in other Roman genres, and part of this self-definition is to do with positioning the subject genre in relation to other contemporary genres as well as to its own generic precedents. In Latin literature of at least the second century BC to the second AD this means especially the relation of the subject genre to epic, although relation to elegy is also an important perspectival marker for bucolic, satire, and Horatian lyric (cf. *Odes* 1.33, 2.9 etc.).

The content of Virgil's *Eclogues* defines the collection as 'bucolic' and also reaches out into the surrounding literary space, particularly into the realms of epic-epyllion, and elegy. There is, however, more to this than meets the eye. The poems acknowledge allegiance to 'Sicilian' or 'Syracusan' poetry (4.1; 6.1; 10.51),[12] but while this points primarily at Theocritus, it is not only the bucolic poems of Theocritus, nor indeed only Theocritus' poetry that is used.[13] Theocritus' poetry presents a considerable variety of content and genre (even if we confine our purview to only those parts of the corpus to which the *Eclogues* explicitly allude).[14] Even if there was a pre-Virgilian collection of Theocritean bucolic as such,[15] Virgil is alluding rather to a cross-generic anthology.[16] However, Virgil still conveys the fictive suggestion that Syracusan poetry is a specific 'kind' of poetry, and specifically the kind that provides a sort of Platonic ideal form of bucolic.[17]

Virgil also makes a point of reminding the reader of another bucolic model – and again one which we could also think of as a generic hybrid – namely two passages of Lucretius' didactic poem, the *De Rerum Natura*.

Quae bene cum videas, rationem reddere possis
tute tibi atque aliis, quo pacto per loca sola
saxa paris formas verborum ex ordine reddant.
palantis comites cum montis inter opacos
quaerimus et magna dispersos voce ciemus.
sex etiam aut septem loca vidi reddere vocis,
unam cum iaceres: ita colles collibus ipsi
verba repulsantes iterabant dicta referri.
haec loca capripedes Satyros Nymphasque tenere
finitimi fingunt et Faunos esse loquuntur,
quorum noctivago strepitu ludoque iocanti
adfirmant volgo taciturna silentia rumpi
chordarumque sonos fieri dulcisque querellas,
tibia quas fundit digitis pulsata canentum,
et genus agricolum late sentiscere, quom Pan
pinea semiferi capitis velamina quassans
unco saepe labro calamos percurrit hiantis,
fistula *silvestrem* ne cesset fundere *musam*.

cetera de genere hoc monstra ac portenta loquuntur,
ne loca deserta ab divis quoque forte putentur
sola tenere. ideo iactant miracula dictis
aut aliqua ratione alia ducuntur, ut omne
humanum genus est avidum nimis auricularum.

Lucr. 4.572-94

When you see this well, you may be able to give an account to yourself and to others how the rocks return the same shapes of words in order in solitary places, when we are looking for straying companions among the shady mountains and are calling them loudly, scattered as they are. I have seen places return six or even seven cries when you sent one forth. In such a way do the hills themselves knock back to hills and repeat words trained to come back.

People nearby imagine that goat-footed satyrs and nymphs occupy these places, and say there are fauns by whose night-wandering noise and humorous play they commonly affirm the unspeaking silence is broken, and that there are sounds of stringed instruments and sweet plaints poured out by the pipe tapped by the fingers of those singing, that the race of farmers far and wide sense it when Pan, shaking the pine-veils of his half-beast head, often runs over the open ends of reeds with his lip curved so that the pipe may not cease pouring out woodland music (*silvestrem musam*). They tell of other signs and portents like this so that they are not thought to inhabit solitary places deserted even by gods. For this reason they toss miracles around in tales, or they are led by some other reason, since all humankind is too avid for ears.

At liquidas avium voces imitarier ore
ante fuit multo quam levia carmina cantu
concelebrare homines possent aurisque iuvare.
et zephyri cava per calamorum sibila primum
agrestis docuere cavas inflare cicutas.
inde minutatim dulcis didicere querellas,
tibia quas fundit digitis pulsata canentum,
avia per nemora ac silvas saltusque reperta,
per loca pastorum deserta atque otia dia.
[sic unum quicquid paulatim protrahit aetas
in medium ratioque in luminis eruit oras.]
haec animos ollis mulcebant atque iuvabant
cum satiate cibi; nam tum sunt omnia cordi.
saepe itaque inter se prostrati in gramine molli
propter aquae rivom sub ramis arboris altae.
non magnis opibus iucunde corpora habebant,
praesertim cum tempestas ridebat et anni
tempora pingebant viridantis floribus herbas.
tum ioca, tum sermo, tum dulces esse cachinni
consuerant; *agrestis* enim tum *musa* vigebat.
tum caput atque umeros plexis redimire coronis
floribus et foliis lascivia laeta movebat,
atque extra numerum procedere membra moventes
duriter et duro terram pede pellere matrem;

unde oriebantur risus dulcesque cachinni,
omnia quod nova tum magis haec et mira vigebant.
et vigilantibus hinc aderant solacia somno
ducere multimodis voces et flectere cantus
et supera calamos unco percurrere labro;
unde etiam vigiles nunc haec accepta tuentur.
et numerum servare genus didicere, neque hilo
maiore interea capiunt dulcedine fructum
quam silvestre genus capiebat terrigenarum.

Lucr. 5.1379-1411

But to imitate the clear voices of birds with the mouth came long before men were able to celebrate smooth odes in song and delight their ears. And the zephyrs hissing through the hollow reeds first taught men of the country to blow into hollow hemlock stalks. Thence, little by little, they learned the sweet plaints which the pipe pours, tapped by the fingers of the singers, once discovered among pathless woods and forest, and glades, among the deserted places of shepherds and divine leisure. [So time brings forth every single thing little by little into common use, and reason lifts it into the shores of light.] These things soothed their minds and delighted them along with fullness of food; for then everything is congenial. Often, therefore, stretched among themselves on the soft grass by a stream of water under the branches of a tall tree, at no great expense did they give pleasure to their bodies, especially when the season smiled and the time of year painted green herbage with flowers. Then there would have been merriment, then conversation, the sweet guffaws; for then the field-muse (*agrestis musa*) flourished. Then joyful playfulness advised them to bind the head and shoulders with woven garlands, with flowers and leaves, and to step forth moving their limbs harshly out of time and to beat mother earth with harsh foot; thence arose smiles and sweet guffaws, because all these things new and wonderful had more vigour then. And when they were wakeful hence came solace for their sleep, to bring forth the voice in multiple wise and bend song and run along the reeds from above with curved lip; hence even now watchmen preserve the tradition and have learned to keep the kinds of rhythm, nor meanwhile do they have any greater fruit of sweetness than the woodland stock of those born of earth had.

Here we have an accumulation of features that will become familiar in the *Eclogues*. In the first passage we have echoes and the presence of nymphs, fauns, satyrs and Pan, and the sound of pipes, pine, and indeed, a *silvestris musa* (4.589; cf. V. *Ecl.* 1.2). In the second, we have pipes, *nemora*, *silvae*, *pastores*, and the use as setting for song of the *locus amoenus* – the lovely grassy place under a tree by a stream, in spring weather, surrounded by flowers and here described as home to the field-muse (*agrestis musa*, 5.1398; cf. V. *Ecl.* 6.8). Lucretius writes as though the conventions were well established, but he is as likely to be thinking of Greek poetry as anything in Latin. His range of allusion is wide (including the same piece of Sappho that his contemporary

21

Catullus used in *Carm*. 51) and his didactic poem incorporates a number of other generic patterns. By alluding to Lucretius,[18] Virgil puts his Eclogue-book retrospectively into a Latin generic grid. In addition, however, we have to carry over into our picture of Virgil's bucolic world some of Lucretius's picture. In the second passage, bucolic song belongs to a primitive happy time in human development (5.1379-1411), but in the earlier picture (4.572-94) it represents human self-deception and a naïve attempt to ward off the realisation of the desolation of the singers' habitat. In this passage, moreover, it is the people of the vicinity (*finitimi*, 4.581) and not Lucretius or his audience, if they happen to pass through, who are deluded into believing in satyrs and nymphs. Here there is a foretaste of the difference between the inside and outside perspective on the bucolic world that we find later in the *Eclogues*.[19]

Other kinds of literature, and well outside the bucolic penumbra, from Virgil's own time form part of the picture too, chiefly epic and elegy. Epic was regarded as the most eminent of genres by both Greeks and Romans. It is marked apart by scale, style, manner, and content.[20] Other genres react to it and set themselves apart from it, as Horace does in *Satires* 1.4, as *recusatio* after *recusatio* does, beginning with Virgil's in *Eclogues* 6.3ff., and as the elegiac programme of 'love (elegy) not war (epic)' does emphatically and repeatedly. But these other genres also use epic content and style when and as it suits their needs. Furthermore, epic is not impervious. It begins to absorb the erotic content prioritised in other genres.[21] We are looking at a picture in which genres jostle and rub off against each other, a picture, moreover, in which surrounding genres take aggressive stances towards the dominant genre, epic, and all genres compete in appropriation of each others' content.[22]

Virgilian bucolic, Horatian satire and lyric, and Augustan elegy all take part in this scrapping with epic, but Virgil and Horace are also in tension with elegy (which in turn sometimes tries to take over bucolic elements, but generally ignores satire). Virgil's treatment of epic and elegy in the *Eclogues* is part of the dynamics of the poetry of his age, and is part of his definition of what bucolic is.

The fourth *Eclogue* conspicuously branches out into epic territory.[23] There is, however, an ambivalence about the relationship between the epic material and the bucolic context (as indeed there is elsewhere, between epic and non-bucolic genres). In the fourth *Eclogue*, iconic epic material is the route by which a new and bucolic golden age will be reached. There is both an attempt to appropriate epic material and a suggestion that epic is not, after all, the ultimate Queen of genres, for it is a distinctly bucolicised Golden Age that is heralded here.

There is more epical material in the sixth *Eclogue*. Towards the end of Silenus' Hellenising and epicising compendium-song, the Roman poet Gallus appears as a Hesiod-like initiate of the Muses (*Ecl.* 6.70), being led away from Permessus' stream (= elegy) and ordered by Linus, the archetypal singer (cf. 4.56) and legendary didactic poet (so, according to Diogenes Laertius, *Lives of the Philosophers* 1.4), to tell of the origin of the Grynaean grove (72). Silenus calls Linus a shepherd (after Callimachus *Aet.* Fr. 27Pf), a typically bucolic role, and Linus hands on to Gallus some archetypically bucolic reed-pipes, which he says Hesiod once owned. Linus is an Orpheus-like figure at 4.56, and Hesiod has an orphic attribute in the passage we are dealing with. In this passage, epic-didactic is clearly being dressed in bucolic colours (and Gallus himself later – in *Ecl.* 10 – acquires a half-hearted bucolic tinge), but this bucolic colouring cannot eradicate the fact of Hesiod's known poetic output – didactic. So Gallus' bucolic-epic contamination in this passage is a masque-costume. He will pass for a bucolic-epic poet for ceremonial purposes, and he is certainly a real poet, but there is something 'dressed up' about his epic-bucolic presentation.[24] Genre here resembles costume.

Servius tells us that the Grynean Grove came from Euphorion. In the light of this, Virgil's use of the word *origo* seems to suggest an aetiological epyllion or something like that – and that fits the epic colour of the other subjects of Silenus' compendium[25] – in which Gallus' initiation appears in sequence – such as the cosmological opening (*Ecl.* 6.31ff.) and the mini-epyllion made of the interlocking stories of Pasiphae and the Proetides (6.45-60).[26] In any case, the figure of Silenus, the narrative of Chromis and Mnasyllus' extraction of a song from him (cf. Aristaeus getting information from Proteus in one of the more epic sections of the *Georgics*, 4.315-558),[27] the subject matter of his song, the trappings of Gallus' initiation – all these conspire to put forms of epic into this *Eclogue*. But this is precisely the *Eclogue* that begins with a Callimachean *recusatio* – in the Callimachean form of an Apolline epiphany – in which Virgil is told not to be doing with the epic matter of kings and battles (*Ecl.* 6.3-12). Furthermore, the epic matter of Silenus' song is only partly brought into Eclogue-land, for it is sung by an outsider in a dream-like setting, and at the end of the poem the song is silenced and put away by the ordinary evening tasks of Eclogue-land (6.84-6). Virgilian bucolic contains epic, but also disposes of it at will.

Epic is the genre usually noticed – and noticed most prominently, and with the greatest friction – by other genres. Elegy, however, figures pronouncedly in the *Eclogues*. The same Gallus that we saw in the sixth *Eclogue* also figures, this time as an elegist, in the tenth, where he pines for the unworthy object of his love, Lycoris, and seems unable to be at home in Eclogue-land, even though he promises to tune (*modulabor;* 10.51) his elegies[28] to bucolic hexameters – before giving up hope in *any* poetry (62-3).

The contrast between this lovelorn Gallus who remains alien in Eclogue-land, and the fully naturalised, hibiscus-weaving Virgil who appears in the same poem makes an assertion about bucolic poetry which will need looking at again when we consider more closely the interior space of Eclogue-land. For the moment, however, it is worth registering that this contrast suggests that elegy and bucolic do not simply share the category of 'new annexations from the Greek generic grid', but appear as two separate brands of Latin literature, even if one of them may seem somehow less adequate than, or its subject matter can be contained in, the other. Stephen Harrison draws a very satisfying picture of the complexities of the generic inclusion symbolised by the bucolic basket (10.70-2) that Virgil has been weaving while 'singing' the tenth *Eclogue*. Metaphorically, the basket is the *Eclogue* itself (as already seen by Servius, ad loc.) and holds within it an icon of Gallan elegy. One genre hosts (as Harrison puts it) another - but not neutrally. The inclusion (as in my term 'competitive inclusiveness') asserts the superiority of the containing genre, and part of the grounds for asserting superiority is precisely this annexation and subjugation of the material of the guest (Harrison's word) genre by its host.[29]

We may now turn more directly to the interior space of the *Eclogues*. There are ten poems in the book, and although they exhibit considerable variety they give a strong impression of having a powerful unity too. This comes partly from the programmatic allusions to Theocritus and the references to the *Eclogues* and their poet made within the *Eclogues* themselves, and partly from formal considerations such as the alternation of dialogue and narrative through the whole set,[30] and – perhaps most of all – the overall sense that both the settings and the *dramatis personae* show a considerable homogeneity. Of course, it does not take us long to find out that place- and personal names have relationships outside the collection, but the settings and characters themselves appear, nonetheless, to show a great deal of uniformity. In the *Eclogues*, there is a general pattern that the herdsmen come together in pairs and sing in a stereotypically attractive setting of shade and water (a *locus amoenus*): there is nothing in Virgil which resembles the failure of Lacon and Comatas (Theocr. *Id.* 5.44-60) to agree on a suitable setting, each steadfastly remaining in his own *locus amoenus*, which the other does not recognise, and singing from there.

Apart from the use of place-names, we are strongly impelled by cumulative detail to think of the settings of the *Eclogues* as having the character of a (more or less) idealised place – largely green, largely warm and free from rain – in which (more or less) idealised characters seem to be herdsmen, but are almost entirely occupied with singing, piping, and being in love. As regards the place-names, however, we find a curious mixture in the collection as a whole – Rome, for example, appearing in the first *Eclogue*, and Sicily in the following one (2.21). Either the setting is not actually unified throughout the collection, or we are not meant to take such references wholly literally. Be that as it may, the landscape, with its flora, fauna, population, and climate, certainly seems to have a uniform character. We are therefore drawn towards regarding the landscape as a single place – a place about the general features of whose geography we can accumulate information. Looked at in one way, this might seem a pedestrian way of ordering the material which Virgil gives us in such an organic mixture, but in fact the steady accretion of references to plants and animals, and the kaleidoscopically shifting patterns of the cast-lists of the *Eclogues* make a powerful cumulative contribution to the reader's overall grasp of the contents of the poems. There is something, then, particularly appropriate about the geographer's approach, so to speak, to a collection of poems whose thematic consistency is so emphatically 'local'.[31]

The nature of the *Eclogues* seems to invite us to conceptualise the *Eclogue*-book as containing a landscape which has its own distinctive features, character, and borders. This is a concept which will need some unpacking as this study proceeds, for the book is highly self-referential and its borders are complex and multiple. There are the partially permeable borders between it and other genres in the literary field, the borders (within the book) between Arcadia[32] and places outside Arcadia, and the borders between Arcadia (the place described in the book) and the real outside world – the world, that is, of Virgil and his contemporaries, a world which itself reaches into the poetic landscape, for example, in the form of the representation of Rome in the first *Eclogue*.

The notion of landscape will also need more probing, but I start with some general observations.

The settings of the *Eclogues* are rural. As such, they are different from the generally urban contexts of a number of coexistent Roman genres – satire, elegy, iambic, and (much) epigram. They are also different from the settings of epic, which tends to have a larger backdrop, ranging from famous and antique poetical cities, through the journey-scapes of its heroes, and extending to the realms of the divine apparatus and poetic Underworld scenes.[33] In epic, in the human sphere, we see cities (notably Troy), and the land and sea outside them are places of journey, transition, storm, or battle. Didactic, because of its subject-based instructional form, does not have the same sort of localised settings as its relative, epic, but its world is still different in kind and presentation from that of bucolic. The difference in this respect of Virgil's *Eclogues* from other genres is an important element of their generic identity in itself. However, this difference also raises the question of what exactly the context of this identity is; the flora and fauna in the *Eclogues* contribute to the definition of what the bucolic world is, but this is both positive and negative, for the bucolic world is both of two things. It is, on the one hand, *not* the world of other-genres, and, on the other, it is also something in itself.

As to that 'something in itself', the landscape of the *Eclogues* is generally benign. It is almost always a nice season there; within the ten poems it is only the elegiac outsider Gallus in the tenth *Eclogue* who really experiences winter. Wind and rain are mainly absent. It is virtually always day time. Mountains quite often appear, but they are generally friendly (Gallus, again in the tenth *Eclogue*, is worried about icy mountains, but they are part of his elegiac baggage).[34] The sea does not have a strong presence (perhaps surprisingly, given comparison with Virgil's model, Theocritus).[35] To all intents and purposes there are no fierce or dangerous animals: wolves,[36] lions, and the like are mainly present only in figures of speech.[37] What we see mainly are useful and more or less domesticated animals: cattle, goats, sheep, and bees. Untamed animals appear only occasionally, chiefly stags and boars. These too are present for their human-related function as hunting quarry, but also as markers of generically alien material (hunting is not a frequent or naturally Arcadian occupation).[38] Poisonous plants and thorny plants are virtually absent.[39] Like the animals, most of the plants found in the *Eclogues* are useful to the shepherds. They provide food, fodder, shade for animals, hedges, or material for making pipes, garlands, and baskets – homely uses. Luxurious spices have a low profile.[40] Birds are rare; this may seem surprising at first sight (especially given their profile in Roman wall painting),[41] but they are probably insufficiently integrated into human usefulness to appear very much in the collection. The people in the *Eclogues* are also comparatively gentle, sociable, and – to a degree – productive; they herd animals, sing of love and song, and tease each other. Their diet appears to consist mainly of ground herbs and leaves, milk, and cheese. They know very little of money. They live in cottages, but although villas appear in the distance (*Ecl.* 1.82), the landscape of the poems is largely free of architectural edifices. The absence of much work, the diet, and the low profile of architecture conspire to suggest a similarity to the Golden Age. The fact that the inhabitants are primarily presented as herdsmen fits this too, since Varro placed herding in the initial stage of human civilisation (*RR* 2.1.4-5), and he says that farmers alone are survivors from the stock of King Saturn (*RR* 3.1.5).

Not only is almost everything in Eclogue-land benign; mostly it is also homogeneous and communal in one or another sense. The most frequent animals are goats, cattle, and sheep;[42] the more individualistic horse[43] is rare, as is the vulgar pig.[44] The individualistic, but useful, dog only occasionally appears.[45] However, we cannot fail to notice the frequency with which the animals that do appear regularly often do so in flocks or herds (*pecus, grex, armentum*).[46] Likewise, trees and the like appear in gardens, orchards, or vineyards (*horti, nemora, arbusta*).[47] There are also cornfields[48] and – on different levels of collectivity and arrangement – quantities of grass and baskets of flowers. Woods are often mentioned (*silvae*).[49] These may not be artificially arranged, but they are still part of an orderly disposition of nature, and they are still functional. Indeed, the *silvae* are a programmatic sign of the bucolic woodland (*silvestris*) Muse.[50] The human inhabitants are frequently herdsmen (*pastores*, another programmatic word in the *Eclogues*):[51] they do not form the human equivalent of orchards or flocks, but they certainly gather in twos and threes (for assessed singing competitions). On a different level, moreover, they are arranged like flowers in a garland, as, for example, in the orderly patterns of names often disposed at the beginnings of the poems of the Eclogue-book. This is perhaps especially the case at the beginning of *Eclogue* 8, but to some extent it happens at the beginnings of all except *Eclogues* 4, 6, and 10. The names themselves are like picked flowers, with an anthology of pastoral antecedents behind them.

In the geography of Eclogue-land, however, there is not *simply* a selection of benign and harmonious elements. There are two respects particularly in which this is to be seen. Firstly, although the ten *Eclogues* conspire to create an impression of bucolic space as somewhere where the typical inhabitants lead a more or less idealised kind of life, various elements in the composite picture are not fully reconciled with each other. Sometimes we seem to be on Sicily, sometimes in northern Italy, but at another level we do not seem to have changed location. For the moment we might – and perhaps naively – say that the text presents a palimpsest in which Italy is real and Sicily is a literary layer. This layering may perhaps also be seen in the temporal as well as the geographical space. Sometimes it seems to be summer in the *Eclogues*, sometimes spring or autumn. In something of the same spirit, we might say that the setting is simply 'not-winter', one season in which the kindly aspects of spring, summer, and autumn coexist. In the second *Eclogue*, Corydon lists floral offerings he would like to make to Alexis. The format and much of the selection is an amalgam of a passage of Theocritus (11.56-9) and an epigram by Meleager (*Anth. Pal.* 5.147), and contains plants that are not in season together.[52] In the Theocritean passage, Polyphemus realises this and steps back from the comic ramifications – thus making the audience aware of the comedy; Virgil, by contrast, leaves Polyphemus' escape route behind when he transfers the rest of the passage. Perhaps the humour is meant to remain, but more subtly, or perhaps we just accept the conglomeration – as in many Dutch still life paintings – as supra-realistic.[53] One might well also note here the resemblance between the diet of the people in the poems and that of another placeless and timeless place without winter, the Golden Age (see further Chapter 5, under 'climate and time' below).

The second feature of Virgil's bucolic geography which goes beyond the merely benign is that many of the elements in the constitution of the *Eclogues* have or acquire programmatic overtones. The more one looks, the longer the list can become: *silvae/silvestris* (woods/woodland), *agrestis* (meadow), *ovis* (sheep), Syracuse/Sicily, *myricae, fagus* (beech), *hedera* (ivy), *pastor/pastores* (herdsman/herdsmen). Sometimes these elements cluster and reinforce each other – *calami, fistula,* and *capella* ('reeds', 'pipe', 'kid'; 8.33), or *florentibus herbis, fontis, umbra, Amaryllis, Tityrus,* and *capellas* ('flowering plants', 'spring', 'shade', 'kids'; 9.19ff.), where other elements besides plants and animals enter the list. Indeed, we come to be able to include Pan, Daphnis, and nymphs too as connotating bucolic poetry and / or song.

2

Flora[1]

It is time to consider some aspects of the flora, geography, and population of the *Eclogues* in more detail, starting with the flora, and specifically beech trees. According to the elder Pliny (*NH* 16.35), the bark of beech trees had a variety of uses among country people – making panniers and baskets, large flat receptacles for carrying corn and grapes at harvest times, and roofing the eaves of cottages. At a simplistic level of correspondence to real life, that makes it an appropriate tree to figure in the *Eclogues*. It does so for the first time right at the beginning of the collection.

> Tityre, tu patulae recubans sub tegmine fagi
> silvestrem tenui Musam meditaris avena;
>
> *Ecl.* 1.1-2

> Tityrus, reclining under the cover of the broad beech-tree, you rehearse your woodland Muse on slender pipe.

In the opening line of the Eclogue-book, a native reclines tooting a woodland (*silvestrem*) song about his love on his slender oat pipe (*avena*) beneath the shade of a beech tree (*fagi*). The woods (*silvas*) resonate. Nature in the *Eclogues* is almost always inhabited, and humans act out their lives in what seem to be natural surroundings. However, the *fagus* in the very first line conceals a puzzle.[2] In Latin a beech tree, in Greek the *phagos* is a kind of oak. Virgil is writing in Latin so that at first when we visualise this highly visualisable scene we see in the mind's eye a beech. But Tityrus (1, 4) and Amaryllis (5) both come from Theocritus.[3] Meliboeus (6) does not, but the meaning of his name ('he has care of the cattle'; Servius) suggests that he is not alien to that background. The tooting of love on an oat pipe is Theocritean too. The poetry is so marked out as Theocritean-bucolic[4] that perhaps we imagine the Greek oak, especially as it is actually found in Theocritus (*Id.* 12.8).[5] But perhaps it is neither beech nor oak, but rather a literary-programmatic tree, a marker of Virgil's similarity to, *and* difference from, Theocritus, a poetic tree specific to Eclogue-land rather than a tree of the sort we can find in the real world.[6] Indeed, it, the *fagus*, is suitably recurrent in the Eclogue-land poetryscape (2.3; 3.12; 5.13), providing, into the bargain, a surface for 'bucolic' songs to be written on (5.13).[7]

Fagi are also particularly noteworthy in the ninth *Eclogue*, a poem which corresponds closely with the first in content. Here some space seems – at first – to have been saved from threat[8] by the songs of Menalcas.

> certe equidem audieram, qua se subducere colles
> incipiunt mollique iugum demittere cliuo,
> usque ad aquam et ueteres, iam fracta cacumina, fagos,
> omnia carminibus uestrum seruasse Menalcan.

Ecl. 9.7-10

> Indeed I had heard for sure that where the hills begin to draw themselves down and slope their ridge with gentle incline right up to the water and the old beech trees – now broken tops –, your Menalcas had saved everything with his songs.

The space described is typical of the kind of landscape the fictional shepherds inhabit. In addition, it is also representative of the kind of space that belongs to or is occupied by the genre invented by Theocritus[9] and transferred into Latin by Virgil. The songs of Menalcas that are referred to have this bucolic suggestiveness as well. At the simplest level, Menalcas is an inhabitant of Eclogue-land. His name is 'Theocritean' too.[10] Although most of the Virgilian herdsmen have Theocritean names, Virgil uses this name for the herdman-singer in *Eclogue* 5 who refers explicitly to *Eclogues* 2 and 3 as part of his own repertoire (5.86-7). The songs of the Menalcas also figure in *Eclogue* 9[11] and again have an integral connection with Virgilian bucolic. When they are characterised and quoted from, their topics and features – Nymphs, flowering herbs, shade and springs – are those of Virgil's *Eclogues* generally. Furthermore, the quoted lines of Menalcas feature Tityrus whose name is prominent in *Eclogue* 1, who figures elsewhere in the *Eclogues*, and who stands in for Virgil himself when Apollo appears to him in *Eclogue* 6. In the ninth *Eclogue*, then, we come close to having one bucolic representation of Virgil (Menalcas) including in his songs another bucolic representation of Virgil under yet another name (Tityrus),[12] just as Virgil's own *Eclogues* themselves incorporate bucolic representations of himself under other names (Menalcas and Tityrus).[13] This space, which seemed to have been saved by a bucolic-singing and bucolically named *alter ego* for Virgil, a space in which the *dramatis personae* of the ninth *Eclogue* walk and sing the bucolic songs of Menalcas-Virgil, is bounded, marked off, and identified by beeches (*fagi*; *Eclogue* 9.9).

The space within *Eclogue* 9 doubtfully saved from the incursions of the real world is an icon of bucolic poetry, and saved (if it is saved at all) by the singing of an icon of the bucolic poet. In that sense it is a doubly bucolic space, its edge, moreover, marked by those peculiarly bucolic *fagi.* Beyond them are danger, the city and all it represents,[14] and a whole outer world.

Before we leave beech trees, we might in this context observe the beechen cups wagered by Menalcas in the singing competition with Damoetas (*Ecl.* 3.36ff.).

> *Menalcas:*
>   pocula ponam
> fagina, caelatum divini opus Alcimedontos,
> lenta quibus torno facili superaddita vitis
> diffusos hedera vestit pallente corymbos.
> in medio duo signa, Conon et – quis fuit alter,
> descripsit radio totum qui gentibus orbem,
> tempora quae messor, quae curvus arator haberet?
> necdum illis labra admovi, sed condita servo.
>
> *Damoetas:*
> et nobis idem Alcimedon duo pocula fecit
> et molli circum est ansas amplexus acantho
> Orpheaque in medio posuit silvasque sequentis;
> necdum illis labra admovi, sed condita servo.

Ecl. 3.36-47

Menalcas: I'll lay beechwood cups, the embossed work of divine Alcimedon, on which a pliant vine, added by his easy lathe, clothes berry-clusters scattered on pale ivy. In the middle are two figures, Conon and – who was the other, who marked out for its peoples the whole world with his rod, what times the reaper should keep, and what the bent ploughman? I haven't yet moved my lips to them, but I've been keeping them in store.

Damoetas: The same Alcimedon made two cups for me too and twined the handles with soft acanthus, and put Orpheus in the centre and the pursuant woods; I haven't yet moved my lips to them, but I've been keeping them in store.

Damoetas claims that he has two cups made by the same Alcimedon as Menalcas' cups, and, although he does not say so, one presumes that they too would be made of beech. In the centre of Menalcas' cups are Conon, the third-century astronomer, and a figure whose name Menalcas cannot remember, but who from the description seems to be Archimedes or the fourth-century astronomer Eudoxus. In the centre of Damoetas' cups is Orpheus, the archetypal poet-singer. All three figures may have poetic resonances. Orpheus' association with poetry is obvious (see *Ecl.* 4.55, 6.30, 8.55). As for Conon, it was he who was credited with naming the constellation which is the subject of Callimachus' *Coma Berenices* and is named both there and in Catullus' version of the poem (Callim. fr. 110.7; Cat. 66.1-72). Eudoxus' *Phaenomena* was the source of Aratus' didactic poem of the same name, which was translated into Latin by Cicero and used by Virgil in the astronomical parts of the *Georgics*. The weight of these poetic connections points towards the unnamed figure on Damoetas' cup being Eudoxus rather than Archimedes. On this reading we would have here an association of beech with symbolic figures showing the universality of poetry (Orpheus) and reaching out from the bucolic context into the broader literary field of Virgil's own time (the *silvae sequentes*, perhaps!).[15]

Apart from the *fagus*, a number of other trees appear in the *Eclogues*: *pinus* (pine; 1.38; 7.24, 65; 8.22; cf. 4.38; 10.14), *ulmus* (elm; 1.58; 2.70; 5.3; 10.67), *salictus/salix* (willow; 1.54, 78; 3.65, 83; 5.16; 10.40), *pirus* (pear; 1.73; 9.50), *castaneae* (chestnuts; 1.81; 2.52; 7.53), *spinetum* (hawthorn; 2.9), *malum* (apple/quince; 2.51; 3.64, 71; 8.37), *pruna* (plums; 2.53), *laurus* (laurel; 2.54; 3.63; 6.83; 7.62, 64; 8.13; 8.82, 83; 10.13; cf. 7.62, 64; 2.54; 8.82), *arbutus* (strawberry tree; 3.82; 7.46), *oliva* (olive; 5.16; 8.16), *quercus* (oak; 1.17; 4.30; 6.28; 7.13; 8.53; cf. *glans* = acorn 10.20), *ilex* (holm oak; 6.54; 7.1; 9.15), *alnus* (alder; 6.63; 8.53; 10.74), *ornus* (rowan, 6.71), *iuniper* (juniper; 7.53; 10.76), *populus* (poplar; 7.61, 66; 9.41), *corylus* (hazel; 1.14; 5.3; 7.63, 64), *fraxinus* (ash; 7.65), *abies* (fir; 7.66); *nuces* (= walnuts, 8.30), *taxus* (yew; 9.30).[16] Of these, the majority are useful to the bucolic way of life in one way or another (for example, providing shade, fruit or other food, supporting vines). The remainder appear in figures of speech or are otherwise exceptional. Some have a degree of special significance attached to them, for example the *salix, pirus, castaneae,* and *malum*, and especially the *laurus, pinus*, and *quercus*.

As well as other general bucolic attributes, the willow flower provides pasture for bees (1.54) which in turn have a connection with song (cf. 7.13), and, through the wax which is used in Pan-pipes (2.32; 3.25), the Arcadian god Pan. The pear tree is mentioned only twice (1.73; 9.50), but the two passages allude to each other and achieve prominence that way. At 1.73 Meliboeus ironically orders himself, now that he is being expelled, to graft pears; at 9.50, the other poem in which the land-confiscations threaten the bucolic way, one of Menalcas' songs (for his connection with Virgil see below) orders the archetypal bucolic figure Daphnis to graft pears so that his grandchildren – unlike Meliboeus' – may pick the fruit.[17] The pear trees stand for a way of life which is fragile. The *malum* (2.51; 3.64, 71; 8.37), another non-meat foodstuff like the chestnut, is regularly associated with love.

The pine appears fairly frequently in the *Eclogues* (1.38; 4.38; 7.24, 65; 8.22; 10.14). On its first appearance at 1.38 it is a typical part of the bucolic setting, but at 7.24 it is sacred and the place where a bucolic pipe will hang, and at 8.22 the connection between music and Arcadia is more explicit (cf. 10.14). At 7.65 and 68 it is part of some figured language rather than setting as such, but the suggestion present that the pine is a typical garden tree is interesting in itself.[18]

The oak too is a tree frequently appearing in the *Eclogues* (1.17; 4.30; 6.28; 7.13; 8.53; cf. *glans* = acorn 10.20); at 1.17 lightning-struck oaks can – if one takes notice – predict the future; at 4.30 in the second golden age they will drip honey; at 6.28 they respond to Silenus' song as oaks conventionally did to Orpheus'; at 7.13 sacred oaks humming with swarms of bees are part of the setting of the famous song contest remembered by Meliboeus; at 10.20 Menalcas, who is more or less identified with Virgil in this poem, comes to remonstrate with the lovelorn Gallus 'from the winter acorn' (*hiberna de glande*).

The laurel, like the pine (7.24) and the oak (7.13) is sacred (see 3.63 6.83 7.62, 64 for the connection with Apollo and song) and at 10.13 is paired with the programmatic *myricae*.[19] Myrtle is paired with laurel at 2.54 and 7.62; in the latter case the connection with Venus explicitly parallels Apollo's with laurel. Song and love are prime pursuits of the bucolic inhabitants.

As well as these significances we might well ask how much correspondence there is between the selection of trees in the bucolic landscape, in Italy generally, and in Pompeian gardens.

Pompeian evidence – either in physical remains or in painting – is absent only for a small number of Virgil's bucolic trees.[20] These are the *abies* (fir), the *alnus* (alder), *ornus* (rowan), *salictus/salix* (willow), and the *taxus* (yew). Of the other trees in the *Eclogues* there is evidence either in painting or in gardens, or in both. Thus, there is evidence of the following in wall paintings (including garden paintings*): *arbutus** (strawberry tree), *corylus* (in tree and nut form; hazel), *laurus** (laurel), *malus** (apple; the fruit is in numerous wall paintings, often in bowels/baskets, but the tree is also found), *pinus** (pine); *pirus* (pear; in fruit and tree form), *prunus* (plum; fruit and tree), *quercus* (oak; branches, leaves, and acorns are common in a variety of art media), and the nut of the walnut.[21] There is evidence that chestnuts (*castaneae*), though not found in extant garden paintings, were found in gardens. Similarly, the shrubs, *myrtus* (myrtle), ivy (*hedera*), and the guelder-rose (*viburnum*) are all found in garden paintings (ivy also being used in topiary).

There is some evidence independent of garden painting for the use in gardens of the pear (*pirus*), apple (*malus*),[22] juniper (*iuniper*), and hawthorn (*spinetum* = *Crataegus* in Jashemski, Meyer, and Ricciardi). The laurel (*laurus*) was popular as a garden plant, and Virgil (*Georg.* 4.141; *Ecl.* 7.65, 68) suggests that this is true for the pine (*pinus*). There is also evidence of the following being used in gardens and/or vineyards etc., in ash-form, probably as fertiliser, or in wood-form, for stakes or props: chestnut (*castaneae*), hazel (*corylus*),[23] beech (*fagus*), ash (*fraxinus*), poplar (*populus*), elm (*ulmus*), and walnut. We are told that the *ilex* (holm-oak) could provide bedding for sheep and cattle (Cato *RR* 5.7-8), winter fodder (Columella *RR* 6.37), and acorns for pigs (7.9.6, 9.1.5). On the other hand, the plane tree (*platanus*), popular as a shade-provider (cf. Cic. *De Div.* 2.30.63; V. *Georg.* 4,146, as a garden tree giving shade to wine-drinkers; cf. Hor. *Odes* 2.11.13-17, Pliny *Ep.* 5.6.20, 28) and frequent in gardens and in wall paintings, is – perhaps oddly – absent from the *Eclogues*.[24] Likewise, the cypress, although mentioned elsewhere in Latin verse (Hor. *Odes* 1.9.11) and popular in gardens and paintings, favoured at estate boundaries (Varro *RR* 1.15), and used in topiary (Pliny *NH* 16.140), appears in the *Eclogues* only in figurative language (*Ecl.* 1.25). Perhaps the association with boundaries (or death; see on Hor. *Odes* 1.9) made it unwelcome in Arcadia.

Admittedly most of the trees were common or common enough in Europe or the Mediterranean area, but the chestnut, apple, pear, and plum (*castanea, malus, pirus, prunus*) were commonly or usually cultivated. We should also bear in mind that Virgil's audience would have considerable first hand experience of gardens and painting, and cultivated areas, and that their knowledge of wilder regions would be less to the forefront of their minds. The audience would, of course, belong to the garden- and art-owning class.

Considered as an assemblage, it looks as though Virgil's trees would be at least as familiar to his audience from art, gardens, cultivated plantation, the fruit table, and sometimes poetic associations as from some wider concept of natural landscape.

Trees, like animals, are frequently in groups in the *Eclogues*; characteristically they appear in plantations and groves (*arbusta, nemora, lucos*), and woods (*silvas*).[25] The latter word is especially interesting: *silvae* frequently connote the woodland Muse (*silvestris Musa*) of bucolic (1.2; see 1.5; 6.2; 10.63; see above for full references) or the Arcadian way of life (8.58), and at 4.3 it is almost an incipient book title for the Eclogue-book.

We may also observe that as in the Roman garden the bulk of the Eclogue-book's plant life is made up of trees and bushes rather than flowers. Flowers were certainly prized. They featured in symposiastic garlands, and appear widely in Pompeian wall paintings; the rosebeds at Paestum that Virgil claims bloomed twice a year (V. *Georg.* 4.119) became well known in Latin verse (see also Prop. 4.5.61; Ov. *Met.* 15.708; Columella 10.37; Mart. 12.31.3), and Virgil's Corycian farmer has lilies, poppies, roses, and hyacinths (*Georg.* 4.130-7). However, even though they are frequent and varied in garden paintings, difficulties of cultivation may have contributed to the limited role of flowers in ornamental gardens.[26] Overall, flowers should be seen as choice highlights rather than as unimportant. Appropriately, in the *Eclogues* they have rather localised, but not insignificant, sites.

The most conspicuous gathering of flowers in the Eclogue-book is that promised by Corydon to Alexis in the second *Eclogue*.

huc ades, o formose puer, tibi lilia plenis
ecce ferunt Nymphae calathis; tibi candida Nais,
pallentis violas et summa papavera carpens,
narcissum et florem iungit bene olentis anethi;
tum casia atque aliis intexens suavibus herbis
mollia luteola pingit vaccinia caltha.
ipse ego cana legam tenera lanugine mala
castaneasque nuces, mea quas Amaryllis amabat;
addam cerea pruna – honos erit huic quoque pomo –
et vos, o lauri, carpam et te, proxime myrte,
sic positae quoniam suavis miscetis odores.
rusticus es, Corydon; nec munera curat Alexis
nec, si muneribus certes, concedat Iollas.
heu heu, quid volui misero mihi? floribus Austrum
perditus et liquidis inmisi fontibus apros.

Ecl. 2.45-59

Come here, o lovely boy! Look, the Nymphs are bringing lilies in full
baskets for you; for you dazzling Nais, plucking pale violets and the tallest
poppies, is joining narcissus and the flower of fragrant dill with them;
then, weaving marjoram in and other sweet herbs, she colours the soft
bilberries with yellow marigold. I will pick apples myself, white with soft
down, and chestnuts, which my Amaryllis used to love; I will add waxy
plums – it will be an honour for this fruit too – and you, o laurels, I'll pick
and you, nearby myrtle, since so placed you mix sweet odours. You are a
bumpkin, Corydon, and Alexis does not care for your offerings, nor, if you
should compete in offerings, would Iollas back down. Alas, alas, what
have I wished on myself, wretch that I am? Damned fool, I've loosed the
south wind on to the flowerbeds and boars into the clear springs.

Narcissus, lilies, marigold, roses, violets, poppies, myrtle, apple, and
plum are all known in Pompeian garden paintings,[27] but over and above
this fact we can see in the passage before us a conflation of Theocritus
and Meleager (see above). Corydon's floral gathering – his metaphorical
anthology – is poetic in another sense too, for it parallels his singing in
that it too is a love-offering despised by Alexis (56 cf. 23ff., 31ff.).
Corydon sees the waste of his efforts as akin to letting the south wind
at flowers or boars at clear springs (58-9). Since the latter cannot fail to
make us think of the Callimachean springs of poetic inspiration, the
former may make us think of poetry too, in the form, say, of poetic
garlands (such as, indeed, the 'Garland of Meleager').[28] Nature, as
generally in the *Eclogues*, is artificially arranged into poetry. Else-
where, the hyacinth (which appears in Graeco-Latin poetry from early
times) is an offering for Apollo (god of poetry) at 3.63; it decorates the
description of Pasiphae's beloved bull in Silenus' song at 6.53 – a
passage with a number of bizarrely transferred bucolic features (see
below); and it is the answer to a riddle at 3,106f.

Unspecified flowers disappear (in a passage of figurative language) at the death of the archetypal bucolic figure Daphnis at 5.38; in general, flowers have a poetic association with spring and rebirth (cf. Lucr. 1.8). Flowers also have a typical function in garlanding the archetypal poet Linus at 6.68. They appear in poetic figurative language at 8.53, and as a metaphor for poetry at 9.19. Flowers are a signifier of the bucolic way of life in one of Menalcas' song fragments[29] at 9.41 (as they are also in 'Lucretian bucolic' at Lucr. 5.1396) and part of the iconography of the programmatic bucolic figure Silvanus at 10.25.[30] There is a persistent association of flowers and poetry, and flowers and bucolic poetry.

Other plants have significance too; reeds and oats (*calamus, harundo, avena*, and *fistula*) all connote bucolic song because of their use as pipes. The tamarisk (*myricae*) is also programmatic. It appears in an archetypal bucolic setting in Theocritus (*Id.* 1.12), and symbolises bucolic at 4.2, 10.13, and especially 6.10.[31]

There is a very considerable range of plant-life disposed throughout the *Eclogues* and it would hardly be possible to consider all named plants here. There are – as we have seen already – cumulative effects (most are benign or useful), but it would be as well to consider the complete assemblage from one eclogue. I use the first, since the opening poem is clearly meant to set the scene in important ways for the rest.

The Eclogue-book opens with the *fagus* whose programmatic resonances have been dealt with already. In the second line the *avena*, also programmatic, appears as the oat-pipe on which Tityrus tootles his bucolic song. *Silvestris* and *silvae* (1.2; 1.5) have already been considered too, although it should now be added that this set of words makes in itself a memorable and highly suggestive assemblage, which will echo through the rest of the collection. In line 10 Tityrus himself refers to his instrument as *calamus*, showing that the programmatic significance of the whole group (*calamus, harundo, avena*, and *fistula*) outweighs the niceties of botanical classification. We later learn that Pan was the inventor of the *calami* (2.32; 8.24). The hazel thickets (14, *densas corylos*) provide shade for kid-bearing goats, and for bucolic singers when they reappear at 5.3; at 7.63-4 they are the subject of bucolic song. The *quercus* (1.17) has been treated above as generally significant for the bucolic setting of the *Eclogues*. The next items (1.25) are the *viburnum* and the *cupressus* used in figurative language to show how much bigger Rome is than other cities. They do not reappear in the *Eclogues*, but typify the way the inhabitants' language is frequently derived from natural-world analogies. At lines 37 and 80 *poma* are part of and typify the bucolic context and way of life. The word recurs at 9.50 in one of the fragments of Menalcas' bucolic song. *Poma* could be apples, pears, or other fruit, and these too appear throughout the Eclogue-book. In the same passage as the first occurrence of *poma* in the poem, the pine (*pinus*; 38) too is found. Its Arcadian and musical connections are outlined above. In the same context we find also *arbusta* (orchards, 39), one of the collectives that appear throughout the book (see above). At 1.48 muddy rushes (*iunci*) cover Tityrus' pasturage. Elsewhere they (2.72) are given a typical bucolic application in the weaving of useful artefacts (cf. 10.71); here, however, the point is rather the fact that Tityrus' land is at least his own, even if not ideal. It is a touch of pathos that while he is being driven out of the bucolic world Meliboeus still pines for it at the same time as seeing it in comparatively unidealised terms. With the willow (1.54; see above) and its pasturage for bees (1.54) and goats (1.78) we are back to the general picture of the usefulness and benignity of nature (cf. also 3.65, 83, 5.16, 10.40). Likewise the elm (1.58) is the home of the turtle dove (*turtur*; cf. the doves (*columbae*) at 9.13 and (*palumbes*) at 1.57 and 3.65; this group of birds has distinct song-connotations). Elsewhere the elm is useful as a support for vines (2.70) and (5.3) as a provider of shade for singers (a significant contrast occurs in Gallus' despairing failed picture of life in Arcadia at 10.67). The *caespes* (sod, 1.68) is useful for roofing the bucolic cottage. Corn (*aristae*, 1.69; 4.28) and cornfields (*segetes*, 1.71; 5.33) are useful and appear spasmodically through the book (including in one of Menalcas' song-fragments; 9.48). Pears (cf. *poma* above) appear here (1.73) and this passage is alluded to in one of Menalcas' song-fragments in the other Eclogue in which land confiscations figure importantly (9.50), thus giving the pear some force as a bucolic indicator. Although there is no sign that the bucolic inhabitants drink wine, vines (1.73) are the object of one of the standard bucolic occupations (2.70; 3.11). They are also associated with Bacchus (5.31; 7.61), figure in one of Menalcas' song-fragments (9.42) and in Gallus' image of bucolic life (10.40). Flowering Lucerne (*cytisum*, 1.78) is the food of Meliboeus' goats (cf. also 9.31), leafage (*fronde*, 1.80) provides bedding (and food for goats at 10.30), and chestnuts (1.81; 2.52; 7.53) are a foodstuff for the bucolic natives.

The general usefulness of the plant-life in the first *Eclogue* is as expected. What is also striking is how many of the items reappear in other the rest of the book, how many have bucolic and or song-associations either here or elsewhere in the collection, how many appear in Menalcas' repertoire in the ninth *Eclogue* (especially significant given the connection between Menalcas and Virgil), and how many become parts of chains of associative plants and animals as the collection proceeds. Some items are plainly programmatic, some cumulatively acquire various degrees of programmatic force in the course of the book. The plants in the first *Eclogue* – and this continues in the rest of the collection – help define bucolic space, and other features reinforce this (e.g. references to occupations, to goats, to Tityrus, and the 'self-quotations' in the text) such that this space acquires a distinct character against which alien elements draw attention to themselves as alien.

3

Fauna

The characteristic animals of the *Eclogues* are sheep (*oves* are found 13 times; *agni* or *agnae* 6 times),[1] goats (*capellae* are found 10n times, including the bucolically typifying 8.33, 9.23, 10.7 and 77; *capri* 5 times, *capreoli* once; *haedi* 8 times; *hirci* twice),[2] cattle,[3] and bees.[4] As already observed, the rarer animals tend to be less in keeping with the bucolic way of life, are wilder or more dangerous, or have other justifications for their exceptional presence. They are, for example, included in figurative language rather than part of the bucolic landscape, or they are part of the iconography of Orpheus (lynxes at 8.3) or Bacchus (tigresses at 5.29),[5] or have too great a degree of individualism for the communal tone of Eclogue-land,[6] where the most significant bucolic animals frequently appear in flocks, herds, or swarms (*greges, armenta, pecudes, pecora, examina*).[7]

Quite often there is a particular point made by reference to animals. As well as being part of the typical setting of Eclogue-land, sheep are ingeniously programmatic in the divine epiphany at the beginning of the sixth *Eclogue*, when Apollo tells Virgil in Callimachean language (cf. *Aetia* 1.1.22f.) that the *pastor* (herdsman/bucolic poet)[8] should feed his sheep fat, but say (*dicere*)[9] a slimmed down song (*deductum carmen*):

> cum canerem reges et proelia, Cynthius aurem
> uellit, et admonuit: 'pastorem, Tityre, pinguis
> pascere oportet ouis, deductum dicere carmen.'
>
> *Ecl.* 6.3-5

> When I was singing kings and battles, Apollo plucked my ear and warned me, 'Tityrus, it suits a shepherd to feed sheep fat, but to say a thin-spun song.'

On a number of occasions sheep are more than setting-elements, but also typify the bucolic way of life, song, or bucolic itself (e.g. 2.33; 6.85; 7.3; 10.16-18).[10] Likewise, goats are sometimes used as pregnant signifiers (e.g. 1.12, 74-8; 2.30, 41; 7.3, 9; 8.33; 9.6, 62; 10.7). Tityrus, who stands for Virgil at 6.4, and may have this colour elsewhere, appears a number of times as the feeder or watcher of the goats while others go about their activity (3.20, 96; 5.12; 6.4; 9.23); on such occasions his name, itself already a bucolic signifier,[11] reinforces the effect. Goats and sheep appear often in Pompeian wall-painting in sacral-idyllic scenes which have various features reminiscent of bucolic poetry (more on this below). Sheep also appear in mythologico-pastoral scenes which also have bucolic connections, especially those involving Polyphemus and Galatea, and Paris.

Bees[12] too are poetically charged. They produce wax for the Pan-pipes (2.32; 3.25) which have a programmatic connection with song and Pan.[13] They also make a soft soothing noise akin to song (1.54; 7.13).

Birds are not as common as one might expect in the *Eclogues*,[14] but some have significance as regards song. The Chaonian doves (*columbae*) at 9.13 connote poetry,[15] and specifically in a contrast with war (symbolised by the eagle, *aquila*), raising the issue of the role of poetry in human circumstances. Also in the ninth *Eclogue*, singing swans (*cantantes cycni*, 9.29) represent the grand poets who will sing Varus' praises if Mantua is spared according to an unfinished (*incondita*) fragment of Menalcas' poetry. In the same poem swans (*olores*) and the goose (*anser*) represent different levels of poetic ability (9.36; cf. swans and owls at 8.55). Although Virgil's selection is a much smaller one,[16] it is noticeable that all of the birds mentioned in the *Eclogues* are found in Pompeian wall and/or garden paintings.

Lizards appear once (2.9),[17] and are not songful or communal, but they are Theocritean (*Id.* 7.22; Virgil's use of the seventh *Idyll* in his ninth *Eclogue* suggests that he thought of it as a key Theocritean poem). If we remember as we read *Eclogue* 2 that Theocritus' reference to the lizard opens the songful Lycidas' part in the dialogue, we may feel that Virgil may be making both the low esteem Alexis has for Corydon's songs (*Ecl.* 2.6) and also Corydon's current solitary songlessness (*incondita*, 'uncomposed, artless'; *Ecl.* 2.4) the more conspicuous.[18]

From the extra-bucolic direction, too, there are significant animal references. Hunting features boars, stags, and dogs[19] (all three animals feature in Pompeian *venatio* paintings). As we have already seen, it is a rather unbucolic occupation (although Daphnis has a bow at 3.12);[20] by contrast, it is both an occupation of the Roman aristocratic audience and a feature (as metaphor and image) in Roman elegy, and elegy is that genre with which Virgil's bucolic seems to have the most fraught relations. In the *Eclogues*, boars, stags, and dogs (and Gallus the elegist) appear in hunting contexts as an index of these tensions.

Boars appear in figurative language at 5.76 and as an offering to Diana in Corydon's song (7.29). At 3.75 they appear as a motif in a song exchange, and are used to express Menalcas' unrequited love for Amyntas. The language is well on the way to being purely figurative. More significantly, boars are a threat to the other Corydon's clear fountains because of his erotic distraction (2.59); we surely cannot fail to think of Callimachean springs here, and this presents the boars as antithetical to poetry. Finally, Gallus envisages hunting boars with his Cydonian arrows and his (!) Parthian bow (10.59-60). The two geographical epithets are strongly unbucolic, and the bow – here called *cornu* which can in other contexts mean 'horn'– is markedly in contrast with the bucolic pipes we see frequently in the collection. Gallus intends to hunt in Parthenian glades (57). The geographical epithet probably also plays on Parthenius, his poetry, and his *Erotika Pathemata* (dedicated to Gallus as they were) and strengthens the impression that what is at stake here is a conflict of poetic ideologies.

Stags appear in figurative language at 1.59 and at 5.60 (in the latter case hunting is explictly present).[21] At 7.30 the antlers of a stag will be Corydon's offering to Diana, along with the boar's head mentioned above. At 2.29 the besotted Corydon unrealistically imagines the sophisticated Alexis living in the country with him (as Tibullus imagines Delia with him; 1.5), herding a programmatic flock of goats and shooting stags.[22] The latter seems much more in keeping with the image of the unbucolic Alexis than with the normal bucolic way of life.

As with plant life, so with animals, a review of the total assemblage in a sample will be useful. Here I choose those two *Eclogues* that push most strongly against the usual boundaries of the bucolic genre, the fourth and sixth.

The animal life of the fourth *Eclogue* is unusually thin, but very striking. We have within its confines goats (4.21) and cattle (4.22) unafraid of lions (4.22), the explicitly verbalised *absence* of snakes (4.24), oxen released from their yokes (4.41). The standard bucolic sheep are replaced with a ram which can change its colour, and vermilion lambs (4.43-5).[23] The assemblage is a version of the standard bucolic assemblage, but heightened, made hyper-bucolic (an analogous case could be made for the poem's plant-life).

In the sixth *Eclogue* also the animal assemblage is meagre. This outlandish version of Eclogue-land is framed by standard – and explicitly programmatic – sheep at its opening (6.4) and some more typically bucolic sheep at the end of the poem (6.85). In between, there are the wild animals (*feras*, 6.27) which respond to Silenus' quasi-Orphic song, and, in the song itself, there are oddities. First there are the *animalia* (a unique word in the *Eclogues*)[24] of cosmogonic myth (6.40). Secondly, there is a cluster of animal-words, all but one of which would be at home in any of the standard *Eclogues* (*armenta, iuvenci, pecudum, grege, bovis, armenta,* and *vaccae,* 6.45-60);[25] what makes these words outlandish here is the fact that they belong to the story of Minos' wife Pasiphae, who fell in love with a bull and produced the Minotaur.[26] In this context, in Pasiphae's neoteric-style speech[27] the word *vacca* (cow) is an emotive debasement of standard bucolic vocabulary. The final oddity is the presence of the metamorphic monsters (6.75, 77) of the Scylla tale.[28] In this *Eclogue* Virgil pushes at the limits of bucolic, but both frames the poem with markedly standard animals, and substan-

41

tially uses standard animals in the main body of the poem, but subjects them to a remarkable translation of context.

Virgil's selection of animals in the *Eclogues* is tiny compared to the Roman knowledge-base derived from provincial government, military expeditions, animal shows in the amphitheatre, and the range of edible animals on the aristocratic dinner table. The animals Virgil uses – like the trees, bushes, and plants – help define bucolic space largely from inside, but also from outside. It is also noteworthy that there are significant points of contact between the animals in the *Eclogues* and those in Pompeian painting. Sheep, goats, and birds figure significantly in these points of contact, but there is another important resemblance on a more general scale. 'If the owner had greater aspirations, he might include in his garden decoration, in addition to fountains, trees, birds, and flowers, also lakes or streams in a mountainous setting full of wild animals' (Jashemski, 2002, 18). By so painting the walls of a garden, the owner creates and enhances a civilised haven of artificially tamed nature within an outer surrounding of wildness, untamedness, and danger. With this we can compare the way in Pliny's description of his Tuscan estate real mountains fringe the view (*Ep.* 5.6.6, 28).

Places in and out of Eclogue-land[1]

Although the dense self-referentiality of the beech passage in *Eclogue* 9 (*Ecl.* 9.7-10) and of the *Eclogues* as a whole gives an impression of a hermetically sealed landscape, bounded by generic markers, it is a landscape whose boundaries with outer worlds are complex and permeable. Both the poetry of the *Eclogues* and the songs of the inhabitants reach out into the wider field of Roman poetry. In addition, both the poetry of the *Eclogues* and the songs of their inhabitants quite often figure the incursions of the 'real' world.[2]

This outside world can be represented in various ways, but first it will be useful to give a preliminary geographical survey of Theocritus' *Idylls* and Virgil's *Eclogues*. The *Idylls* of Theocritus make up a mixed collection which includes a significant bucolic element, but also urban mime, court-poem, and framed mythological narrative. The poems are not always clearly located, but *Idyll* 15 is set in Alexandria, and the bucolic poems when the setting is evident are variously set in Cos (7.1-2), southern Italy (4.17; 5.2, 72), and (most frequently) Sicily (1.117; 8.56; 9.15; cf. the bucolic-mythological hybrid 11.7; Bion 2.1). We are faced with a variegated compilation in which different poems have different settings, even when we narrow the scope to the bucolic poems alone. However, if we allow ourselves to think of the world of Theocritean bucolic in general we begin to see differences and similarities between his poetic world and that of the *Eclogues*. Virgil takes the world of Theocritean bucolic and both makes it more imaginary and also, paradoxically, brings more real contemporary life into it.

We may think of Virgil's landscape as idealised, but by contrast the devastated and impoverished state of Sicily and south Italy in Theocritus' time does not figure in the latter's poems at all, whereas troubles arising from the Augustan land-confiscations are prominent in the first and ninth of Virgil's *Eclogues*. The figures in Theocritus are aware that people move around the Greek world, and are themselves sometimes presented as coming from this or that named place;[3] on the one hand, this cumulates in a general impression that Theocritus' bucolic world is part of – or partly coterminous with – the real Greek world of the time, but at the same time there is nothing in Theocritus' bucolic landscape to match Virgil's presentation of Rome in the first *Eclogue*. On the other hand, the coarse gossip, the pricking of thorns, and the variety of occupation and geography that we see in Theocritus are very much reduced and shaped in Virgil.

Places outside Greece and Italy

Places outside Greece and Italy are mentioned in the *Eclogues*, but generally connote poetry or regions closed to the inhabitants of Eclogue-land – regions of danger, madness, and extremes.

As with plants and animals, we must make a distinction between figurative language and the referential language of description and narration. When Tityrus mentions a cluster of remote and savage places in the first *Eclogue* (1.62f.; Arar, Parthia, Germania, Tigris), it is merely in a figure of speech and they are not conceived as places either within or outwith Eclogue-land.[4] Likewise, the lions and tigers, themselves alien in the bucolic landscape, at 5.27ff. are Phoenician and Armenian, but here too we have highly figured language and a distinctively poetical register, used in this case to indicate the universal scale of grief for Daphnis. At 5.17 and 7.32 'Phoenician' is no more than a poetic word for 'red'.[5] Assyrian cardamoms will grow freely in the new Golden Age at 4.25; here the whole trope depends on this mythopoetical register rather than being part of the depiction of the bucolic visual field.

To an extent, insofar as these places are part of the language of Eclogue-land, they belong imaginatively to that world. However, all this is very different from Meliboeus' reference to Africa, Scythia, Oaxes, and the Britanni (1.64ff.). Here, Meliboeus and others like him cease to be inhabitants of Eclogue-land and are obliged to go to remote, harsh, and alien, but real, regions outside the bucolic world. In contrast with the poetic places mentioned a moment ago, the very reality (for the Roman audience) of the places to which Meliboeus refers arguably helps locate them outside the bucolic world of native inhabitants. Analogously, when Gallus tries to enter Arcadia in the tenth *Eclogue* his attempt is burdened with the mention of various remote places (Alps and Rhine at 10.47; Parthia at 10.59; the Thracian Hebrus[6] and Sithonia, and Aethiopia at 10.65-9) and his attempt is ultimately unsuccessful. Again, although at *Eclogues* 8.43ff. the Thracian Tmaros and Rhodope (cf. V. *Georg.* 3.351 for the remoteness of Rhodope) and the African Garamantes might be considered part of a piece of figurative language (for Amor's inhumanity) rather than as actual geographical designations for places in the world of the *Eclogues*, these places are in any case harsh and dangerous (it is this that justifies the supposition that Amor could have been born there). Likewise, Pontus (8.95, 96) is also used as a marker of the extreme and remote: it is the source of magic poison for the love-crazed woman in the eighth *Eclogue*.

A sense builds up that Eclogue-land is contained in a temperate zone, bounded and closed in on itself by a ring of climatic and geographical extremes (but also that poetry can reach out from within it to a larger imaginative world). The range of places named in the fourth *Eclogue* (itself exceptional in other respects too) belong partly to the grander scope of that poem - Cumae, Assyria, Troy, and (suggesting Orpheus) Thrace.

Places in the Greek world

Places in Greece or the Greek world are different. On the one hand, like some of the references to remote places, they tend strongly to produce figurative texture rather than evoke geographically realised places (cf. *Ecl.* 5.17 and 7.32, as mentioned above, for 'Phoenician' as no more than a poetic word for 'red'). On the other, although there is no route-map, so to speak, showing how a native of the *Eclogues* might reach Syracuse, Hybla, Parnassus, or such places, they are generally mentioned as though they are somehow not too far away. Tityrus' bees, for example, are Hyblaean (1.54) in a poem in which Rome is, if remote, still accessible. The epithet suggests both the excellence of the honey the bees produce, and also the poetry-scape of Theocritean bucolic.

In the fifth *Eclogue* Menalcas promises (5.71) to offer the deified Daphnis Ariusian wine – wine from the north of Chios, a region whose wines were prized by real Romans (Pliny *NH* 14.73). In the same passage (5.72-3) three bucolic natives, Damoetas, Aegon, and Alphesiboeus, will sing and dance; all three names are found elsewhere in the *Eclogues*, two are in Theocritus as well, and the remaining name, Alphesiboeus, suggests the bucolic world because of its meaning ('producing a good yield of oxen').[7] Among these stereotypical eclogic names we notice that Aegon is described as Lyctian, i.e. from Crete. Numbers of characters in the more open and mapped world of Theocritus are said to come from named places; however, although nouns in the *Eclogues* are not infrequently supplied with largely decorative Greek place-names, the overall sense of mappedness is much weaker in Virgil's bucolic world than in Theocritus', and we should be receptive to the extra-geographical colour when the singing Aegon is here connected with a place associated with the cult of Apollo (Callim. *H.* 2.33), the god of poetry.[8]

In the seventh *Eclogue* we find Hyblan thyme implying honey (7.37; cf. 1.54) in a decorative, poetic comparison made by Corydon in a bucolic song competition. 'Sardinian herb' (probably celery) at 7.41 is the corresponding (and contrasting) comparison in Thyrsis' response to Corydon's lines. Cyrnean yews (= Corsican; 9.30) make another figured and decorative reference (to bitter honey).[9] In the second *Eclogue* Corydon says that his songs are the ones that Dircaean Amphion sang on Actaean Aracynthus while calling his cattle (2.24). Here the bucolic singer (Corydon) has through his songmaking a contact with a broader poetic world, and one familiar to the Roman poetry-audience. Although he naturalises Amphion by representing him as a bucolic figure, Corydon is somehow in touch with the repertoire of mythological poetry (as other natives of Eclogue-land are too), and is able to use it figuratively as material for comparison and exemplum. In the same poem he uses Dardanian Paris (2.61), cast as yet another bucolic figure – a 'shepherd'[10] on Ida – as a parallel for himself. In the same poem, the Libethrian nymphs (7.21) are the Muses, since there was a town called Libethrum or Libethra in the Pierian region (the home of the Muses), and a mountain called Libethrium in the Helicon complex (where there were shrines to the Muses and the Libethrian nymphs; Pausanias 9.34.4; Strabo 8.410).

There is a more complex set of places named in *Eclogue* 6. The bulk of the poem is Silenus' Roman-sounding song-cycle. Near its end, two archetypal poets Linus and Hesiod, one mythical and the other real, figure in the inauguration of the Roman poet Gallus. Linus is presented in bucolic guise as a 'shepherd (*pastor*) of inspired song' (6.67); Hesiod is referred to as the 'old man of Ascraea' (*Ascraeo seni*; 6.70), to whom the Muses have given some typically bucolic reedpipes (*calami*). Like *Ascraeo,* other place-names and adjectives derived from them contribute to the net of poetic connotations in Silenus' song: Parnasian (6.29; cf. 10.11, Theocr. *Id.* 7.148), Permessus (6.64), Aonian (6.65, 10.12), Eurotas (6.83), and the Greek but remote Rhodope (6.30; 8.44) and Ismarus (6.30) variously have associations with Apollo, Orpheus, poetic inspiration. Other place-words come from poetic contexts. Mt Dicte (6.56) was the home of the nymphs who nursed the infant Zeus (Callimachus *Hymn* 1.46); Gortyn (6.60) is part of the setting of the story of Pasiphae; the Grynean grove (6.72) was, according to Servius, the place where Mopsus defeated Calchas in a divination contest, and is to be the subject of a poem by Gallus; Dulichium (6.76) was part of Odysseus' kingdom (Homer Odyssey 1.245-6) and in Propertius and Ovid 'Dulichian' is used as synonym for 'Ithacan' in reference to Odysseus (cf. Propertius 2.14.4; Ov. *Met.* 13.107).

In the tenth *Eclogue* there is another dense cluster of place-names (and derived epithets) which deserve to be considered *en bloc* (see below, *Arcadia* (iii)), but relevant here is the use of Cydonian (10.59 = Cretan) for Gallus' allegedly bucolic arrows (in the same line his bow is a very unbucolic 'Parthian'). Although the archetypal bucolic figure Daphnis has a bow at 3.12-13, hunting is not a normal activity for the natives of Eclogue-land. 'Cydonian' here is another word with probable poetic provenance,[11] but in this case this does not represent the outreach of the eclogic native into Latin literature, but rather hints at Gallus' status as coming into Eclogue-land (or trying to) from outside – hunting was familiar to Romans of high social standing, and Latin literature was their cultural heritage.

4. Places in and out of Eclogue-land

A good number of the Greek-world place-names, as has already been seen, belong to a distinctly poetical linguistic register. These places stand out, of course, from the world of real herdsmen, but they become part of the world and the language of Eclogue-herdsmen.[12] Many have specific or overt poetic connotations into the bargain. The 'poetry' in these poetical references is twofold: sometimes we are directed towards poets from the real world – from various degrees of proximity to the Roman literary context – and sometimes to 'poetry' in the more absolute or generalised sense. Thus, 'Ascraean' refers to Hesiod in Gallus' poetic initiation at 6.70. Also connected with Gallus is his 'Chalcidic' verse (10.70), which alludes to Euphorion or perhaps Theocles.[13] 'Thracian' describes Orpheus at 4.55, and Rhodope[14] and Ismarus (6.30) are given (and thereby give to Silenus' compound song) a specifically Orphic connection.[15] Apollo is alluded to by way of Parnassus (cf. Theocr. *Id.* 7.148) in the same passage (6.29) and again at 10.11 (in connection with Gallus). Apollo appears in the context of Permessus and Aonia (and Gallus) at 6.64-6. Apollo again is connected with the Eurotas at 6.83, and Aonia connotes the Muses at 10.12 (in the same context as Parnassus and Pindus (cf. Theocr. *Id.* 1.67), and Gallus). At 9.13 Chaonian doves stand for poetry (alluding to the oracle at Dodona), and Cumae at 4.4 refers to the Sibylline verses.

Two Greek places remain, and are of particular importance: Arcadia[16] and Sicily (*Ecl.* 4.1; 6.1; 10.51). They are frequently named and generally associated with poetry, specifically bucolic.

Sicily

Theocritus originated from Syracuse, the chief city of Sicily, and in the *Eclogues* Sicily and Syracuse primarily connote Virgil's Theocritean poetic affiliation rather than places as such. The Muses addressed in a clearly programmatic passage (4.1-3) also mentioning programmatic myrtles and woods – *myricae, silvae* – are specifically described as Sicilian; Virgil's verse is programmatically described as Syracusan at the beginning of the sixth *Eclogue*; at the generically self-referential beginning of the tenth *Eclogue*, there is an address to the Arcadian-Sicilian (*Sicanos*, 10.4) nymph-river, Arethusa, and later in the same poem Gallus uses 'Sicilian' (*Siculi*, 10.51) along with other generic marker-words (*pastoris, avena*) in another generically significant passage. The reference to Hyblaean bees in the first poem of the book (1.54) is perhaps also a reminder to the audience of Theocritean Sicily.

One other reference to Sicily remains, Corydon's at 2.21. The second *Eclogue* is based on one of Theocritus' mythological caprices (*Id.* 11) rather than a pastoral poem as such. However, the *Idyll* has various pastoral trappings and is set – as chiefly in Theocritean pastoral – on Sicily (47). Virgil replaces Theocritus' Polyphemus with Corydon, whose name is a well-attested bucolic one (cf. Theocr. *Id.* 4; 5.6; V. *Ecl.* 5.86; 7), and so can be seen as consciously bucolicising the situation.[17] In the course of bewailing Alexis' scornful attitude to his love, Corydon complains that all his sheep on Sicilian mountains (21; *Siculis in montibus*) ought to make Alexis less scornful of him. Does this reference set the poem on Sicily? In that case, would we be obliged to take Corydon's implied but implausible claim to own a thousand sheep seriously?[18] Alternatively – and more pointedly – the reference can be seen as part of the generic drama that is played out in the poem between ('Sicilian') bucolic as represented by Corydon, and sentimental love-poetry as represented by Alexis.[19]

On balance, the word *Siculis* at *Eclogues* 2.21 seems analogous to the use of epithets such as Hyblaean, Ariusian, and Phoenician for their poetic connotations or stylistic level rather than to refer to particular places. It does not strongly urge a particular geographical location on the poem as a whole, but reminds the audience of Theocritus and specifically of the Sicilian Polyphemus, whose name Virgil has removed because it would bring memories of the Homeric monster too closely to the surface. A Polyphemus would look grotesque among the Virgilian bucolic natives.

Arcadia (i)

The other Greek place-name requiring special attention is that of Arcadia. Arcadia is not used as a bucolic setting in Theocritus or other Greek pastoral earlier than Virgil. On the other hand, in a poem addressed to Virgil, Horace refers to Arcadia in an allusion to the *Eclogues*:

> dicunt in tenero gramine pinguium
> custodes ovium carmina fistula
> delectantque deum cui pecus et nigri
> colles Arcadiae placent.

Hor. Odes 4.12.9-12

> In the tender grass the guardians of fat [Callimachean!] sheep sing with the pipe and delight the god who loves the flock and the dark hills of Arcadia.

In the Eclogue-book itself Arcadia has a strong presence, though not uniformly spread through the whole collection. There are references to Arcadia at 4.58-9 and 10.26, and Arcadians at 7.4, 26, and 10.31 and 33. Places in Arcadia are also named. *Maenalus*, the mountain and favourite haunt of Pan (Theocr. *Id.* 1,124) is named in the eighth and tenth *Eclogues* (8.21; 25, 28a, 31, 36, 42, 46, 51, 57, 61; 10.55). In the latter instance, the reference comes in Gallus' 'bucolic' song. Another Arcadian mountain is found at 10.15 (*saxa Lycaei*) and yet another at 10.57 (*Parthenios saltus*).[20] It is evident when one looks at these lists that there are concentrations in *Eclogues* 7, 8, and 10, and that these are late in the Eclogue-book. While this may lead one to doubt that the identification of the bucolic setting as Arcadia can be generalised, it is also evident that there is a repeated connection between Arcadia and Pan, and this may point in the other direction. There is also the complex question of Arcadia's relationship with the Italian landscape.

The latter question will have to be deferred for the moment. As to the irregular distribution of references to Arcadia, one might consider the partial analogy of human names.

At *Eclogue* 6.4 Tityrus represents Virgil in a brief speech by Apollo in a Callimachean epiphany to the poet, but what about Tityrus' appearance in the first *Eclogue*, when the reader has not yet come to the sixth? In the fifth *Eclogue,* however, it is Menalcas and not Tityrus who stands for Virgil, since Menalcas' repertoire includes the second and third *Eclogues* (5.86-7); in the ninth, Menalcas is a bucolic songster whose songs encompass the themes and motifs of specifically Virgilian bucolic.[21] What, then, are we to make of Corydon's reference to a Menalcas as a possible alternative for his affections in the light of Alexis' scorn (2.15), or the appearance of a Menalcas as one of the songsters competing in *Eclogue* 3 (where he knows, or knows of, Virgil's contemporary, Pollio; 3.86)? Do Tityrus and Menalcas only become Virgil at particular points in the book, earlier than which they are merely Tityrus and Menalcas, or does the reader who has read the whole book wonder if, for example, there is an element of overlap between Tityrus and Virgil in the first poem (as Servius thought)? The ambivalence of the tree mentioned in the opening line of the collection (beech / a kind of oak / a Theocritean or bucolic tree) is somewhat similar. In the light of these ambiguities, it is quite possible that we could identify the bucolic landscape as a whole, and in the whole book, retrospectively as Arcadia, even though references only appear when the book is under way.

Pan has a special place in the *Eclogues* and often appears in connection with Arcadia. He is its presiding god (10.26; cf. Theocr. 1.14ff.) and also the inaugurator of bucolic practices (2.31ff.); he is the inventor of the panpipes (8.24; cf. [Theocr.] *Id.* 8.18-19), a sort of presiding song-god (4.58), and the ambassador of joy at the elevation of the archetypically bucolic figure Daphnis (5.59). The Arcadian mountain Maenalus is Pan's mountain (8.22ff.). Another Arcadian mountain (*saxa Lycaei*; 10.15) was a centre of worship of Zeus and Pan (cf. Theocr. *Id.* 1.123-4). He is the recipient also of a dedication by two Arcadians, Glaucon and Corydon, in an epigram by Erucius (*Anth.Pal.* 6.96). He is associated with the *phagos*, that especially bucolic tree (Philemon ap. Athenaeus. 2.52e), a tree which marks the boundary of bucolic space at *Eclogues*

9.9, and whose bark bears a bucolic songscript at *Eclogues* 5.13. Elsewhere, Pan is associated with idealised landscape (*h. Hom.* 19; Eur. *Hel.* 167-90) and with love and music making (*Anth. Pal.* 5.139). Arcadian Pan's special place in the bucolic world of the *Eclogues* goes some way to reinforce the impression that that world can indeed be called 'Arcadia'.

Places in Italy

The relationship of Arcadia with Italian place-names still needs to be considered, but the matter of Italian geography needs prior discussion in its own right. The river Timavus and Illyricum (8.6-7), Rome (1), Cremona (9.27) and Mantua (9.27,28), and the river Mincius (7) are the Italian places most requiring to be dealt with here. Cumae (4.4) has already been treated as Greek, although it could be considered as either Italian or Greek.

Timavus and Illyricum

Damonis Musam dicemus et Alphesiboei.
tu mihi, seu magni superas iam saxa Timavi
sive oram Illyrici legis aequoris, – en erit umquam
ille dies, mihi cum liceat tua dicere facta?

Ecl. 8.5-8

We shall sing of Damon's and Alphesiboeus' Muse. But you – whether you are already conquering the rocks of the great Timavus or coasting the Illyrian sea, – say, will that day ever come when I may be allowed to sing your deeds?

The real-life boundaries between the Greek and Roman worlds, and between them and the realms beyond, are complex and elusive, but from the perspective of the *Eclogues* we might well see the Timavus and Illyricum (*Ecl.* 8.6, 7) as on – or just beyond – the edge of Eclogue-land: they are associated with the addressee, C. Asinius Pollio (who appears anonymously in the introduction rather than the body of the poem),[22] and they are therefore arguably part of the frame rather than the picture. They connote alarming scenes of the great deeds in the real world towards which Pollio is heading,[23] and are thus an appropriate marker for what is beyond Eclogue-land. However, the contrast between real and poetic is perhaps not straightforward, for it is arguable that there is also a generic boundary here. According to the *Aeneid* (1.242-9), the Trojan hero Antenor reached the Illyrican bay and sailed past the Timavus to found Patavium (Padua).[24] One might infer that Pollio (coming from Rome) would be travelling in the opposite direction to Antenor (coming from Troy). Treating the Antenor story as a founda-

50

tion myth, one could see Antenor entering history while Pollio enters the world of epic from which the former is coming.[25] At another level again, in geographical terms, the two names, Timavus and Illyricum, define the transition point between Italy and not-Italy. The Timavus enters the sea at the extreme north east of Italy, and Illyricum, the first province on the east outside Italy, lines the east of the Adriatic sea.

The Timavus and the Illyrican sea are liminal, but they seem to be so in more than one way, and the different levels interfere with each other. The two place names mark the border between the poetic world of Eclogue-land and the real world of Virgil's contemporaries; they mark the border between the real world of Virgil and Pollio and the epic world into which he can be seen to be moving; one might overlay these two divisons on top of each other to generate another border, between bucolic and epic; finally, one can also align the use of the threshold places Timavus and Illyricum with Virgil's use of places outside Italy and the Greek world as markers of remoteness, strangeness, extremes, and danger. The relationship, or the degree of overlap, between the bucolic world and the Graeco-Italian world becomes ambiguous and hard to pin down.

Rome

Rome has a more ambivalent position.[26] It is within the reach of one of the natives of Eclogue-land, Tityrus, in *Eclogue* 1, but from Meliboeus' reaction it is clear that going to Rome is an exceptional move. Rome is outside the sphere of the generality of bucolic inhabitants. On the other hand, it certainly exercises an influence on Eclogue-land and its inhabitants.[27] Two other Italian cities appear in the *Eclogues*, Cremona and Mantua. They do not appear directly, but as the subject in the ninth *Eclogue* of a song by Menalcas (who stands, on the one hand, for Virgil, but is, on the other, a fellow native of the shepherds of the poem, Lycidas and Moeris, and one that they can hope will turn up (67)). Cremona and Mantua have a rather indeterminate relationship to the bucolic landscape, but their troubles, the subject of Menalcas' song, stem, like those of the bucolic natives in the ninth *Eclogue*, from Rome. Rome is named in the first *Eclogue*, and looms in the atmosphere of the ninth, but with it need also to be considered the occasional anonymous references to 'the city.'

There is no explicit mention of the city in the second *Eclogue*, but its presence can still be felt. Alexis, Corydon's beloved, has a name which comes from outside bucolic, and indeed his general portrayal suggests the urban genre of elegy and/or urban epigram.[28] Alexis' sophistication reminds us of urban values and is an anti-bucolic strain that lies behind the unrequitedness of Corydon's love.

Love rather than the city is the more directly responsible agent of

51

unhappiness in the eighth *Eclogue*, but the city is felt there all the same, and as an anti-bucolic presence in the scorn in which Nysa holds the bucolic way: Nysa's[29] husband Damon complains[30] that she scorns, along with him, his way of life represented by the bucolic natives (all of them: *omnis*, 32), and the programmatically bucolic *fistula* ('pipe') and goats (33f.). Love here is portrayed as an inhuman and alien influence (*nec generis nostri ... nec sanguinis*, 45), born on unbucolic rocks in places remote from any of those representing Eclogue-land (Tmaros, Rhodope, *extremi Garamantes*, 44); Love's inhumanity and disruption of bucolic stability aligns it with the city as a dangerous and alien presence.

In the same *Eclogue*, a girl (her part is sung by Alphesiboeus) laments (repeatedly, since it is in the refrain: *Ecl.* 8.68, 72, 76, 79, 84, 90, 94, 100, 104) that the city is keeping her beloved Daphnis away from her. Insoluble questions lurk here. Is Daphnis – elsewhere an archetypal bucolic character – drawn like Alexis to the values and sophistications of the city? Alternatively, is he just a few minutes late and the girl overworried? Perhaps the dog barks for some other reason than Daphnis' appearance: the girl's magic has failed and Daphnis has not come back at all. We are left not knowing. The scale and effects of the city's intervention in bucolic love are impossible to gauge in this case, but the city's availability evidently remains a source of worry to Daphnis' lover.[31]

The city is clearly much more dangerous in the ninth *Eclogue*. It lies behind the disturbances (pointing at the land-confiscations of 42 BC onwards) which nearly cause the deaths of Moeris and Menalcas (9.16). The road to the city is itself ominous,[32] marked as it is by the low profile of roads in the other *Eclogues*[33] and by the presence by the roadside here of one of the two tombs firmly placed in Eclogue-land.[34] In this poem, the city is also the source of a number of words located in a social framework that is both alien and potentially hostile to Eclogue-land – *advena, possessor, coloni* (immigrant, owner, tenant-farmer; 9.2-4), and *lites* (14). Words of a similar class have already appeared in that other poem concerned with the land-confiscations, *Eclogue* 1 (*libertas* (liberty; 27, 32) *peculium* (savings; 32) *aere* (bronze = money; 35, the only reference to money in the *Eclogues*), *servitio* (slavery; 40), *finis* (boundary; 67), *miles* (soldier; 70), *barbarus* (barbarian; 71), and *civis* (citizen; 71)),[35] and together with the explicit presence of Rome in that poem this lexical overlap puts the shadow of Rome firmly in the ninth *Eclogue* too.

Rome – named in the first *Eclogue* and felt in the ninth[36] – is the most striking instance of the way external reality impinges in the world of the *Eclogues*.[37] In the first *Eclogue* this presence is ambiguous. On the one hand, it lies behind Meliboeus' displacement; on the other Tityrus has done an unbucolic thing and gone to Rome with the result that he is able to stay in Eclogue-land (something it is not certain that Menalcas' songs in the darker ninth *Eclogue* achieve). It is not impossible, but it is not easy for the natives of Eclogue-land to retain their way of life in the context of the real Roman world; there is clearly a tension between the needs of Rome and Arcadia, and successful compromise perhaps rubs something away from the bucolic patina. However, one should not too easily fall into believing that the bucolic ideal is meant to be taken as overriding the imperatives of the Roman context.[38] We should not forget that if we come to the Eclogues from Lucretius, we have already seen an outsider's pictures of the bucolic experience and of the Golden Age (Lucr. *DRN* 4.572-94; 5.925-1010) – nor should we forget the elements of comedy in the presentation of Virgil's plaintive hexameter-singing shepherds.[39]

After the battle of Philippi in 42 BC Octavian needed to settle tens of thousands of soldiers, and privately owned land had to be confiscated. At least 18 Italian towns were affected, some drastically.[40] The process, however, was necessary and by the time, some five or ten years later than the *Eclogues*, that Horace recalls Octavian's settlement of veterans on confiscated land, it is noticeable that complaint is positively rejected in the speech he puts into a dispossessed landowner's mouth (*Satires* 2.2.112-36).[41] By contrast, Meliboeus' picture of dispossessed smallholders driven to the extremes of the four quarters of the world (Africa, Scythia, Oaxes, and Britain; 64-6) is a clearly grotesque exaggeration stemming from the geographically topsy turvy figure of speech Tityrus has just used (59-63).[42] When Tityrus says that exiled (61) Parthians will drink the Arar and Germans the Tigris before he forgets the young man who has saved him, Meliboeus ironically suggests that such are the places where he and others like him will be going to. Though his situation is unfortunate, this is not a literal complaint. Furthermore, although it may be no consolation to Meliboeus, Tityrus is not alone (*Ecl.* 1.45) in gaining a reprieve, so we may feel that Virgil is drawing attention to the availability of at least some sort of mitigations process.

There was, however, certainly discontent. According to Suetonius (*Aug.* 13.3) Augustus (then still Octavian) satisfied neither the landowners nor the veterans.[43] The next major settlement (after the defeat of Pompey in 35 BC) involved land outside Italy rather than confiscations and sent a message that citizens would no longer find themselves deprived of their land (Eck 2003: 26-7). In the *Res Gestae* (3; 16) Augustus emphasised the later, kinder settlements to the point that the earlier confiscations are invisible. Soon after the settlement following the defeat of Pompey, Horace's account of the uncomplaining Ofellus, dispossessed in the earlier confiscations (*Satires* 2.2.112-36) is already taking part in this adjustment of historical memory. The account is firmly located in a quite distant past (112-13),[44] and Ofellus' fortitude and spirit also suggest (for those with still uneasy memories) that even at the time the confiscations were able to be endured with fortitude and spirit.

53

Behind Virgil's presentation of Rome there is also the use of the town and country contrast in the wider literary sphere: the country symbolises hardy Roman manliness and values, whereas the town connotes luxury and foreign contamination (cf. Varro *Agr.* 2.1; V. *Georg.* 2.467ff.).[45] The different backgrounds pull against each other, leaving the reader aware that nothing is ever perfect. One can read the later manifestations of the bucolic idea in Virgil's *Georgics* and *Aeneid* as interpretations of, or revisitations to, the *Eclogues*, and here too there is not a clear cut weighting in favour of either side of the balance.

In the first book of the *Georgics,*[46] we learn that Jupiter willed work on humans to sharpen their intelligence, and there is a contrast with a Golden Age where land boundaries were unknown, everything was held in common, and the earth itself provided for human needs without need of work. The picture is not, however, a pure Utopia, but negatively characterised as slothful. Moreover, to lead mankind to generate skills, boat-building, hunting, fishing, iron, and tools, Jupiter removed fire and added features untypical of the world of the *Eclogues* – snakes, wolves, and the stormy sea (121-46). The advance of civilisation – even apparently at the price of Caesar's death, civil war, and chaos (466ff., 489ff., 510ff.) – is worth more than the kind of world the bucolic shepherds might find themselves at home in. By contrast, however, the second book presents something like the bucolic experience in a positive light. Here the loveliness of Italy (2.143-76) is adorned with fruit, olives, cattle, perpetual spring/summer, orchards, crops, and the absence of unbucolic lions, tigers, and snakes, and Italy is addressed as the Golden Age land (*Saturnia tellus*, 'Saturnian land'; 2.173). There are, indeed, some unbucolic features that are not negatively presented – wine, horses, triumphs, cities and so forth – but Italy is clearly presented with a strong and positive bucolic colouring. Later in the book, the loveliness of spring likewise has a strong bucolic flavour, with woods, fruits, birds, herds, love, grass, vines, cattle, and a resemblance to the dawn of world. Later again, traces of the Golden Age, with which the world of the *Eclogues* is aligned, appear in the praises given to the life of the farmer (2.458-74); a life far from war, and for which the earth lavishes easy livelihood, a life in which there is no urban extravagance, nor the absurdities of the morning social round of visiting patrons (*salutation*), but peace, innocence, and a life lived in a landscape which has the bucolic trappings of caves, cattle, sleep under a tree, and the last traces of the Golden Age.

Later again, in the *Aeneid*, we see a tension between the bucolic and the Roman. In Book 7, Latinus' kingdom clearly has Golden Age features (Latinus' people are the children of Saturn and lack a penal code; 7.202ff.), but it is his agrarian people (*agrestis*, 8.482) that is used by Allecto to start the conflict between the Trojans – urban, since they come from Troy – and the Italians, and she summons the latter (farmers according to 7.521; *agricolae*) with a herdsman's horn-signal (7.513, *pastorale signum*). In Book 8 (337-61), the simplicity of Evander's kingdom (the site of the future Rome) is contrasted with Rome's ultimate architectural splendour (cf. Prop. 4.1.1-38; Ov. *AA* 1.103-8; 3.113-16). Herds wander and cattle low where one day the Forum and elegant Carinae will be (360-1); where will be the Capitol, there are woodland bushes (347-8). Evander tells Aeneas that the Arcadians (the inhabitants of the region, who have followed the Arcadian Evander; 8.51-4) believe they have seen Jupiter there (352-4). The site of Rome had once been the wooded home of native Fauns and Nymphs (314), and a race of men without civilisation or ancestral customs (*mos, cultus*) who lived off fruit and hunting until Saturn brought them together and gave them laws and established the Golden Age (315-27). Progress and decline, innocence and civilisation, and the bucolic past and the unbucolic present are inextricably intertwined and confused throughout this material.[47] The bucolic worlds of Latinus and Evander are too fragile to stand against the realities which the *Aeneid* presents them with.

While the *Eclogues* predate the full flowering of Augustus' radical transformation of the conceptual and physical fabric of Rome,[48] this magnificence already seems to be immanent. Some twenty years before the appearance of the *Eclogues*, the rousing conclusion of Cicero's second speech against Catiline (63 BC) urges his audience to implore the gods to defend 'the city they wished to be most beautiful, most flourishing, and most powerful' (*quam urbem pulcherrimam florentissimam potentissimamque voluerunt*; Cic. *in Cat.* 2.13.29). While the architecture of Rome bleeds ambivalently into much Augustan poetry, the city was still magnificent[49] and pregnant with meaning for its citizens (as in the symbolism of the Capitol for Rome's power and immortality: Hor. *Odes* 3.30.8; V. *Aen.* 9.448).[50] Moreover, as well as the actual city at any given time, we should also take into account the inhabitants' image or perception of the city, and at another level again a sort of Platonic idea of the city, which individuals may strive to realise or move towards. This individual vision (or, indeed, competing individual visions) incorporates a kind of precognition of possible futures and lies behind the Augustan building and restoration programme.[51] In Ovid's celebration of the New Rome (*AA* 3.113-28) there may be a note of mockery of the past which Augustus might find embarrassing, but the celebratory tone nevertheless finds an echo in Augustus' pride at finding a brick Rome and leaving a marble one (Suetonius *Divi Augusti Vita* 28) and in his account of the programme in the *Res Gestae* (19-21).

> simplicitas rudis ante fuit: nunc aurea Roma est,
> et domiti magnas possidet orbis cpes.
> aspice quae nunc sunt Capitolia, quaeque fuerunt:
> alterius dices illa fuisse Iovis.

Curia, concilio quae nunc dignissima tanto,
   de stipula Tatio regna tenente fuit.
quae nunc sub Phoebo ducibusque Palatia fulgent,
   quid nisi araturis pascua bubus erant?
prisca iuvent alios: ego me nunc denique natum
   gratulor: haec aetas moribus apta meis.
non quia nunc terrae lentum subducitur aurum,
   lectaque diverso litore concha venit:
nec quia decrescunt effosso marmore montes,
   nec quia caeruleae mole fugantur aquae:
sed quia cultus adest, nec nostros mansit in annos
   rusticitas, priscis illa superstes avis.

Ov. AA 3.113-28

Before, life was rough and plain: now Rome is made of gold, and owns the great wealth of a tamed world. See what the Capitol is now, and what it was: you'd say they belonged to different Jupiters. The Senate-house, which now is most worthy of such a council, was made of wattle when Tatius held the kingship. The Palace which gleams under Phoebus and our leaders – what was it but pasture for oxen about to plough? Antiquity may please others: I congratulate myself for having been born in this time. This age suits my ways. Not because now pliant gold is drawn out of the earth, nor because pearls come, picked from remote shores, nor because mountains shrink as marble is dug out, nor because blue waves are put to flight by moles, but because refinement has come, and countrified ways have not lasted into our times, to outlast our ancient grandsires.

The *Ars Amatoria* postdates the *Eclogues* by some 40 years, but Rome's emergent splendour was already in the mind of Virgil's audience, and Virgil makes this manifest in the opening *Eclogue*.

urbem quam dicunt Romam, Meliboee, putavi
stultus ego huic nostrae simile, quo saepe solemus
pastores ovium teneros depellere fetus.
sic canibus catulos similis, sic matribus haedos
noram, sic parvis componere magna solebam.
verum haec tantum alias inter caput extulit urbes
quantum lenta solent inter viburna cupressi.

Ecl. 1.19-25

The city they call Rome, Meliboeus, I thought – fool as I was – was like this one of ours, to which we shepherds are used often to drive the tender offspring of the sheep. Just so I knew puppies are like dogs, kids like their dams; just so I used to compare great things to small. But this city lifted[52] its head among others as much as the cypress-trees among the pliant guelder-rose.

For a moment the Roman audience can see Rome through Tityrus' eyes and can both laugh at his simplicity and empathise with his awe-struck amazement (*Ecl.* 1.19-25): Virgil's audience is native to a city which astounds other people, and rightly, they may feel. The same device of conveying the force of something amazing by looking through another perspective is used in Ovid's *Metamorphoses,* when the apparently (and, of course, actually) impossible feat of human flight is performed, and the sense of how astonishing this would be is conveyed not simply by describing the impossible – and therefore hard to imagine – act but by presenting it through the emotional lens of an amazed bystander (*Met.* 8.217-20).

Cities (*urbes*) generally, or 'the city' (*urbs*), are mentioned only in *Eclogues* 1, 8, and 9.[53] In the *Eclogues* – though not in Theocritus' *Idylls,* where civilised urban contexts are quite often present – they are at the fringe of the bucolic world and most imminent in those *Eclogues* which can be considered to be on the *outside* of the collection, 1 and 9 (if we take 10 – in which Virgil has entered Arcadia and Gallus has with only partial success – as a portal outside the set of rings made up by the other nine). This inner and outer division repeats itself at large in the use of place-names. Outside Eclogue-land (but referred to in the Eclogue-book), are places that are remote or dangerous, or both, mythical (= poetic) places, or places appearing only in figures of speech rather than as places with a location in any relationship with the settings of the *Eclogues.*

Cremona and Mantua

Cremona and Mantua should be mentioned here as threatened by the very same land-confiscations which in the symbolism of the *Eclogues* stem from the city as represented by Rome. They are also pointed up as real places in the real world by means of their appearance in an unfinished song which is addressed to the real Varus (*Ecl.* 9.26) and sung by a Menalcas who here stands for Virgil. It might be objected that the ontological status of these two cities in Eclogue-land is reduced, because the evidence for them is indirect or second-hand. However, the issues of reality and embedded representation will be treated further, along with the appearance inside the *Eclogues* of Virgil and other poets, and therefore it will be enough here to observe that their appearance at least cuts against any simplistic polarity between town and country in the book. They are affected by the reality of Rome just as is the woodland habitat of the bucolic natives.

The Mincius

The Mincius is very different from either the Timavus or Rome. The Timavus is both an entity inside the Eclogue-book, and a place in the real world of the book's audience. Virgil's reference to it in the eighth *Eclogue* marks an edge between the world described in the poems and the real world outside the poems. Within the *Eclogues,* it marks also the edge between the benign landscape inhabited by the bucolic natives and the harshnesses outside – which of course reflects the context of the real world. Both inside the book and in the real world outside, the Timavus contributes to defining the limits of bucolic space. Somewhat similarly, Rome is the real place in which the audience of the *Eclogues* lives,[54] and a place referred to in the poems. Within the book, it is not part of the bucolic landscape as such, but has an influence which reaches into the heart of that landscape and disturbs it. Outside the book, in the real world, Rome's influence also reaches into Italy – an Italy which includes the Cremona and Mantua referred to inside the book (*Ecl.* 9.27-8). The space inside the poems reflects the space in which the poems exist; representations of the latter reach into and become part of the former. However, while there is a sense in which the Timavus and Illyricum mark the bounds both between Italy and not-Italy and between inside and outside the bucolic world, Rome can be seen as both Italian and *non*-bucolic. By contrast, the Mincius – another real place, the North Italian river on which Mantua stands – appears not only inside the Eclogue-book, but actually within its bucolic landscape, and is, moreover, fully harmonised with and integrated into this landscape.

In the seventh *Eclogue*, Meliboeus tells an unspecified audience[55] how at some time in the past he heard, at Daphnis' instigation, a song competition between Corydon and Thyrsis. According to the wish of the Muses, he now relays this competition to the audience. Near the start of the poem, Meliboeus tells us what Daphnis said in order to encourage him to come and listen, and Daphnis' words include a description of the Mincius (complete with a deictic *hic*, 'here').[56] This poem, however, also contains references to Hybla, Sardinia, and Arcadia, which can only coexist with the Mincius in a poetic and not a geographical sense.

If we take the references to Hybla (7.37) and Sardinia (7.41) as merely poetic comparisons, i.e. as more or less figurative language, we ought still to have some residual curiosity about the language of shepherds who barely ever seem to travel beyond the local town, and even that only rarely, but whose talk and song is laced with decorative allusions to Mediterranean locations.[57] However, we might additionally wonder if there is a Sicilian tinge even about the Mincius, on the grounds that the poetry of the *Eclogues* as a whole is emphatically and repeatedly Sicilian poetry.[58] If a tree can be both a beech and a Theocritean oak, or if Menalcas can be both a Menalcas and Virgil (and likewise Tityrus), a place can be two (or three) places at once as well.

Arcadia (ii) *and the Mincius*

Be that as it may, the references to Arcadia seem much more obtrusive in the text than those to Hybla and Sardinia; they pose more of a problem and oblige the audience to be aware of the geographical disharmony. We need, therefore, to have a close look at the opening of the seventh *Eclogue*.

> *Meliboeus:* forte sub arguta consederat ilice Daphnis,
> compulerantque greges Corydon et Thyrsis in unum,
> Thyrsis ouis, Corydon distentas lacte capellas,
> ambo florentes aetatibus, Arcades ambo,
> et cantare pares et repondere parati.
> huc mihi, dum teneras defendo a frigore myrtos,
> uir gregis ipse caper deerrauerat; atque ego Daphnim
> adspicio. ille ubi me contra uidet: 'ocius' inquit
> 'huc ades, o Meliboee; caper tibi saluos et haedi,
> et, si quid cessare potes, requiesce sub umbra.
> huc ipsi potum uenient per prata iuuenci;
> hic uiridis tenera praetexit harundine ripas
> Mincius, eque sacra resonant examina quercu.'
> quid facerem? neque ego Alcippen, nec Phyllida habebam,
> depulsos a lacte domi quae clauderet agnos,
> et certamen erat, Corydon cum Thyrside, magnum.
> posthabui tamen illorum mea seria ludo.
> alternis igitur contendere uersibus ambo
> coepere; alternos Musae meminisse uolebant.
> hos Corydon, illos referebat in ordine Thyrsis.
>
> *Ecl.* 7.1-20

By chance, Daphnis had settled under the rustling ilex, and Corydon and Thrysis had driven their flocks together, Thyrsis of sheep, Corydon of goats with udders distended with milk, the two of them flourishing in youth, Arcadians both, and ready and matched to sing and respond. This is where, while I shielded the tender myrtles from the cold, the he-goat of the flock himself had wandered off to, and I noticed Daphnis. When he saw me in front of him, 'Quickly,' he said, 'come here, Meliboeus – your goat and kids are safe – and rest under the shade if you can take the time. The bullocks will come here by themselves through the meadows to drink. Here Mincius edges the green banks with tender reed, and bees are humming from the sacred oak.' What was I to do? I had no Alcippe or Phyllis at home to pen the weaned lambs, and it was going to be a great contest – Corydon with Thyrsis; I postponed my serious stuff for their play. Therefore, they both began to contend in alternating verse; the Muses wanted alternate verse recalled. Corydon delivered these, Thyrsis those, in turn.

The poem begins with a conspicuously typical piece of bucolic iconography. Daphnis,[59] whose death and apotheosis is somehow central to the bucolic myth and figures in the opening poem of Theocritus' *Idylls*, is sitting under a tree just as Tityrus does at the opening of Virgil's Eclogue-book. Nearby are the flocks of the two most typical bucolic animals, sheep and goats. They are the flocks of Corydon[60] and Thyrsis,[61] two names which tell Meliboeus that their singing will be a great contest (7.16), and we recognise here the song contest as an archetypal bucolic situation. Both, Meliboeus tells us, are at the peak of their power, *florentes aetatibus* (7.4), and both, he says, are Arcadians.[62] This additional detail prepares for the description of their readiness to take part in song-exchange: rather than telling us that Corydon and Thyrsis are international singers whose tour has brought them near Mantua,[63] Meliboeus indicates that they are simply exceptionally, or perhaps archetypally, good singers. Meliboeus tells us, moreover, that Corydon has lived up to his performance ever since (7.70): there is no hint that he belongs, or came from, anywhere else (or had to return there subsequently). People around the Mincius can *be* Arcadian, and Arcadian here means paradigmatically representative of bucolic natives. This is reinforced a little later in the poem (7.26), when Thyrsis uses the word almost synonymously, as it were, with the programmatic *pastores*. The place where the bucolic natives live is a single place characterised repeatedly by typifying representation[64] and by its uniform flora, fauna, population, economy, culture, geography, and climate; it can be either Italy, Sicily, or Arcadia, or any two or three at once, just as it shows signs of being spring, summer, or autumn, or all three combined, but not winter (except for Gallus).

Arcadia (iii), Gallus, and Eclogues 10

Arcadia is mainly referred to late in the Eclogue-book[65] (though references to Pan may be felt to reinforce such presence as it has[66]). One might perhaps argue that such is the timelessness and homogeneity of the bucolic world that the force of the reference in the seventh *Eclogue* extends retrospectively, but the matter is complicated rather than simplified by its appearance in the tenth *Eclogue*.

More places are named in the tenth *Eclogue* than any other, and therefore there is a case for treating them *en bloc*.[67] The figure is 18; elsewhere the range is from 0 (*Ecl.* 3) to 13 (*Ecl.* 6, itself an exceptional poem in other ways, not excluding the fact that Gallus features in this poem too). The average figure is 6.4 per eclogue, and there is a mode of 6, and in terms of absolute figures 6 is the number of place-names that is more frequently recurring. Of the 18 in the tenth *Eclogue*, 11 – already a high number – are in Gallus' speech.

Virgil begins the poem by addressing in his own voice a Sicilian spring[68] (suggesting a Theocritean-bucolic source of inspiration) and asking for permission to do one more song, this one for Gallus. After the introductory gambits Virgil indulges in a geographical fantasy in which Gallus is neither quite in Arcadia, nor not, apparently.

> quae nemora aut qui uos saltus habuere, puellae
> naides, indigno cum Gallus amore peribat?
> nam neque Parnasi uobis iuga, nam neque Pindi

ulla moram fecere, neque Aonie Aganippe.
illum etiam lauri, etiam fleuere myricae;
pinifer illum etiam sola sub rupe iacentem
Maenalus et gelidi fleuerunt saxa Lycaei.
stant et oues circum; nostri nec paenitet illas,
nec te paeniteat pecoris, diuine poeta:

Ecl. 10.9-17

What groves or what glades held you, Naiad girls, when Gallus was dying in a love he did not deserve? for not the ridges of Parnassus, nor of Pindus held you back, nor Aonian Aganippe. But even the laurels, even the tamarisks wept for him: even pinebearing Maenalus and the rocks of chill Lycaeus wept for him, lying beneath a lonely cliff. The sheep too stand round; they are not ashamed of us, do not you be ashamed of the flock, divine poet:

The passage starts with a reworking of Theocritus:

Begin, my Muses, begin the herdsman's song. I am Thyrsis from Etna, Thyrsis whose voice is sweet. Where were you, Nymphs, where were you when Daphnis wasted away? In the lovely valleys of Peneus or Pindus? Certainly you were not frequenting the great stream of Anapus, nor the watch-tower of Etna, nor the sacred water of Acis.

Theocr. *Id.* 1.64-9

In Theocritus the setting is clear and specific: Sicilian Thyrsis laments Sicilian Daphnis, and wonders in what other place the Nymphs were when Daphnis wasted away. Virgil, however, has transferred the scene to a new poetic context in which it is simply not possible to localise Gallus, the Naiads, and Virgil in relation to each other in a spatial or geographical sense. If the Naiads were not 'there' for Gallus, it does not mean we place in a relationship with each other the (bucolic sounding) groves and glades which detain them and the (equally bucolic sounding) laurels and tamarisks which – in some sense – *are* 'there' for him. Even line 14 does not unequivocally place Gallus at or near the Arcadian mountains of Maenalus and Lycaeus. The setting is literary-poetic and symbolic rather than a representation, however stylised, of a real or poetic location.[69] In the foreground we have two figures, Gallus and Virgil, playing the parts usually allotted to the singing herdsmen of Eclogue-land. The one's address to the other (via the Naiads) is Theocritean – indeed, it is more than simply Theocritean: it is archetypally Theocritean, and archetypally bucolic too. In the *Idyll* on which Virgil is drawing, Thyrsis and an unnamed goatherd meet in a pastoral setting, and Thyrsis is encouraged with the promise of three kids and a carved cup to repeat the lament for Daphnis which he used in contest with one Chromis of Lybia. Thyrsis is said to be the best of herdsman-singers (20), the poem alludes to the form of the song-competition (23), and Daphnis is both the legendary originator of bucolic poetry, and its authoritative subject matter (cf. V. *Ecl.* 5). Furthermore, this poem, *Idyll* 1, appears to have been regularly placed first in ancient collections of Theocritus' poetry, and Virgil himself uses a transformation of the motif of the carved cup in *Eclogue* 3 (36ff.). The whole of Virgil's passage (and the rest of the *Eclogue* too is essentially a development of this) takes two generically distinct poetic figures, sets them in the context of the iconography of poetry, and weaves them into an intertextually poetic texture so that Gallus is cast as the dying Daphnis.

If we ask where Gallus was when he was perishing from love at the outset of *Eclogues* 10, the answer would have to be something like 'in his poetry.' For the Roman audience Gallus was an elegist, soon to become one of Ovid's four canonic elegists (Ov. *Tr.* 4.10.63ff.; cf. Quint. 10.1.93; cf. Prop. 2.34). Here, however, the Naiads – who seem to be Muses (cf. *Eclogues* 7.21) – fail to assist the love-poet Gallus.[70] At the same time, Virgilian bucolic does provide at least commiseration or a lament, both in the sense that this *Eclogue* is Virgil's lament for Gallus (just as Theocritus gives us Thyrsis' lament for Daphnis), and in the sense that Virgil depicts bucolic icons – the tamarisk (*myricae*),[71] Maenalus,[72] sheep – in mourning poses. Within the tenth *Eclogue*, bucolic and elegy are being weighed up against each other.

There is clearly an awareness of generic difference, of difference between Virgilian and Gallan poetry here.[73] It is enhanced by Virgil's injunction to Gallus not to be ashamed of sheep (= bucolic; 17), and by the procession of clearly bucolic visitors who tell Gallus off for his elegiac folly: a shepherd (*upilio*, 19), swineherds (*subulci*, 19),[74] Menalcas (= ?Virgil, 20), Apollo (21),[75] Silvanus (24), and Pan, the god of Arcadia (*Pan deus Arcadiae*; 26) – whom Virgil has himself seen (26-7) –, all of whom together are addressed by Gallus as singing Arcadians (31-3).

We should not visualise these Arcadian visitors as coming from Arcadia to another place where Gallus is. Rather what matters is the symbolism of different kinds of poetry, specifically bucolic and that other kind in which the poet is mad with love (21-2) and besotted with a woman (Lycoris) who pursues another man through the contemporary Roman world of snow and military camps. The divide is not total, for Pan illustrates his understanding of love problems with bucolic imagery, but even so the Arcadian world and bucolic song remain – for Gallus – enviable but alien (the mountains belong to the Arcadians, not to him; 32). Gallus wishes forlornly that he might have had the bucolic lifestyle (35-43), but his vision of the bucolic world is irredeemably contaminated with that other wish-figure of his, Lycoris,[76] and he expresses a desire that the Arcadians might have sung his love – or his elegies (*amores*, 34)[77] on the bucolic pipe (*fistula*). Gallus' bucolic aspiration is defeated by being unable to free itself from elegiac baggage.

62

4. Places in and out of Eclogue-land

Lycoris, who belongs recognisably to elegy, is set in a harsh, unbucolic real-world of Alpine and Rhenish cold (47). These place-names are perhaps even more inimical to the bucolic ideal than the presence of Rome is in *Eclogue* 1. They belong to the Roman world – and that is part of their alienness in the *Eclogues* - but they belong to the part that is – doubly ironically – both alien in the elegiac tradition (they are located well outside Rome), but also present (we are told) in Gallan elegy.[78] A complex net of othernesses builds up here, and, entangled, Gallus falls between the two stools of elegy and bucolic.

This betweenness persists, and goes on manifesting itself through place-names.

> ibo et Chalcidico quae sunt mihi condita uersu
> carmina pastoris Siculi modulabor auena.
> certum est in siluis inter spelaea ferarum
> malle pati tenerisque meos incidere Amores
> arboribus: crescent illae, crescetis, Amores.
> interea mixtis lustrabo Maenala nymphis,
> aut acris uenabor apros; non me ulla uetabunt
> frigora Parthenios canibus circumdare saltus.
> iam mihi per rupes uideor lucosque sonantis
> ire; libet Partho torquere Cydonia cornu
> spicula; tamquam haec sit nostri medicina furoris,
> aut deus ille malis hominum mitescere discat!
> iam neque Hamadryades rursus nec carmina nobis
> ipsa placent; ipsae rursus concedite, siluae.
> non illum nostri possunt mutare labores,
> nec si frigoribus mediis Hebrumque bibamus,
> Sithoniasque niues hiemis subeamus aquosae,
> nec si, cum moriens alta liber aret in ulmo,
> Aethiopum uersemus ouis sub sidere Cancri.
> omnia uincit Amor: et nos cedamus Amori.'

Ecl. 10.50-69

I will go and practise the songs I composed in Chalcidic verse on the reed of the Sicilian shepherd. It is fixed: I prefer to endure in the woods among the dens of wild beasts and carve my love (*amores*) on tender trees: as they grow, you too will grow, my love (*amores*). Meanwhile, among the Nymphs I will range on Maenala or hunt fierce boars. No cold will forbid me surrounding the Parthenian glades with hounds. Already I seem to myself to go over the cliffs and sounding groves, I want to shoot Cydonian arrows from my Parthian bow (*cornu*) as if this could be medicine for my madness, or that god could learn from the ills of men to grow mild. Now no more do Hamadryads nor songs themselves please me; again, you woods, give in. My toil cannot alter him, not if I should drink from Hebrus in midmost cold and undergo Sithonian snows of watery winter, nor if, when dying bark dries on lofty elm, I steered Aethiopian sheep under the constellation of Cancer. Love conquers all: I too must give in to Love.'

In this passage, Gallus says he will modulate his Chalcidic songs on the reed pipe of the Sicilian shepherd (50-1).[79] *Avena* and *pastor* are thoroughly established as programmatic words by now and definitively indicate bucolic; 'Sicilian' (51) refers to Theocritus. 'Chalcidic', however, refers to a different kind of poetry, that of Euphorion (or perhaps Theocles, founder of elegiacs), and so Gallus shows a similar kind of crossgeneric confusion to that earlier in line 34 (*amores* vs *fistula* = elegy vs bucolic). His decision is fixed (*certum est*, 52) and described in terms abounding in bucolic apparatus, but also containing a number of oddities. The carving of poems on trees (53-4) may resemble the bucolic texts on *fagus* at *Ecl.* 5.13, and is located in the woods (*in silvis*; 10.52). *Silvae* are programmatic elsewhere in the *Eclogues*, and the word is suggestive of a title at 4.3 (cf. also 6.2), but the text here is Gallus' very elegiac sounding (and perhaps titular) *amores*. By writing his love(s) on trees in the woods, will he turn his *Amores* into a *Silvae*? He will, moreover, range over Maenalus (55), or hunt boar (56), but hunting boar is a low-profile activity elsewhere in the *Eclogues*. He will, besides, be hunting with dogs (dogs are rare in the *Eclogues*, and no others are hunting dogs) in Parthenian glades (56-7). *Parthenius* may be an Arcadian mountain, but the adjectival form used surely allows us to think also of Parthenius, author of the collection of synoptic mythological love stories dedicated to Gallus (the *Erotica Pathemata*) and said in the dedicatory epistle to be suitable for him to turn into hexameters and elegiacs. Gallus' interest in hunting is very emphatic, and in itself rather odd in Eclogue-land, but in addition his bow is Parthian (59) and his arrows are Cydonian (59); both places belong to the Roman world rather than the world of bucolic. As the passage proceeds, Gallus' dream evaporates. He cannot be delighted by nymphs (62),[80] by song, or by *silvae* (63; again connoting bucolic poetry).[81] He ends, hopelessly, by envisaging lack of consolation from drinking water from the river Hebrus (65), enduring Sithonian (66) snows or herding Ethiopian (68) sheep, and with these names – all more at home in other genres – he strays further and further away from names natural to Eclogue-land.[82]

The final picture is of Virgil, in his own person and in his capacity as poet (70), performing the bucolic activity of weaving hibiscus (71) – fully at home, that is to say, in the world of the *Eclogues*, and dramatically contrasted with Gallus, whose bucolic attempt he has, for a while, hosted.[83]

Places: Conclusion

The Eclogue-book contains a space; everything in the book is – in one sense – part of the space. Paradoxically, on the other hand, the Eclogue-book builds a picture of bucolic space; in this sense, the book contains in itself elements that are both inside and outside the space with which it is concerned. Place-names help plot what is inside and what is outside the bucolic ideal. On the inside we find Mincius, Sicily, and Arcadia. 'Arcadia' is chiefly important in precisely the speech of a character who hankers after the ideal, but cannot realise it. This bucolic space as a whole does not have a single name. Rather, several names are used in order to build layers in the depiction, and to suggest things about the complexities of its boundaries.

Climate, Time, Geology, Geography

There is more, of course to the geography of Eclogue-land than flora, fauna, and place-names. In this section I consider climate and the natural geography of bucolic space,[1] and, as a necessary corollary, time.

Climate and time

Time has a more transparent and contingent profile in Classical literature than in modern. Although the fleetingness of human existence is a recurrent Classical motif, there is nothing in Classical literature like Proust's variety of perspectives on the psychology of the perception of time. There is nothing like the hero's obsessive tracking of clock-time – while, ironically, the action is virtually stagnant – that we see in Knut Hamsun's *Sult* (*Hunger*, 1890). In Classical genres, time is the medium for the events of narrative, biography, history, and seasonal change. However, partly for this very reason, that it manifests itself largely as conditioned by generic features, it is not uniformly treated, and generic differences make themselves felt.

There is a number of ways in which time in the *Eclogues* is generically distinct. First of all, the seasons in the collection are significant; one poem is in one season, one in another.[2] The seasonal profile, however, is not uncontrolled or random. Rain and wind are not foregrounded,[3] and winter is almost completely absent except in the tenth *Eclogue*, where it has an insistent presence in connection with Gallus the elegist.[4] In *Eclogue* 2 there is a hint that the seasons are – as in Dutch flower painting – somewhat amalgamated in a uniform benignity. This impression fairly easily translates itself to the level of the collection as a single organic unity rather than a set of individual poems (as with the issue of the autonomy of the individual eclogue as regards place and characters).[5] But over and above this, time itself is different in this genre from others.

The *Eclogues* contain traces of narrative time, but they are few compared to most other genres. There are no Kalends or Ides in the *Eclogues*, though there are in the more urban genres, satire, elegy, and Horatian iambic. There are signs of the whole elaborate temporal framework of urban culture, covering hours, days and dates, months, and years, and the patterns of time usage,[6] in these other genres; their absence from the *Eclogues*, as well as the synchronicity of the seasons that we have already noticed, fosters the impression of a partial identification of the temporal setting, the 'now', of the *Eclogues* with the Golden Age.[7] We note the benevolence of the climate, geography, and 'economy' of the poems; we see how the diet and way of life of Arcadia are strongly redolent of the Golden Age. It is true that the wooden cups wagered by Menalcas bear post-golden age insignia (the images of the Hellenistic Conon and the measuring rod of the other carved figure; *Ecl.* 3.41), but they still have the air of belonging (for the bucolic native as well as the reader) to a *quasi-golden* past. This is partly a matter of the value accruing to these (and other) bucolic items (cf. 2.36-7 and 5.85-90),[8] and partly a matter of the patina of antiquity borne by the *wooden* cups which can in themselves represent a remote and rather 'golden' past for Virgil's contemporaries (like the beechen bowl in Ovid's account of the hospitality offered by the pre-flood Baucis and Philemon to Jupiter and Mercury; *Met.* 8.653).[9] The elder Pliny writes that vessels made of beech were prized by men of old (*antiquos; NH* 16.185). In the context of the 'golden' indications in the *Eclogues*, the occasional appearance of – for example – money and land-confiscations seems discordant, but can be seen as anomalous disturbances of an ideal.

On a smaller level, one might take notice of temporal indicators. Epic is sprinkled with time-periphrases marking narrative shifts and stages. Satire is varied in form, sometimes narrative, sometimes discursive, sometimes in dialogue form, but if we look at a sample book there is a variety of time-references.[10] In Horace's *Satires* we find prominently the account of a journey from Rome to Brundisium (*Sat.* 1.5) in which the stages of the journey are plotted in distances and times in a variety of ways. In another satire we find the outline of a day (*Sat.* 1.6.111ff.). In yet another (1.9) we find the stages of a walk through Rome marking the transition of time, and in both 1.6 and 2.6 there is also the demarcation of stages involved in establishing a friendship with Maecenas. In Catullus' short poems in various metres (*Carm.* 1-61), temporal indications are many and extremely varied (although individual poems may lack them entirely), and the position in Horace's *Epodes* and *Odes* is comparable. In elegy too we find a range of temporal structures (see e.g. Prop. 1.3; 4.7). The *Eclogues*, by contrast, are very sparing in this regard.

At the end of the first and second *Eclogues*, the shadows lengthen (1.83; 2.67; here the oxen also return home), providing – in the second – a sense of time wasted on pining away. Silenus bears traces of yesterday's drinking at 6.15, and the poem closes, with the end of the song, with Vesper's appearance (= evening), and with the counting of the flock (6.85-6). The seventh *Eclogue* begins with a rather striking narrative pluperfect tense (*consederat*, 7.1) which resembles a Virgilian narrative introduction (cf. the same tense at *Ecl.* 8.14, *decesserat*), and the poem also contains the idea of work postponed or put later (in favour of song;

7.17). The eighth takes place soon after dawn (8.14-15). The ninth *Eclogue* remembers Moeris singing at the threshold of night (9.44) and has the stages of its journey to town as temporal indications (9.59, 62), and approaches night (63). The ninth *Eclogue* is in this respect both darker[11] and more temporally marked than the generality, and this is in keeping with its greater exposure to the troubles of the outside world. Only Gallus, the elegiac outsider in the tenth, rivals it. Mostly, time in the *Eclogues* indicates the transitions between bucolic work, such as it is, and bucolic song, or the timelessly and eternally repeated close of day.

There is also the relationship between bucolic time and Roman time implied by the openings of the even-numbered *Eclogues*. As we know, the odd numbered *Eclogues* are pure dialogues, whereas the others have a more or less narrative frame. In the introductions to the fourth, sixth, eighth, and tenth (all, that is, except the second, where his presence is more implicit) Virgil makes his own presence as a Roman poet palpable. In the introductions to the fourth, (Pollio), sixth (Varus), eighth (Pollio), and tenth (Gallus) other contemporary Romans also have their presence made felt. What is the temporal relationship between these Roman frames and the bucolic content? We notice that the bucolic action is staged in the past tense in the second (2.1), sixth (6.14), and eighth (8.14) *Eclogues*. On the other hand, the fourth and tenth *Eclogues* represent a bucolic reality contemporary with the poet's own. In the tenth, Gallus tries to live among the bucolic natives, and Virgil portrays himself in the conclusion (10.70ff.) as at home in Arcadia; in the fourth, the bulk of the poem is a prophecy relating to the future from the perspective of Virgil's and Pollio's present time. Thus, the even-numbered poems present an Arcadia which, although it can be described with the past tenses of simple narrative, is also in some sense coexistent with the contemporary world. The intervening poems, inasmuch as they are pure dialogues, present themselves as belonging to a present which is not fixed in a temporal location and is therefore compatible with the timeless 'past' of the bucolic matter in those eclogues with narrative introductions.

The seventh *Eclogue* muddies the water somewhat. Here a speaker resembling the Virgil of the even-numbered poems, but who turns out in line 9 to be Meliboeus, tells of a bucolic occasion in the same kind of narrative past as Virgil does in – say – *Eclogue* 8. On the whole there is little to disturb the bucolic synchronicity of the representation of Arcadia, but its relation to the contemporary Roman world remains ambivalent. The same is perhaps also true if we consider the relationship between the bucolic natives' time and the poet's time. Shadow is closural for the natives at the end of the first *Eclogue,* where it marks sleep-time and the end of the poem (*umbrae*, 'shadows', is the final word); it marks the end of Corydon's wasted day at 2.67 (although he proposes to do at least something practical in compensation even at this late stage; 70-2). On the other hand, shadows also mark time for the Virgil in both his capacity as a bucolic singer and as the bucolic poet and author of the *Eclogues* at the end of the tenth *Eclogue* (10.75-6) where they are again a closural marker. Here, as elsewhere, for example in his appropriation of the roles of Menalcas and Tityrus, Virgil straddles the Roman and the bucolic worlds.[12]

Within the poems there are also traces of 'biographical' time, but again slight. Menalcas is older than Mopsus (5.4) and Damon remembers a scene from his childhood (8.39). Corydon and Thyrsis (*Ecl.* 7) seem to belong to an unidentifiably remote past and there is Alcimedon whose carving of Hellenistic astronomers (3.36ff.) possibly suggests that his artefacts have been treasured like heirlooms. Tityrus in the first *Eclogue* is called *senex* ('old man', 1.46) and recalls an earlier stage in his life (1.27-35). Most, however, seem young,[13] and such 'narrative' as is implicit in poems or parts of poems is fragmentary, giving the impression of a timeless present which contains embedded snippets of past (a childhood memory at 8.37ff.; a famous song contest in *Ecl.* 7; eclogic heirlooms at 2.36-8, 5.85ff.; a past love in the first *Eclogue* (1.30). The death of Damoetas (2.38) is a good test case; the same name recurs in the following *Eclogue*, where, although he is one of the singers, there is no sense of flashback to an earlier time (unlike the set-up of 7).[14] Likewise, the future (represented in, for example, the bleak future of Meliboeus in the first *Eclogue*, or Menalcas' impending arrival in the ninth) does not have a high profile in the bucolic world. The land disturbances figure prominently in the first and ninth *Eclogues*, but this is a structural rather than a narrative or temporal arrangement.

On the larger scale – between the poems, so to speak – there is even less sense of time. Obviously, in a poem like the *Aeneid* there is a narrative time extending from book to book over the whole frame; even in collections such as the individual books of Tibullan or Propertian elegy there is a sense that the individual poems, while they may not be rearranged into dramatically chronological order, still belong to a love-story which has the narrative shape of autobiography. By contrast, there is no sense that the events in the ninth *Eclogue*, say, are palpably earlier (or later) than those of the first.[15] Indeed, there is no impelling temptation to see any eclogue as in that kind of temporal relationship with any other. The impression of a timeless – or detemporised – palimpsest within whose levels the reader burrows is sustained throughout.[16]

Geology and geography

Cornfields, groves, orchards, vineyards, grassy spaces, trees, woods; these are the typical foregrounded elements of the bucolic visual field. They come to represent the bucolic way of life. There are, however, other elements, especially mountains, rocks, rivers, and the sea.

5. Climate, Time, Geology, Geography

Mountains

The unknown (*ignaros*) mountains that appear in the cosmogonic part of Silenus' song (*Ecl.* 6.40) are remote from the normal bucolic world. So too, the wild (*feri*) mountains at 5.28 seem as remote as the Phoenician lions whose mourning for Daphnis they and the woods (*silvae*) attest. The mountains among which Pasiphae wanders pining for the bull (6.52) are more equivocal. The story is a travesty of bucolic love and contains a number of 'normal' features of bucolic flora and fauna translated into the new mythological-erotic context. At 8.59 a mountain provides a place for the lovelorn Damon to jump into the sea from; it is part of Eclogue-land, but also a way out of it. At 1.83 the context – albeit disturbed by land-confiscations – approaches more closely the bucolic standard. Here too, however, the mountains from which shadows fall in the last line of the *Eclogue* seem to mark the edge of Eclogue-land; they are the boundary which Meliboeus will have to cross on his way towards some hostile and remote place like Africa or Scythia.

Elsewhere, however, mountains usually seem to be a friendly and natural part of the bucolic visual field. At the beginning of the second *Eclogue*, Corydon laments to the mountains and woods (2.5), somewhat as Tityrus sings about Amaryllis to the woods at the opening of the first poem. If this seems to allow a friendlier light to be thrown on mountains, mountains seem even more clearly not to be unfriendly at 5.8 where Amyntas is the only one 'in our mountains' (*montibus in nostris*) to rival Mopsus at singing, or at 10.32 where Gallus imagines the Arcadians (*Arcades*) singing of his love 'in your mountains' (*montibus ... vestris*). Mountains throw their voices to the sky in joy at the bucolic Daphnis' apotheosis (5.63) and are the scene of the partially bucolicised Hesiod's Orphic singing at 6.71. Mountains appear as typifying bucolic props at both 2.21 and 7.56.[17] Mountains are, besides, part of the normal world of Theocritean pastoral (cf. *Id.* 7.73-4; Bion *Adon.* 32ff.), as their epithet, Sicilian, at *Eclogues* 2.21 reminds us.

As well as *montes*, there are rock formations – perhaps analogous to those in the sacral-idyllic scenes of Pompeian painting (on which see below). Here also there is a degree of indeterminacy. They may be the typical haunts of bucolic goats (1.76) and boars (5.76), or comprise part of the bucolic visual field (1.56), but there are other more complex references (5.63; 6.29; 10.14, 58).

As well as these generalised references to mountains and rock formations, there are various named mountains. Predominantly these are poetic, and sometimes specifically bucolic (although there are some significant anomalies). The threshold of Olympus (5.56) appears as poetical language for the entrance to the upper world of the gods in the context of Daphnis' apotheosis. Parnassus (cf. Theocr. *Id.* 7.148), Rhodope, and Ismarus (6.29-30) all have poetic associations via Apollo

71

(*Parnasia rupes*, 6.29) or Orpheus. Maenalus (8.22 and the refrain at 21 etc.) is Arcadian and a favourite haunt of Pan (Theocr. *Id.* 1.124); in the eighth *Eclogue* it is used to refer to and characterise Damon's bucolic song. At 8.44f., however, Tmaros and Rhodope (remote at Theocr. *Id.* 7.77) signify the harshness of love. Another literary trope in Damon's song is Hesperus' desertion of Oeta (8.30). In the tenth *Eclogue*, Parnassus and Pindus (10.11) have poetic connotations and Pindus in addition alludes to Theocritus (*Id.* 1.67-8), and a little later we find more poetic mountains, Maenalus and Lycaeus (10.15; cf. Theocr. *Id.* 1.123-4). Later again, the Parthenian glades (10.57) are probably also poetic, by way of echoing the poet Parthenius' name, although the hunting Gallus imagines indulging in there is a doubtfully bucolic occupation.[18] In between, the Alps (*Alpinas ... nives*, 10.47) are part of the characterisation of Gallus' profoundly unbucolic elegy. As well as the geographical distinctiveness of these mountains (which belong to the world of Roman military expeditions), there is also the unbucolic snow, and the possibility that the lines relate somehow to themes or even a passage in Gallus' poetry (Servius ad loc.).

Overall, a doubt hangs about mountains, named or otherwise, and rock formations. They are often part of the bucolic visual field, and sometimes are iconic for bucolic poetry, but they may also hover at the fringe of the bucolic world. Indeed, one might suspect that bucolic poetry and the bucolic poet are themselves somehow outside Arcadia looking in through the spectacles of the Roman poetic field. Once, indeed, the mountains come from a double otherworld, that of contemporary Roman life and Gallan elegy. In addition, the mixture in the same book of the vocabulary of mountains and of cornfields has a clear element of artificiality about it.

Caves, woods, springs, rivers

Various apparently natural features in the *Eclogues* turn out not to be unequivocally natural. First, caves. These first appear in the opening poem. In Meliboeus' nostalgic depiction of his lost bucolic life, he sees himself (1.75-6) as stretched in a green cave watching his goats hanging from a thorny crag (*dumosa ... rupe*). The image is strongly symbolic of the bucolic life. At *Eclogues* 5.6 a cave, sprinkled with woodland (*silvestris*) vine, is a possible setting for the song exchange Menalcas and Mopsus. At line 19 they have entered the cave for the singing. With Menalcas becoming Virgil in this poem (see 86-7), the poem's placing at the end of the first half of the book and in the centre of a set of pairs (1 and 9, 2 and 8, etc.), and the iconic subject matter of Daphnis' death and rebirth, this passage puts the cave as a locus for song at the heart of the bucolic world.[19] Gallus' picture of the caves of wild beasts as part of the setting for elegiac verse (10.52) is strongly contrasted in its generic trappings, in the wildness, and in the use of a different word (*spelaea*, not *antrum*).[20] Thus, not only do we have the cave as a locus for bucolic verse at the heart of the Eclogue-book, but it is also implicated in the generic conflict with elegy which is a major presence in the book. There is another significant cave, the one in the ninth *Eclogue*. Here it is part of the depiction of an ideal bucolic setting to which the sea-nymph Galatea is invited in one of Menalcas' song fragments (9.41; the passage is based on Theocritus 11.42-7).[21] The cave is important as an element of bucolic iconography. We might think of Calypso's cave in the Odyssey (*Od.* 5.68-74), but given the contrast with the 'wild' Gallan caves we might well also think of the artificial caves of Roman gardens.[22]

Woods, too, are suggestive of poetry. As already observed, woods (*silvae*) are strongly programmatic in the *Eclogues*. They appear in a generically defining scene in the opening lines (*Eclogues* 1.5), both as setting and as content – content, that is, of both bucolic song (Tityrus' *silvestrem Musam,* 2), and also, by extension, of bucolic poetry as well. *Silvae*, again as already observed, appear almost to be becoming a book title for the *Eclogues* at 4.3 (perhaps 6.2 also). A number of the trees mentioned individually in the poems also have poetic connections (see under *flora* above), especially the beech. Here one should add that woods are the settings for bucolic caves, but also that on a number of occasions they appear in conjunction with the somewhat ambivalent motif of mountains (2.5; 5.28; 6.39-40; cf. 5.63; 7.66), and, finally, that at 10.63 Gallus' ultimate resignation of any joy in the woods implicates this motif, like that of caves, in the bucolic-elegiac struggle.

Springs and rivers, like caves and woods, have poetic connections. With springs we think immediately of Callimachus. *Fontes* first appear in the *Eclogues* in the opening poem (in which many motifs that will recur throughout the book are first seen). Meliboeus imagines Tityrus among familiar rivers (*flumina*, 1.51) and sacred springs (*fontis sacros,* 52) seeking cool shade. In the *Eclogues*, this situation suggests preparing to sing; the sacredness of the springs, furthermore, makes us think of the famous springs of poetic inspiration. In the second *Eclogue*, Corydon wastes his efforts – including song - on Alexis, just as though he had let wind among the flowers and boars into the springs (2.58-9), and we think especially of pure Callimachean springs. Springs are found numerously thereafter (3.97; 5.40; 7.45; 10.42). Of these passages the last is interesting in that we find yet another bucolic motif taking part in the Virgilio-Gallan generic struggle.

Rivers too (*flumina*) can bear Callimachean signification, but it is not always quite so ready to hand (see 1.51; 3.96; 5.25, 84; 6.64; 7.52, 56; 8.4; 9.40; 10.18). However, the association of song with natural power at 5.84 is very striking. Streams (*rivi*) are strongly poetic at 3.111 and 5.47, but not at 8.87, 101; 10.29 (nor is *amnis* ('stream') at 5.25, or riverbanks (*ripae*), at least in themselves, at 3.94 and 7.12. One should also be mindful of the fountains in Roman gardens, and the stream running through the *Horti Sallustiani*, Sallust's (died 35 BC) garden complex on the north-west side of Rome.[23]

Named rivers can be very strongly suggestive of poetry, but there are complications here. The Permessus (6.64) is the scene of Gallus' poetic initiation. It flowed down and around Helicon, the scene of another poetic initiation, that of Hesiod (*Theog.* 22-3) whose reed pipe is now being handed by Linus to Gallus (6.69-71). Additional stages in the handing down may be inferred by the reader from Callimachus (*Aetia* fr. 2) and Ennius (*Ann.* 1-12V), and later the motif appears in Propertius (2.10.25-6). Of course the Virgilian passage shows regard for Gallus, but one may wonder about this matter of inheritance. Certainly, inheritance is one of the models of how poetry works in the *Eclogues* (see below). However, to the extent that Virgil's sheep earlier in this poem (*Ecl.* 6.4-5) imply any assimilation of Virgil's role to Hesiod's tending his lambs at the foot of Helicon (*Theog.* 22-3), one may be curious about the relative standing of Virgil and Gallus when they both seem to appear as heirs of Hesiod in one and the same eclogue.

The Permessus rose from the spring Aganippe, and Aganippe features in another Gallan context at *Eclogue* 10.12. Neither Parnassus, nor Pindus, nor Aganippe detained the Muses when Gallus was dying of an unworthy love (on this passage see above). In the same poem Virgil associates himself with another poetic spring, Arethusa (10.1), invoking her aid in composing something for Gallus (something which Lycoris too might read). In this poem in which Gallus tries to be a bucolic poet, Virgil is also trying to perform some of the functions of an elegist, and to contain elegiac poetry inside bucolic.

There is another river in *Eclogue* 6. Here the Eurotas (6.83) appears in connection with Apollo's singing: all that Eurotas heard from Apollo is now the matter of Silenus' poetry, summarised in turn by Virgil in the sixth *Eclogue*. Here the poetic river appears to be an all-encompassing repertoire of material for later poets to draw on. Harrison (2007: 47-8) suggests that Silenus represents Parthenius; if so Parthenius is himself being presented as a compendious source of material for later poets.

Apart from these Greek and poetic rivers, there are also the Timavus (8.6) and the Mincius (7.13). These two rivers belong to the real rather than, or as well as, the poetic world. The former points towards glorious public deeds, the latter to bucolic poetry as a Roman phenomenon. If we think of these two rivers, albeit referred to in different *Eclogues*, together, we may see something of the war vs poetry polarity that appears again and more explicitly at 9.11-13 (and in different forms often in elegy). Indeed, we may see this as figuring the public-private polarity that is deeply enmeshed in all Augustan poetry, including the *Eclogues*.

5. Climate, Time, Geology, Geography

Caves, woods, springs, and rivers all enfigure song and poetry. With caves and woods the connection specifically with bucolic poetry is stronger, although the tension with elegy is also visible, whereas with springs and rivers the connection with poetry as a sort of universal abstract is more present, although here too tensions with elegy are visible.

Bogs, mud, stones, sand

Bogs, mud, stones, and sand are exceptional in Eclogue-land. We find bare flint (*silice in nuda*, 1.15) and bare stone and bog with muddy reeds (*lapis nudus* and *limoso palus iunco*, 1.47-8) in the first *Eclogue*. This is, indeed, the most emphatic presence stones have (we do not count mountains and cliffs, which have a category of their own). In this *Eclogue* other exceptional natural problems are also visible: infections and bad pasture are recognised (1.49-50), sickness (1.13), and problems of birthing (1.15). Mud is only elsewhere found at 8.80 (in a magical rite). There is a pathos in the fact that Meliboeus, who is being driven out of Eclogue-land, feels the loss acutely, despite the fact that it is in his speeches that the bucolic idealising tendency is most prone to show cracks. It is also noticeable that the opening Eclogue sets the tone for both the bucolic and the anti-bucolic elements in the rest of the collection.

The remaining stone passages are miscellaneous. At 5.84 rivers in stony valleys, the hissing of the wind, and the beating of waves on shore all fail to delight Mopsus as much as Menalcas' song. These comparisons suggest nature's power is in some respect comparable to poetry. At 7.31 Corydon promises Diana a marble statue as an offering (Thyrsis caps this with promise of a gold statue for Priapus, 7.36).[24] At 8.43 bare rocks (*nudis cotibus*) are the putative birthplace of harsh love. At 10.15 the rocks (*saxa*) of cold Lycaeus are the site of Gallus' dying Daphnis performance.

Sand is found only at 3.87, being pawed by a bull in such an abstract picture (a hypothetical offering) that one cannot say whether the sand is natural ground, or in a preparatory stall.

Bad ground, then, makes its presence felt strongly only in the first *Eclogue*. It makes a dramatic impact in a poem otherwise so determinedly and self-definingly bucolic – apart, that is, from the land disturbances, the proximity of Rome, the impact of soldiers and civic discord (70-1), and villas (82).

Sea

The sea is generally at some remove from Virgil's bucolic world (whereas it appears not infrequently in Theocritus). Sometimes it merely figures in the songs of the inhabitants, or in figures of speech.

75

At other times it is a boundary marking the edge of the bucolic world. In this regard there is a clear difference from the Theocritean world, where one finds both the sea and fishing.

In the first explicit reference to the sea in the *Eclogues*, Corydon sees his reflection in the still sea (2.25-6)[25] in a passage based on lines from Damoetas' Polyphemus-song (Theocr. *Id.* 6.34-8) and in a poem based on Theocritus' own Polyphemus-song, the sea-girt eleventh *Idyll*. In an earlier implicit reference to the sea, Meliboeus and his like, driven out of the bucolic world, may end up in – among other places – Britain, 'separated from the whole world'; here the sea is an emphatic liminal marker. In the last reference to the sea in the collection, in a poem in which the bucolic world is clearly threatened and overshadowed (*Eclogue* 9), it emerges that the road to town (1) passes both Bianor's tomb and the sea (57-60; perhaps see also water, *aquam*, at 9.9).

All other references to the sea are, in one way or another, more remote from the direct experience of standard Arcadians. In *Eclogue* 4 a new heroic age, complete with ships (including a new *Argo*), will precede the new and shipless bucolic Golden Age (4.31-9); at *Eclogue* 5.83 the sound of the sea is one of the comparisons for the delight given to Mopsus by Menalcas' poetry; Silenus' unbucolic song contains a treatment of Scylla and Odysseus (6.74-7); in *Eclogues* 7 Corydon has a quatrain in a song-contest in which he plays the Polyphemus role (although keeping his own name) and addresses the sea-nymph Galatea (37-40); in Thyrsis' response (7.41-4) seaweed is part of a hypothetical and quasi-proverbial (cf. Hor. *Sat.* 2.5.8; *Odes* 3.17.10) comparison, although one which may play at sustaining the sea-setting of the Polyphemus and Galatea motif; at *Eclogue* 8.7 the Roman frame of the poem refers to the Illyrian sea in the context of Pollio's expeditions; later in the poem, Damon's deranged song of unrequited love contains an implicit sea reference in an adynaton figure (8.56), an exaggerated wish to see the world submerged (58), and a profession that he will commit suicide by hurling himself from a mountain into the sea (59-60) – although there is a precedent in the posturing of a Theocritean victim of unrequited love (*Id.* 3.25-7),[26] the Roman reader might also see an echo of the story of the love-sick poetess Sappho's suicidal jump from the Leucadian promontory, and might then infer that Damon's distraught condition has pushed him beyond the bounds of bucolic into the more extreme genres of love-poetry;[27] at *Eclogue* 9.39-43 Moeris recalls a song inviting the sea-nymph Galatea to leave the sea for a bucolic-sounding land world. Here Polyphemus seems to be in the air again, and again the sea is 'other'.

In his use of the sea Virgil draws on a huge mass of material in Graeco-Roman literature in which the sea is a threshold on this side of which one finds the sensible world of experience, but going onto it or beyond it is dangerous or even transgressive.

Natural geography: Conclusion

Flora, fauna, and geographical features make three strands that run through the *Eclogues* in kaleidoscopic permutations. In each set there is a comparatively small number of typical or typifying items which reappear with some frequency. In each set there is also a sprinkling of – so to speak – anti-bucolic items (poisonous plants, dangerous animals, bogs, for example). These circulating and intertwining elements form the setting and content of the inhabitants' singing, and of Virgil's bucolic poetry – they create a bucolic space. However, although the visual field of the *Eclogues* has, in this sense, a uniformity or harmony about it, the selection of natural elements is coherent in literary rather than realistic terms, and the contrast with wildness strongly indicates an artificial landscape.

Cornfields, groves, orchards, vineyards, grassy spaces, trees, woods, and springs map out the typical lie of the land. Woods in particular represent bucolic in various ways. Rivers and caves are part of the programmatic presentation of the bucolic landscape in their capacity as props in the setting for bucolic song, but they are also part of the presentation of bucolic *poetry* (in its capacity as part of the Roman literary field). Caves and woods are implicated specifically in the tension between bucolic and elegy. Some features, however, tend to enter the bucolic picture more ambiguously. Mountains sometimes seem to be a natural part of the setting, but sometimes they seem liminal, pointing to the surrounding worlds of Roman poetry or of non-bucolic. The sea is another boundary, whether between Eclogue-land and the real world, or between it and that which is dangerous (the two divisions are not entirely separate). Some features suggest the intrusion into bucolic space of painful extra-bucolic or even extra-poetic realities. They come from outside the purely bucolic landscape. Stone and mud, for example, suggest the discordant and potentially painful intrusion of real world elements into the ideal landscape.

Geographical place-names are also part of this 'inside-outside' pattern. Remote place-names are used to characterise what lies beyond bucolic space. Here, however, things start to become more complex. On the one hand, remote place-names belong to the 'outside' both for the bucolic inhabitants and for the Roman audience. Inside the *Eclogues*, their otherness helps to define Eclogue-land, but for the Roman audience outside the book they are also implicated in the world of Roman public duties, expeditions, ruling the world. On the other hand, there is a degree of subjectivity about what actually is remote. For the bucolic inhabitants, Rome is itself remote (though the Mincius is not) and ambivalent, whereas for the Roman audience not only is it emphatically present in the Eclogue-book (and indeed bucolic space may itself be seen as peripheral from this Roman perspective), but it is also the centre of their individual and corporate lives.

6

Human Geography

The patterns of human occupation, dwelling, diet, societal structures, and human geography in general are as generically shaped as the natural geography of the Eclogue-book.

Occupations and social roles

The standard animals in the *Eclogues* are sheep, goats, and cattle, and these imply certain kinds of typical occupation. The natives are frequently called herdsmen (*pastores*), and there is also milk and cheese production, and the sale (1.35) of the latter at least. There are sheep-pens and penning. Milk and meat do not seem to be significant products of the cattle, but bulls are yoked, which implies ploughing (cf. 1.45; 2.66; 4.41), and there are cornfields. Vines are grown, trained on elms, pruned, but there is no mention of wine (or eating grapes). There is a variety of fruit.[1] Olives have a Theocritean background (*Id.* 5.31f.) and are fit for bucolic use, but remain in low profile (5.16, 8.16). All this suggests a set of stylised literary images of farmland life – and a generically constrained set at that (there is more detail and variety, where we might expect it, in the *Georgics*): the typical manifestation of the natives – resting and singing while perhaps Tityrus watches the herd – is quite other than the other Roman stereotype of the hardy small-holding farmer ready on the instant to become a soldier or general. On the other hand, the Eclogue-book's apparently indiscriminate amalgam of farming types is perhaps not unrepresentative of small-scale farming.

Both before and after Virgil's time the typology of farming in Italy was varied, but some generalisation is possible.[2] In the south, relatively large-scale cereal cultivation (using chain gangs of slaves) and large-scale stockbreeding with seasonal transfer of stock between summer (upland pastures) and winter (coastal plain stations) probably predominated. In central western Italy (the region around Rome and its main ports), the predominant form was that of the villa estate, with intensive production on medium sized estates of wine, olive oil, wheat, fruit and other cash crops. However, a full picture of Roman farming and agriculture would be much more complex and variegated. We know, for example, of vineyards of various sizes, orchards, and a flower industry actually within the city walls at Pompeii.[3] Outside the cities, smallholders continued to be found, especially in hillier areas and the Po valley. In the Augustan period peasants increasingly became tenants rather than owners of small farms (cf. Hor. *Sat.* 2.2). However, the model of smallholdings on which peasants held a few sheep, an ass (entirely lacking in the *Eclogues*, but present in Pompeian wall-painting), and a plough, and sowed their land with cash crops while pasturing their animals in local scrub and woodland (*OCD*³ s.v. 'pastoralism, Roman' for references) appears in Cato, Varro, and Columella,⁴ and matches fairly well the general impression of work patterns given by the *Eclogues* – insofar as work is represented there at all.

Nevertheless, we should be wrong to think of the Virgilian bucolic landscape as simply an idealised stylisation of real smallholdings, or just an amalgam of Theocritean-style poetry and the farming patterns of parts of Italy. The importance of social life, especially represented by song-exchanges, and the low profile of farming work conspire to make us think rather of villa-estates which the Roman aristocrat would own, visit, and entertain at, and at which farming would take place, but as spectacle and background rather than as a livelihood-providing occupation. Moreover, within the Eclogue-book various polarities can be seen to coincide in the depiction of Eclogue-land (e.g. inside-outside, safe-dangerous, domestic-public, native-foreign), some of which fit the idea of a garden better than they fit either a farm or an estate.

We can easily list the working activities mentioned in the Eclogue-book. Picking fruit (apples at 8.37f., grapes at 10.36), grafting fruit trees (1.73; 9.50); leaf-stripping (9.61) and pruning (1.56; 2.70) are all seen in the background. There is cheese-related activity (1.35, 81); Corydon might do some basket weaving (2.72) and Virgil himself (in his bucolic guise) does so at 10.71. Hunting or the trappings and equipment of hunting are mentioned by bucolic natives (2.29; 3.12-13; 5.60-1; 7.29-30) and by Gallus (10.56), but hunting is not actually performed. By contrast, activities concerned with sheep- and goat-herding (2.30, 33) are much more foregrounded (tending cattle is played down in comparison) – watching and leading sheep or goats (3.1ff.; 5.12; 7.1ff.; 9.1-6; 9.23) are commonly mentioned. Indeed, watching sheep is a bucolic icon (see especially 6.4-5, Virgil as Tityrus; 10.14-15, Virgil's advice to Gallus), and *pastor* is a heavily laden word. At 1.21, it is Tityrus' word for bucolic natives; at 6.4, in its Callimachean context, it almost stands for 'contemporary Roman poet'; at 6.67 it describes Linus, at 10.51 Theocritus. In between these poles are 2.1, 5.41, 59, 7.25 (where it is virtually synonym for *Arcades* – 'Arcadians'), 8.1, 23, and 9.34, and some programmatic connection with bucolic song is often at least in the air. The emphasis on this word is clearly a stylisation with programmatic intent, for the prime occupation of the bucolic *pastor* is singing rather than herding.

Analogous occupational words are rare. Very odd is the presence of the unbucolic word for *pastor*, *upilio* (10.19) and even more odd – given the absence of pigs in the *Eclogues* – is a solitary reference to *subulci* ('pigmen', 10.19). The Gallan contamination of the passage in which these words are found may be relevant. Although Gallus is not the speaker in these lines, we may feel that the bucolic idea is here seen through his outsider's eyes. *Upilio* and *subulci* may reflect Gallan-elegiac difficulty in fitting in with the world of the *Eclogues*, just as the *silvestris/agrestis Musa* (1.2; 6.8; cf. 1.10) becomes *rustica* in a concession made by Damoetas to Pollio's imagined urban susceptibilities (3.84). Perhaps a little surprising because of its rarity rather than because of its presence is *agricola* ('farmer'), only used at 5.80 and 9.61. Fishing is absent altogether (fish appear in figured language at 1.60 and 5.76), despite its appearance in Theocritus.

Against this background, in *Eclogues* 1 and 9 we have clusters of words which stand out starkly in the bucolic context; *libertas* (liberty, 1.27), *peculi* (savings, 1.32), *aere* (bronze = money, 1.35), *servitio* (slavery, 1.40), *miles* (soldier, 1.70), *barbarus* (barbarian, 1.71), *civis* (citizen, 1.71),[5] *advena* (immigrant, 9.2) *coloni* (tenant-farmer, 9.4), and *lites* (lawsuit, 9.14).[6] All these indicate a set of social and economic structures that clearly belong to the Roman context, and are difficult intrusions in the bucolic world. The soldier in particular – given the tension between war and poetry at 9.12-13 – is almost a polar opposite to the programmatic *pastor*. We should not too single-mindedly think from the perspective of the bucolic native (a perspective in which the general absence of such social conditions seems to suggest a Golden Age simplicity); neither *Eclogue* should be taken as a veiled critique of the land-confiscations. On the other hand, we should be aware of the extra-bucolic tension between poetry and war. This tension is much stronger in elegy (where it is represented as an opposition between elegy and epic) than in bucolic, and this difference itself is an index of a further, ideological, difference between the two genres (perhaps also in the air in the picture of Gallus, especially around *Eclogues* 10.44-5). As Roman aristocrats (and Virgil's audience), we can feel sorry for the bucolic natives, but need not feel that we are therefore obliged to oppose the real-world land-redistribution (any more than Horace does at *Satires* 2.2.112-36).[7]

The concentration in the *Eclogues* on the *pastor*-figure is an obvious differentiating factor from other genres, but so too is the rarity or absence of Roman social words. Such social types and terms are prominent in satire, comedy, lyric, and elegy, but not in the *Eclogues* (though note 'masters' – *domini* – at 2.2 and 3.16). Female entertainers are variously visible in lyric, satire, and elegy. Legalities appear in satire, Catullus, elegy, but in the *Eclogues* only at 9.14 (where the rustic notion of 9.15 makes the mention of lawsuits all the more striking). Perhaps most strikingly of all, the vocabulary of *amicus* and *amicitia* (friend, friendship), which is thematic in the *Satires, Odes,* and *Epistles* of Horace, and in the elegists, and represents a core social function in the world of the late republic and early empire, is also absent from the *Eclogues.* Again, in the short poems of Catullus we see, among other types, mistresses, slaves, provincial governors, an assemblage not unlike that of Lucilian and Horatian satire or Roman elegy, but altogether unbucolic.

Occupations, then, in the Eclogue-book are very strongly based on a generically marked picture, and contribute to the artificial nature of its natural geography.

Familial roles

Familial relationships have only a low-level presence in the *Eclogues* (much lower than in Theocritus). Marriage makes an unstable – and destabilising – appearance at 8.17-35, in the exchange-song of Damon in which his character ultimately contemplates suicide (59-60). In the same song, Damon has a recollection of his childhood beloved picking apples with her – or perhaps his – mother (in the corresponding Theocritean passage it is definitely Polyphemus' mother; *Id.* 11.25-8). Menalcas has a father and stepmother at home (3.33). Otherwise, the chief relationships are non-familial: the bucolic natives have transient loves, and as singers they inherit poetic pipes (see 2.36ff.; cf. 5.85ff.) or assume something like master-pupil roles (cf. 5.4, 48).

As well as being in flagrant contrast with the social organisation of Rome, this picture is also in very strong contrast to other literary genres, where familial relationships are significant – often highly significant – presences, even if not always frequent ones. Horace's father in the *Satires* (1.4) is strongly foregrounded (he is, in effect, a model for Horace as satirist), but as well as this there are in the texture of the *Satires* examples of sons, fathers, in-laws. In the *Odes* there are wives, brothers, and children. The personnel of elegy is thinner, largely because the elegiac mistress takes up more attention, but here too familial relationships are found (e.g. Delia's mother at Tib. 1.6.57ff.; Nemesis' dead sister at Tib. 2.6.29ff.; Tibullus' sister at Tib. 1.3.7; Cynthia's sister at Prop. 2.6.12; cf. also Prop. 1.21-2). Virgil's Pollio appears as his brother's brother in Catullus (*Carm.* 12), and elsewhere in Catullus there are uncles, in-laws, fathers, mothers, wives, Catullus' own brother (repeatedly and emphatically), as well as the paternal relationship with which he compares his feelings for Lesbia (72). If we consider in addition the various friends and friends of friends in these genres, a complex social geography emerges, which is very different indeed from that of the bucolic world. In Theocritus too there is a much greater presence of familial and social structures.

Dwellings

In the *Idylls* of Theocritus there is a variety of architectural evidence: there are neighbours (2.71), houses (2.76), gymnasia (4.7), people who live in towns (7.25), and individually owned farms (7.132; 10.16). Architecture of any kind is extremely sparse in the *Eclogues*. Tityrus and Menalcas both have homes (*domum*, 1.35; *domi*, 3.33). Tityrus has an altar, as has the unnamed female sung by Alphesiboeus (8.64, 74, 105), which also suggests a home. Meliboeus has a cottage (*tuguri*, 1.68) with sod-roof (and corn, pears, and goats), and Corydon imagines life with Alexis in a cottage (*casas*, 2.29). The bed Tityrus offers Meliboeus is made of leafage (1.80). Damoetas has a neighbour (*vicinus*, 3.53), which suggests regular abodes, and the guard dog and threshold (*limen*, 8.107) of Alphesiboeus' female role suggest a dwelling place. For the sake of thoroughness, one might add the tomb of Bianor (9.60). Apart from these, there are only – and it is a very remarkable contrast – the villas whose smoking tops are visible at the close of the – in other ways equally remarkable – first *Eclogue* (1.82).

If we think more broadly of the city as an abode, we observe that in extra-bucolic verse, while it may sometimes be the locus of luxury, it is often also a sign of civilisation – the gathering together of humans in mutual protection. In a quasi-Golden Age Eclogue-land, the city is threatening and liminal, whereas for Virgil's audience it is home – and the home of Virgilian poetry readings.[8]

Diet

The social activity of the herdsmen centres on song exchanges: there are no dinner parties (*cenae*) in the *Eclogues*, though they were important in Roman life and in some non-bucolic poetry (especially satire). There is food, however, and this is quite different from that of contemporary aristocratic life and other literature.

There is no visible meat- or fish-eating in the *Eclogues*.[9] There is almost no sign of wine-drinking (at 5.71 wine appears as a ritual offering). The reader is given the impression that the staple foodstuffs are milk, cheese, chestnuts, herbal mix at *Ecl.* 2.10-11 (cf. the anonymous *Moretum*), honey, and fruits. The strawberry tree (*arbutus*) appears at 3.82 and 7.46, in neither case as food for humans. Lucretius places the use of its fruit as food in the Golden Age (*DRN* 5.941; cf. V. *Georg.* 1.147-9, 2.520). Pliny, Columella, and Dioscorides provide corroborative evidence that it was not highly regarded by contemporaries as an edible for humans,[10] and it is unlikely to have been a feature of gardens,[11] although it features in the garden paintings in two houses at Pompeii.[12] By contrast, the strawberry (*fraga*) was eaten by humans. It is picked by children in the *Eclogues* (3.92). Ovid uses picking both the *arbutus* and the strawberry (along with acorns) as a Golden Age marker (*Met.* 1.102-6; cf. Lucr. 5.939-42), and Juvenal refers to stawberries (together with acorns) in a parodic account of the Golden Age (Juv. 13.57).[13] Corn and cornfields are a standard part of the eclogic scenery, but there is no great suggestion that bread – a post-Saturnian food – is eaten. The composite picture assimilates the bucolic natives to standard depictions of the pre-urban Golden Age. Moreover, food is a frequent element in the Roman moralising tradition and a major motif in satire; in both of these literary arenas meat easily becomes suspect, and fish is regularly stigmatised. On the other hand, we notice that vegetarianism could be an issue for some Romans, as later we find Senecas's father putting a halt to his son's foolishly idealistic vegetarianism (Sen. *Ep.* 108.22). The bucolic natives (again) are ideal, but a somewhat amusing ideal.

We can also ask the reverse question: as well as noting what is present by way of food in the *Eclogues*, we can look outside to find what is absent from them. Figs, lemons, and grapes are well attested in art and literature,[14] but although there are vines in the *Eclogues* there is neither wine nor eating of grapes. There is but one reference to walnuts in the *Eclogues* (*Ecl.* 8.30), but only for throwing at a marriage (although this is a Roman custom: cf. Catull. 61.124-8), and not as a foodstuff. There are no mushrooms in the *Eclogues*. Indeed, there is a wealth of food material absent from the collection. The Romans knew of a variety of meats and fish, and none appear here. Also absent are cabbage, turnip, porridge, chickpea, carrot, asparagus, fig, lentil, eggs, mallow, leek, cherry, peach, pomegranate, and radish. It emerges that what is absent is actually very much a hotch-potch of different kinds of food: luxury foods are absent, but so too are many of the simple-life foods of the Roman moralising tradition, and many elements of the standard Roman diet of the upper class and of the large Roman literature of dining. That returns us to what is present in the book, with an increased awareness of the Goldenness of the selection.

Human geography

The visual field in the *Eclogues* often contains fields, orchards, vineyards, groves. Of these, fields in particular are marked out as iconic of the bucolic sphere (cf. *agrestem musam,* 6.8, 'fieldland Muse'). All these are clearly also features of the Italian countryside rather than the geography of the Golden Age. In varying degrees they are compatible with both the world of the Roman *colonus'* smallholding (which features also in the approximately contemporary verse-book of Horace's second book of satires; 2.2) and also that of the aristocratic estate. Thus there is in the visual field of the *Eclogues* an element which can be seen as compatible with the stereotypical image of the countryside as a home for traditional values of decency and hard work. The fences, pens, and folds which appear occasionally belong to the same kind of world (1.33; 1.53; 8.37).

Roads are somewhat more ambiguous. *Via* is only found at 9.1, 23, 59, and 64. Of these, the more prominent and 'real' road leads Lycidas and Moeris to the *urbs* (the other is an innocent part of one of the song fragments of Menalcas; 23). Crossroads (*triviis*, 3.26) are the imagined setting of Damoetas' squawky singing and piping (*stipula* is uniquely and mockingly used for a bucolic pipe only here) in the bantering abuse of Menalcas, and its unbucolic character is therefore appropriate. The existence of roads can be inferred from – for example – Tityrus' journey to Rome, but in such places they remain unverbalised and unvisualised. Where they become part of the reading experience, they, and cross-roads, are largely a discordant element in the bucolic world.

Roads might be seen as joining places, and to this extent they might seem functionally different from boundaries, whose function is separa-tion, but this difference is actually rather illusory. Roads and boundaries belong to the chartered world in which the *Eclogues* were composed rather than being part of the pure bucolic experience.[15] Inside the bucolic world, boundaries (*fines*) are found only in the first *Eclogue* and are signifiers of Meliboeus' loss of and forthcoming exclusion from the bucolic world (1.3, 61, 67).[16] Boundaries – and specifically bounda-ries in the Roman world – are also implicit in the word *patria* ('native land'): this word and the related form *patrios* occur only in proximity to these anomalous *fines* (*Ecl.* 1.3; 1.67) and – in the context of another dislocation – at *Eclogue* 10.46. That is to say, the concept of a homeland separate from an outside most strongly raises its head when loss of that homeland is looming most strongly. It is very striking that at 1.3, at the very outset of the collection, the unbucolic vocabulary of *patriae fines* interrupts the programmatic, indeed iconic, representation of bucolic given in the opening lines: even at the outset of the *Eclogues* bucolic contains an alien perspective.[17]

Nymphs, fauns, and satyrs

Before proceeding to the named people in the *Eclogues*, it seems appro-priate here to consider briefly – and by extension of the notion of human geography – the extent of the presence of nymphs, fauns, and satyrs.

Named nymphs are Nais (2.46), Aegle (6.20-1), Galatea (7.37, 9.39), Arethusa (10.1), and Doris (10.5). None of these is strongly woven into the texture of life of Eclogue-land's inhabitants. Arethusa and Doris are part of a Virgilian introduction, Galatea appears as a sea nymph in exchange-songs, and Nais is a piece of imaginary decoration in Cory-don's love-apostrophe to Alexis. Aegle is the closest to an exception. She turns up to help Mnasyllos and Chromis bind Silenus in the sixth

Eclogue, but the sixth is arguably the least bucolic of all the *Eclogues*, and her role is very slight. Moreover, Aegle has no antecedent in pastoral, nor does she occur elsewhere in the *Eclogues*. On the other hand, she is found outside bucolic, as she was one of the seven Hesperidean nymphs (Ap. Rhod. *Arg.* 4.1428).[18]

Unnamed nymphs – *nymphae* – are also referred to. They can be found at 2.46, 3.9, 5.20-1, 75, 6.55-6, 7.21, 9.19, and 10.55 – not infrequently, in other words. Corydon refers to them together with Nais and they figure in the banter of Damoetas as witnesses to Menalcas' unspecified activity in a shrine (3.9); they appear in exchange-songs and in Pasiphae's neoteric speech in Silenus' song; they are presented as typical Menalcan bucolic content by Lycidas at 9.19, and by Gallus at 10.55. The Libethridan nymphs are the Muses in Corydon's song at 7.21 (cf. Theocr. *Id.* 7.92).[19] However, although not infrequently referred to, nowhere do unnamed nymphs interact directly with bucolic natives in plain description. They do not, in this sense, figure significantly in the 'real' bucolic world at all – and yet they *are* presented as typical inhabitants of the natives' bucolic song. They are a symbolic second-level reality. Likewise, tree-nymphs (*dryades*, 5.59; *hamadryades*, 10.62) hint at, or even stand for, rather than actually contribute to, bucolic content. The sea-nymphs (*naiades*, 6.21) and fauns (*fauni*, 6.27) in the sixth *Eclogue* are quite distinctly alien, appearing as part of the iconography of Silenus, but sea nymphs (*Naides*) can – as other nymphs – stand for the muses (10.10). Satyrs appear at 5.73 as a jolly dance theme in celebration of the rebirth of Daphnis.

In Theocritus, nymphs have a perhaps somewhat higher degree of presence in pastoral *Idylls* than in the *Eclogues*, chiefly in the language of the herdsmen (e.g. 1.11, 65ff.; 5.17, 53, 71), as does Pan (e.g. 1.3, 16; 5.58) and satyrs (4.63). Pan, indeed, appears to be imminently present in the herdsmen's world at *Idylls* 1.14ff. Nymphs have a strong presence in the mythological thirteenth *Idyll* (Hercules' loss of Hylas to some water-nymphs) and Galatea is a sea nymph in the eleventh (see especially 11.62). Much more prominent again, however, is the profile of satyrs, nymphs, and fauns (and Pan) in what seems to be a parody by Lucretius of apparently already existing bucolic conventions (4,572-93; see esp. 581-9). By contrast with this bucolic prominence, the satyrs, nymphs, and fauns have lost some of their presence in Eclogue-land itself, but seem to retain some emblematic force in the texture of the Eclogue-book.

Fauns, nymphs, and satyrs belong in the world of literature, but not *any* literature. They do not belong in the urban genres of comedy, elegy and satire; in lyric they are admitted on a limited basis (see e.g. Hor. *Odes* 1.4). Apart from such evidence as there is for their presence in pastoral-bucolic, they are chiefly at home in Callimachean and post-Callimachean epic-epyllion (they appear in *Aeneid* and Ovid's

Metamorphoses). Despite their role in 'Lucretian bucolic', the casting of nymphs as something like an embodiment of bucolic content seems inappropriate if this is the whole of the background. On the other hand, they also figure in Roman art and – in the form of statues – in the literary allusiveness of the Roman garden, and this is certainly an important contributory factor.

The human geography of the *Eclogues* suggests, under the literary guise of poems about herdsmen, a world that has much in common with the world of the Golden Age coloured with the literary allusiveness of the Roman garden. It is, however, not altogether free from the inroads of the real world.

Named People

The contrast between Virgil and Gallus dealt with earlier is very important, but part of a larger pattern of named people in Eclogue-land. The repertoire of names is a major generic indicator,[1] and it is therefore no surprise that a substantial number of the figures in the Eclogue-book have Theocritean names, and mostly from the pastoral *Idylls* rather than the mythological, court, or other poems. There are, however, significant anomalies, some differences of usage between the two poets, and some puzzles which need a closer look. The material is arranged under the following headings:

Bucolic names
Recurrent names
Non-bucolic names
Special figures – Virgil, Daphnis, and Polyphemus and Galatea
Special figures – Romans
Bucolic charades
Poetry and poets in Rome and Eclogue-land

Bucolic names

The people in the *Eclogues* are primarily herdsmen (*pastores*) who engage chiefly in singing, piping, and singing competitions (*Ecl.* 3, 5, 7, 8, cf. 9). They sing about song and love and on the whole they transfer their loves easily. According to Lipka,[2] at least eighteen people in the collection have Theocritean names (and the figure can be increased by including Theocritean-style names), often retaining Greek inflexional endings. Individual names frequently recur in different poems, where they may or may not represent the same character. Then again, when characters in the *Eclogues* take up Theocritean roles, they may actually assume Theocritean names that are not those of the original Theocritean characters whose parts they are playing: at the beginning of the third *Eclogue* the general outline is Theocritean, but the names come in fact from a different (though still pastoral) Theocritean context.[3] One might think of the effect as like that of a dramatic show in which the performers assume their roles and then take up masks from a small stock, and do so more or less at random since the identities involved are so manneristic.

Recurrent names

Many of the names in the *Eclogues* recur over the collection. The effects of this are rather complex. At one level, there is the cumulative effect of a succession of different patterns – one might think of garlands made of assorted flowers providing something of an analogy (and remember that garland, as anthology, has a metaphorical application which is also relevant to the *Eclogues* as a collection). One might additionally track who is in love with whom as the collection proceeds. Here one finds a kaleidoscopic shifting of patterns as pair-members are shuffled and reshuffled. Usually this occasions no great heartbreak (as in the fluid trio of Damoetas, Menalcas, and Phyllis implied at *Eclogues* 3.76-9 and 106-7), but rather resembles the way the names of love-objects are changed from epigram to epigram in the *Greek Anthology*, its precursors, or, later, in Horace's *Odes*. Against this background, we can see Catullus' use of Lesbia as a marked innovation (one subsequently taken up by the elegists). Then there is also the question of continuity of character. To take some relatively extreme examples, the various appearances of Amaryllis show a high degree of congruity (1.5, 30, 36; 2.14; 3.81; 8.77, 78, 101; 9.22), whereas it is not at all universally accepted that either Menalcas (2.15; 3; 5; 9.10, 16, 18; 10.20) or Tityrus (1.1, 4, 18, 38; 3.20, 96; 5.12; 6.4; 8.55; 9.23, 24; Servius makes this point explicit) *always* stands for Virgil. To the extent that we find a certain indeterminacy of identity attaching to individual names, there is an enhancement of the effect of swapping Theocritean names for Theocritean roles as noted in the preceding section.

Some other test cases will flesh out a range of possibilities.

One of the contestants recalled by Meliboeus in the seventh *Eclogue* is called Corydon. It is a name which has already appeared in the *Eclogues* (*Ecl.* 2),[4] and in both poems the Corydon is in love with a beautiful Alexis (cf. 2.1; 7.55). We may now recall that the Corydon in the second *Eclogue* refers to his sheep being on Sicilian mountains (2.21), whereas the Corydon in the seventh seems to be located in North Italy, around the Mincius (7.13). There is an issue of some complexity here. We might believe that there is one Corydon, who has changed location between the two poems. Alternatively, we might believe that the two Corydons are not actually one person at all. Or we might argue that there is only one Corydon and that one or other (or both) of the geographical identifications is not literal.

None of the three possibilities is free from difficulties. The first, that one Corydon has moved from Sicily to North Italy (or *vice versa*), is out of character with the 'ethnography' of the *Eclogues*. Whereas the attribution of places of origin to a number of people in Theocritus' poems does indeed suggest an awareness of individual mobility, there is little or nothing in the *Eclogues* that resembles this (certainly not the quite different relocation of Meliboeus in the first *Eclogue*). As regards the second possibility, that we have two different Corydons in two different places, this seems too pedestrian and pedantic, especially given the recurrence of Alexis in connection with both. This impression is further strengthened when we recall that Corydon's love for Alexis becomes a virtual symbol of bucolic song when Menalcas quotes the opening of the second *Eclogue* at the end of the fifth (5.86). The third possibility, that the geographical pointers are not an insuperable problem, transfers the question from human to geographical names. Given the emblematic nature of the geography of Eclogue-land and of its place-names, the problem may not be considered very great, the question of identity with recurring names still remains an issue, and one made more complex by the use of both Tityrus *and* Menalcas to stand for Virgil, and at least apparently neither of them always. I have, however, already suggested that this last qualification need not be taken so strongly,[5] and one may certainly observe benefits in particular cases of name-recurrence.

When, for example, in the ninth *Eclogue* Menalcas[6] was visiting Amaryllis and singing on the way the song 'Tityrus, feed the goats till I get back' (9.23) we may wonder whether it is *just* a song,[7] or whether we can think of it as enacting actual instructions to Tityrus. But we may recall that it was Tityrus who was paired with an Amaryllis in the opening *Eclogue*. Perhaps now in the ninth we may see Tityrus as a rival whom Menalcas is interested in keeping out of the way while he makes his visit. Making links between the names can add another dimension to the poems, even if we do not think of the namebearers as fully continuous dramatic entities.[8]

We do not need a reading in which some homonymous characters retain the same identity and others do not, nor one in which all (or no) homonymous characters do so. We want rather a reading in which the details from the contexts in which names occur can be remembered in other poems in which the same names are found. Corydon is neither the same person as another Corydon nor not, but he *can* be looked at from certain directions in either way. We should think of fancy dress parties and rapid changes of dress for swapping parts.[9] The recurrence of names is a much stronger feature in Virgil than in Theocritus[10] and can add piquant possibilities in local instances. In addition, however, it has a cumulative effect, adding to the sense of patterning and artistic composition and arrangement that is manifested in many ways throughout the *Eclogues*.

Non-bucolic names

Some twenty mythological names appear in the *Eclogues*;[11] they are concentrated heavily in the new heroic age prophesied in *Eclogue* 4 and the strangely Hellenistic song of Silenus in *Eclogue* 6. Silenus himself is a mythological figure, and is exceptional in that he is connected with bucolic natives in the narrative of the *Eclogue* in which he appears (*Ecl.* 6). Elsewhere, mythological names may show that the learning of the natives of Eclogue-land reaches out into the world of first-century BC Roman poetry (as with Amphion, Paris, and Pallas at 2.24 and 61). Somewhat similarly, a handful of archetypal poets (including some real ones) are likewise referred to; viz. Orpheus (*Ecl.* 3.46; 4.55; 6.30; 8.55), Linus and Hesiod (in connection with Gallus' initiation at *Ecl.* 6.67-70), Sophocles (in connection with Pollio's tragic writing in the frame of the eighth *Eclogue*; *Ecl.* 8.10), and Arion.

Some ten real-world figures, historical and contemporary, also appear. Personages of Hellenistic science are within the range of the bucolic inhabitants' knowledge (Conon and the anonymous figure at 3.37ff.).[12] Similar, but perhaps more striking and discordant in a world of Greek names, are the references to Roman poets, Pollio, Gallus, Varius, and Cinna, and perhaps also the two bad but unknown poets, Bavius and Maevius (3.90).[13] Virgil's bucolic natives know of most of these figures, and Gallus is a candidate for entry into Eclogue-land, especially in the tenth *Eclogue*. Lycoris, the name used for his mistress in his poetry by the elegist Gallus, is a name that remains forcefully located outside Eclogue-land, and indeed she is a large part of the reason why Gallus fails to settle in Arcadia. As well as Roman poets, a very small number of other Roman figures appear in the book. Pollio, who appeared as a poet in *Eclogues* 3, appears as consul in the fourth *Eclogue* (12-13). Varus is named in two poems (6.7, 10, 12, and 9.26f.). Not a poet at all, he is Alfenus Varus the jurist who served on the land-commission dealing with the settlement of veterans in Cisalpine Gaul (41 BC). There are also the anonymous child in *Eclogue* 4 and Caesar, offstage, in one of Menalcas' songs half remembered in *Eclogue* 9. These Roman figures will be dealt with below.

After we have registered the presence of these categories of non-bucolic names, and observed how they tend overwhelmingly not to integrate with either the bucolic landscape or its population – they are mostly neither inhabitants nor dialogists –, we may turn to a special category: those names attached to natives of Eclogue-land or to their acquaintances, but which do not have a background in Theocritean or other pre-Virgilian Greek pastoral.

Twenty non-pastoral names are attached to figures who seem either to inhabit Eclogue-land on a more or less equal footing with the Theocritean characters or to interact significantly and more or less directly with these natives: Meliboeus (*Ecl.* 1; 3.1; 7), Phyllis (3.76, 78, 107; 5.10; 7.14, 59; 10.37), Alphesiboeus (5.73; 8.1, 5, 62); Galatea (1.30; 3.64, 72; 7.37; 9.39), Thestylis (2.10, 43); Alexis (2.1 etc.; 7.55), Iollas (2.57; 3.76), Neaera (3.3), Damon (3.17, 23; 8.1 etc.), Lycisca (3.18), Palaemon (3.50, 53), Delia (3.67),[14] Mopsus (5.1, 10; 8.26), Stimichon

(5.55), Mnasyllus (6.13), Aegle (6.20, 21), Nysa (8.18, 26), Moeris (8.96, 98; 9.1 etc.), Hylax (8.107), and Bianor (9.60).

In addition to the twenty listed above, a further four non-pastoral names will also be discussed in the following paragraphs. These belong to figures whose integration in the bucolic context is more equivocal. Alcon and Codrus, who appear along with the Phyllis referred to at *Eclogue* 5.10-11, are possibly off-stage bucolic natives, but could be mythological figures.[15] Alcimedon, the craftsman who produced the beechen cups wagered by Menalcas at *Eclogue* 3.36-9, will also need to be considered since his relationship with the Arcadians is not entirely clear. Fourthly, there is also Lycoris (*Eclogue* 10.2, 22, 42) who is drawn into the collection in the penumbra of Gallus.

These non-pastoral names may be considered in four groups: those that, while not pastoral as such, may be Theocritean or appropriate in some way, those that come from other genres, those that remain opaque to us, and, fourthly, the two dogs.

First, there are the non-bucolic names which may have some bucolic connection or compatibility. *Meliboeus, Phyllis,* and *Alphesiboeus* all have names whose meanings are so harmonious with the bucolic world that, even if they are not attested, they nonetheless fit in.[16] Given the prominent siting of Meliboeus' appearance in the emblematic opening of the first *Eclogue* – and the presence of so many programmatic pointers in the first lines – one might wonder if the audience is meant to construe the fact that Meliboeus is a bucolic-type, but not actually a Theocritean name, as indeed a programmatic indication of Virgil's intent to *rework* Theocritean material.

Galatea (1.30; 3.64, 72; 7.37; 9.39) is likewise arguably only partially unharmonious. She appears in Virgil both as a sea nymph and also as a bucolic native; in Theocritus she only appears as a sea nymph, but in the strongly bucolicised eleventh *Idyll*.[17] The sea is definitely less integral in Virgilian bucolic than in Theocritus' *Idylls*, and in the appearances of the sea-nymph Galatea in the *Eclogues* there is generally some sense of the polarity of bucolic and non-bucolic ways of life. This, indeed, is true also in the relationship between Corydon and the Galatea-substitute, Alexis, in the second *Eclogue*. In conclusion: on the one hand, Galatea does have precedent in Theocritus; on the other, it is not in fully pastoral Theocritus. It looks as though the name in Virgil dramatises the tension between bucolic and non-bucolic and hovers on the marine border between the two.

Somewhat likewise, *Thestylis* (2.10, 43) does not appear in Theocritean bucolic, but does appear in the *Idylls*, in that urban mime (Theocr. *Id.* 2) which Virgil turns into a bucolic song in the eighth *Eclogue* (although Virgil does not use the name in that poem). In the second *Eclogue* (where Thestylis makes her only appearance in the book), Virgil seems to make little or no use of any potential alienness in the name. Her role here is as a food-preparer (2.10-11) and as a possible replacement for the alien and ornamental Alexis in Corydon's affections (2.43).

We also find a number of characters who interact with the bucolic inhabitants in some degree, but whose names come from genres other than bucolic and contribute to a subtle index of alienness. *Alexis (Ecl.* 2.1 etc., 7.55) is the first such name in the collection.[18] It is not Theocritean, but is found at *Anth. Pal.* 7.100 (Plato) and 12.127, 164 (Meleager), and suggests strongly the attractive male erotic object of epigram. Not every epigram, by any means, is explicitly urban – or necessarily urban at all –, but many have details of urban culture, and the genre as a whole may be said to acquire an urban resonance. Thus, the different generic affiliations of 'Corydon' and 'Alexis' portend ill for the love of the one for the other, both in the second *Eclogue* and in the reminiscence of it in the seventh (7.53-6).

Neaera (Ecl. 3.3) is perhaps an analogous case:

> *Menalcas*: dic mihi, Damoeta, cuium pecus? an Meliboei?
> *Damoetas*: non, verum Aegonos; nuper mihi tradidit Aegon.
> *Menalcas*: infelix o semper, oves, pecus! ipse Neaeram
> dum fovet ac ne me sibi praeferat illa veretur,
> hic alienus ovis custos bis mulget in hora,
> et sucus pecori et lac subducitur agnis.

Ecl. 3.1-6

> *Menalcas*: Tell me, Damoetas, whose flock? Is it Meliboeus'?
> *Damoetas*: No, but Aegon's; Aegon just now handed it over to me.
> *Menalcas*: O what an unlucky flock, you sheep! Himself fondles Neaera and fears that she prefers me to him, meanwhile this outsider milks the sheep twice an hour while he's watching over them, and robs the flock of sap and the lambs of milk.

Neaera's name is not found in earlier pastoral, but is found elsewhere as a name for mythological nymphs (e.g. Hom. *Od.* 12.133). Probably of much more significance is the fact that the name is found in Parthenius' *Erotica Pathemata* (18).[19] Parthenius dedicated this collection of tales of love-sufferings to Gallus, explicitly recommending them as material for poems in hexameters and elegiacs. We cannot tell what use Gallus made of the collection, but clearly Parthenius did not think such a dedicatory epistle would look absurd. Furthermore, the collection was a literary work, not simply a private document for Gallus: it also had a larger audience among the Greek-reading literate classes of the Romans in mind, and it is this kind of erotic material that becomes more and more important in the Latin poetry of the late republic and Augustan periods. Perhaps Neaera figured in Gallus' work; perhaps by virtue of its being in the *Erotica Pathemata* it might have been possible for

Virgil to think of it as a Gallan-style name. Certainly the story that Parthenius provides gives us a Neaera who adds resonance to Menalcas' love story of Aegon and Neaera. In Parthenius' account, Neaera falls for, seduces, and pursues her husband's friend; in Virgil's context, Aegon is afraid of Neaera preferring Menalcas to himself (at least so Menalcas says).

The name Neaera occurs also in Horace's *Epodes* (15) and later the *Odes* (3.14.21). It was also borne by *hetaerae*, including the heroines of comedies, a background which reinforces the possibility that we may have in Neaera a name characteristic of the kind of love-poetry archetypically represented in Rome by elegy (like the Glycera and Mystes referred to in Horace's *Odes* – 1.33 and 2.9 – as elegiac love-objects). We would have in this case a scenario in the third *Eclogue* resembling that of the Arcadian Corydon in the second, worrying that the generically alien Alexis prefers Iollas to himself. The Menalcas-Aegon-Neaera triangle is not exactly the same as the Corydon-Alexis-Iollas triangle, for both of the rivals in the former, Menalcas and Aegon, have legitimate Theocritean names,[20] whereas in the second *Eclogue* the feared rival, Iollas, is as generically alien as the beloved Alexis. Nevertheless, it is arguable that erotic fear is engendered in both Aegon and Corydon by figures whose names may associate them with love poetry rather than bucolic.

Lycoris' name (*Ecl.* 10.2, 22, 42) is more palpably alien. It specifically signifies Gallan love-elegy, being the name used by Gallus for his poetic mistress.[21] In the eclogue in which she is referred to, Gallus has an ambiguous position. In his capacity as the dedicatee of the tenth *Eclogue* (10.2-3), he is – like Varus in the sixth and Pollio in the eighth – part of the contemporary Roman audience and therefore outside the bucolic setting of the poetry; however, in the tenth *Eclogue* he figures more largely in the body of the poem itself, and, what is more, as someone both surrounded by bucolic trappings and visited by various Arcadians. His inclusion in the bucolic world, however, is not complete – he merely wishes he had been an Arcadian (10.35) and promises rather unconvincingly (50-1) to become a bucolic singer/poet. It is clear that his obsession with Lycoris is the prime factor in preventing his integration. Lycoris is portrayed as outside, and incompatible with, the bucolic world, its values and geography. Hers, rather, is the world – both Roman and elegiac – of *patria* (46), Alps, the Rhine, military expeditions, unbucolic snow, and quasi-adulterous infidelity (10.22-3, 46-9), and her irredeemably elegiac provenance shows Gallus' bucolic aspirations to be sham: for him the bucolic life has no value unless Lycoris comes with it, but the two will not go together. The values embedded in elegy are antithetical to those of bucolic.

There are some names whose provenance and point remain opaque. *Iollas*[22] (2.57, 3.76) figures in the second *Eclogue* as Corydon's appar-

95

ently successful rival for Alexis' heart, and is presented in the manner of an elegiac *dives amator* (cf. Tib. 1.5.47-8, Prop. 4.5, and the comic Thraso in Ter. *Eun.*). Whereas the name Alexis is clearly appropriate for his anti-bucolic role, the implications of Iollas' name are not clear. Although we can say that it is at least unTheocritean, that does not take us very far. Iollas appears again in the third *Eclogue* (3.76, 79), where he figures in Damoetas' couplet as someone who might send Phyllis to him, and in Menalcas' responding couplet as part of a complex triangle involving Phyllis, himself, and Menalcas (or, especially given what is said at 107, a rather more complex geometric figure involving Damoetas too). Iollas' power to send Phyllis casts him as a somewhat unbucolic 'master' type (as in the second *Eclogue* too).

Damon (3.17, 23; 8.1, 5, 16, 62) is not found in earlier pastoral (though the name is common in Greek generally), but figures in apparently archetypically bucolic situations in the *Eclogues*. In the eighth, he is one of the two shepherd-singers, (along with Alphesiboeus) both of whose singing has a bucolic-Orphic quality (2-4), and who take part in a bucolic song-exchange. In the third *Eclogue*, he is an off-stage character in a passage related to the opening of the fourth *Idyll*, but with altered, though mainly Theocritean names. Virgil's dialogists Damoetas and Menalcas stand in for the Battus and Corydon of *Idylls* 4; likewise, Meliboeus replaces Philondas, but Aegon remains the same. Thereafter, the inconsequential banter in the two poems goes in different directions. The point of Damon's name in either the second or the eighth *Eclogue* – if indeed it has one – is hidden from us.

Alcimedon is the craftsman who produced the beechen cups wagered by Menalcas at *Eclogues* 3.36-9. Although Damoetas claims that Alcimedon made two cups for him too (3.44), this could be taken as his comic, or perhaps comically inappropriate, attempt to upstage Menalcas.[23] In this reading, Alcimedon does not actually interact with the Arcadians. The cups wagered by Menalcas, at any rate, figure Conon, who certainly belongs to the third century BC. The other figure represented on Menalcas' cups is anonymous. From what is said about him, he could be Archimedes (also third century) or Eudoxus (fourth century BC). Although the world drawn in the *Eclogues* has an air of timeless undatability, contemporary features such as the *impius miles* in the first (1.70), the proximity of Pollio in this poem, the third (3.84-8), and the major incursion of Gallus in the tenth provide enough of a modern atmosphere for these cups to seem to be treasured from the past – like the pipes given to Corydon by the dying Damoetas at 2.36-8 or perhaps the valued pipe and crook at 5.85-90. However, we do not recognise Alcimedon's name as that of a Hellenistic artist.[24] For Coleman and Clausen the name remains opaque. Lipka[25] suggests an allusion to a mythical Arcadian cave-dweller whose story is summarised by Pausanias (8.12.2-5). However, the story (an Alcimedon's exposure of his daughter and her child by Hercules, and their rescue by Hercules) seems remote both from the bucolic context, and from the Virgilian figure of a craftsman carving Hellenistic astronomers. This name too, therefore, remains mysterious.

Also in the third *Eclogue*, there is the late arrival, *Palaemon*, who judges the song contest (3.50, 53) – an archetypical bucolic role – and who is a neighbour (53) of the contestants. His name, not in Theocritus, is elsewhere that of a sea-god (Plaut. *Rud.* 160; V. *Aen.* 5.823; Ov. *Met.* 4.542). This may seem unexpected, given the small role played by the sea in the *Eclogues* (see above), but we should note how the sea nymph Galatea recurs (see below), how the Polyphemus-Galatea scenario bleeds out into the collection (see below), and how in the sixth *Eclogue* Silenus' role resembles that of the sea-god Proteus in the later *Georgics*. However, it has to be recognised that this does not take us very far.

In the same poem again, in one of the contest-songs themselves, Menalcas refers to two others of his loves before the Phyllis he apparently shares with Damoetas (3.76, 78, 107), namely the Theocritean Amyntas (see *Id.* 7.2) and *Delia*. The latter name is not used for a human in earlier pastoral (or elsewhere in the *Eclogues*).[26] Since Menalcas' couplet responds to and tries to cap Damoetas' brief account of erotic success with Galatea (64-5), we do not look for truth in Menalcas' claim to have two admirers, and one of each gender at that. The absurdity is appropriately increased if we take Menalcas to be suggesting playfully that he has a sort of goddess as admirer (rather as the 'golden apples' – ten already, and another ten tomorrow – that he gives to Amyntas remind us of the famous Hesperidean ones).[27]

Mopsus, not found in extant Greek pastoral, is the name of a mythological seer (Hes. *Scut.* 181; Ap. Rhod. *Arg.* 1.65-6, 3.916-26).[28] His two appearances in the *Eclogues* are quite different from each other. In the fifth *Eclogue* he is one of the two participants in the song exchange into which that poem leads. Song exchange is one of the core scenarios of the bucolic genre, and Mopsus' song is archetypally bucolic, a lament for the death of Daphnis (Mopsus' teacher, according to Menalcas at 48).[29] To this extent it may be a surprise that Mopsus' name – unlike Menalcas'[30] – is without bucolic precedent. This surprise is reinforced at the end of the poem. Here Menalcas and Mopsus exchange gifts in return for their respective songs. Both gifts, arguably, have poetical/bucolic significance: Menalcas (whose repertoire identifies him as the bucolic Virgil at 86-7) gives Mopsus the pipe he learned to sing on,[31] and Mopsus gives Menalcas-Virgil the crook which Antigenes – the name of a friend of Theocritus (*Id.* 7.3) – failed to get from him.[32] Mopsus is a worthy native of Eclogue-land despite his name. Perhaps his importance in the fifth *Eclogue* is itself what legitimises him as an Arcadian native; it would, certainly, be excessively mechanical if Virgil had only used for his bucolic inhabitants names attested in Theocritean pastoral.

The name Mopsus reappears in the eighth *Eclogue* – and in a rather different light. In a song exchange with Alphesiboeus, Damon sings of his doomed love, lamenting that his wife (or 'sweetheart'), Nysa, is now going to marry Mopsus. Damon regards himself as typically bucolic. When he suggests that his beloved Nysa despises the bucolic way and therefore suits his rival Mopsus, it seems appropriate that neither Nysa nor Mopsus has a bucolic name. It is, however, tricky to impute significance to this, given that (a) Damon's own name has no bucolic precedent apart from Virgil's own third *Eclogue*, and that (b) in that respect Mopsus' appearance in the fifth gives him just as good a bucolic precedent as Damon has. Perhaps one could see a subtle wit in the issue of bucolic identity arising among characters whose questionable legitimacy seems more or less equal.

If the implications of Damon's and Mopsus' names remain unresolved, the appearance of *Nysa* (8.18, 26) in the same context adds interesting complications. Her name too does not feature in earlier pastoral, and occurs nowhere else in the *Eclogues*.[33] While the childhood love-story of Damon and Nysa has a Theocritean model (*Ecl.* 8.37-41; cf. Theocr. 11.25-8),[34] the current situation is epigrammatic (cf. Dioscorides, *Anth. Pal.* 5.52) and the concept of marriage is unbucolic. *Coniugis* (18),[35] *uxor* (29), and *marite* (30) all occur only in this *Eclogue* (cf. also *coniuncta viro*, 32).

The situation in which Damon, Mopsus, and Nysa find themselves in the eighth *Eclogue* puts all three of them at some strain in the bucolic context (as may be said also of the anonymous female enacted by Alphesiboeus in the second half of the poem), and their intangible bucolic status may echo this theme.

Phyllis, Alcon, and *Codrus* appear together at *Eclogue* 5.10-11. None occurs in earlier pastoral. The Virgilian context seems to define them as a group in at least some sense. Menalcas asks Mopsus to take the lead in their exchange of songs if perhaps he has to hand any 'flames' (*ignis*) of Phyllis, 'praises' (*laudes*) of Alcon, or 'altercations' (*iurgia*) of Codrus. This looks like an imaginary 'preliterary' generic categorisation of the literary field of bucolic natives – traditional types, as it were, of bucolic songs. We might imagine them to correspond roughly to elegy, epic, and satire or iambic. Beyond this, the names themselves do not seem to help in further defining these imaginary songs.[36]

Elsewhere the topics of song of the bucolic natives are very substantially bucolic, but there are exceptions to this tendency. The major song exchanges in *Eclogues* 3 and 7 are substantially bucolic in content;[37] likewise the songs on the death of Daphnis in *Eclogue* 5. Subject to qualification, this can also be said of the two songs in *Eclogue* 8. The half-remembered snatches of song in the ninth *Eclogue* may be said to be Virgilian or eclogic rather than purely bucolic as such, and a similar proviso obtains with regard to Gallus' attempt at bucolic song in the tenth. Nevertheless, these are still recognisable as bucolic-related. The main contrast to this bucolicising tendency in the songs of the natives is Silenus' song in the sixth *Eclogue*. It is flagrantly mythological, but unlike, say, Menalcas in the fifth *Eclogue*, Silenus in the sixth is not a typical bucolic character; he could be seen as an alien figure. The semi-mythological pair, Polyphemus and Galatea, figure variously in the *Eclogues* and in the songs of the inhabitants, but this is again a special case (with a clear Thecoritean background, in particular in the eleventh *Idyll*). All in all, a mythological reading of the names of Phyllis, Alcon, and Codrus is not excluded so far, but is certainly not particularly favoured.

On the other hand, the internal relations of bucolic natives are recurrent elements of the bucolic repertoire, and two of the three names in question are found elsewhere in the *Eclogues*. Phyllis – potentially a topic for love song here (5.10-11) – appears also in the third, seventh and tenth – always as a stereotypical love-interest-name (3.76-9, 107, 7.14, 59, 63, 10.37, 41). Codrus – here the potential topic for abuse poetry – appears also in the seventh as a bucolic songster Corydon regards well and hopes to equal, and Thyrsis to trounce utterly (7.21-8). This gives at least some support to reading the three as bucolic natives rather than as mythological subjects.

There is a possible countervailing argument. We should bear in mind that in this poem Virgil identifies himself with Menalcas by having Menalcas claim authorship of *Eclogues* 2 and 3 (*Ecl.* 5. 86-7). Mopsus is also drawn special attention to: he is worthy of the Menalcan-Virgilian pipe, and he is the holder of a crook with a Theocritean association (via Antigenes, 5.89, one of the friends of Theocritus in the opening of the seventh *Idyll*). When Menalcas wonders if Mopsus has any poems to hand, the fact that he has here become Virgil may carry a playful suggestion that Mopsus also here stands for a real figure in the Roman literary world. In this case, Phyllis, Alcon, and Codrus still need not be coded references to real poems potentially known to the audience,[38] but the fact that a Phyllis appeared in Callimachus and Alcon in a Hellenistic model underlying Manilius would certainly flesh out the feel of a Roman literary context – as indeed would the idea that Codrus stood for another real Roman poet[39] – without obliterating the bucolic significance of the use of Phyllis and Codrus elsewhere in the *Eclogues*.

In the same poem there is another figure without Theocritean or pastoral precedent, *Stimichon* (5.55). Having heard Mopsus' song, Menalcas (Virgil) praises it and offers his in turn; Mopsus is eager to hear it and observes that Stimichon has already praised it. Servius reports opinions that Stimichon represents Maecenas or Theocritus' father (DServ. at 5.55).[40] Given the literary penumbra about the whole poem – an archetypal lament for Daphnis which in some degree figures also as a Caesar-poem, uttered by a pair of songsters one of whom is identified as a bucolic Virgil, and the other perhaps another dressed-up Roman poet, someone whose repertoire, at any rate, certainly has connections with the Roman literary context – given all this, it is certainly very tempting to read Stimichon as standing for someone of literary-judgemental significance in the Roman world. Maecenas (Servius' suggestion) figures in the *Georgics*, but not elsewhere in the *Eclogues*. Pollio, however, is an attractive candidate. He appears under his own name elsewhere in the *Eclogues*, bucolic natives have heard of him in the third *Eclogue*, and Servius tells us that he instigated Virgil's compositon of *bucolicum carmen* ('a bucolic poem' or perhaps 'bucolic poetry'). Virgil's appearances in the *Eclogues* as Menalcas and Tityrus may tempt the audience to look for other charade-figures, and Pollio seems to have a reasonable degree of fit with the role of Stimichon.

Mnasyllus (6.13) is not found in earlier pastoral. Virgil uses him in the eccentric sixth *Eclogue* as one of the two characters who find Silenus and extract from him a compendious mytho-Gallan song quite unlike the bulk of the bucolic song in the *Eclogues*. The other of the pair is Chromis. It is striking that, whereas Mnasyllus has no pastoral background, Chromis does appear in Theocritus as a contestant in a singing competition remembered by the anonymous goatherd who competes with Thyrsis in *Idylls* 1 (24). The name Mnasyllus also occurs in Homer (*Il.* 2.858; cf. V. *Aen.* 11.675)[41] and it is possible that Virgil wanted a name with some epic resonance[42] to balance the bucolic leaning of Chromis' name, and there may be some significance in the placing of such a name between the Callimachean game with epic with which Virgil begins *Eclogue* 6 and the epic-affiliated material of Silenus' song: as a pair, the names Chromis and Mnasyllus may be wanting to negotiate a space between bucolic and epic. *Aegle*, who appears in the same passage (*Eclogue* 6.20-1), perhaps contributes to this effect. She has no pastoral background and does not occur elsewhere in the *Eclogues*, but is – unusually in Eclogue-land – explicitly referred to as a nymph and has a nymph-name (Ap. Rhod. *Arg.* 4.1428; Paus. 9.35.5; Serv. *ad Aen.* 4.484)); she joins in with Mnasyllus and Chromis to help them as though from epic rather than bucolic.

Moeris too lacks a pastoral background. He appears in two *Eclogues*, the eighth and ninth. His role in the eighth is small: the anonymous female impersonated in Alphesiboeus' song, deranged through love, resorts to magic to bring her beloved Daphnis back from the town. For this purpose she has grasses and poisons gathered for her by Moeris in Pontus (8.95-6) – that Moeris, whom she has herself seen turning into a wolf, calling up ghosts from graves, and transferring crops to other fields (97-9). There is a clear concentration of unbucolic detail here, which is thematically related to, and symptomatic of, the lovelorn woman's derangement. Her indulgence in magic is Theocritean, but not pastoral (*Id.* 2, the source of this section of the *Eclogue*, is urban), and wolves are hardly seen in the *Eclogues*, let alone werewolves;[43] likewise, ghosts do not belong in Arcadia, where death is hardly mentioned, and elsewhere only significantly exceptional graves are mentioned (5.42 and 9.59); Pontus, geographically, marks nonbucolic territory very clearly; finally, the transferring of crops is an unbucolic travesty of the power of Orpheus to draw trees after his song – a power which in its untravestied form is emblematic of Arcadia (*Ecl.* 3.46). Moeris' name is related to Greek *moira* 'fate', and appropriate for the magician's role. Its lack of a bucolic antecedent is also appropriate for a marker of how deranged the character sung by Alphesiboeus is.[44]

The relationship between Moeris' name and role in the ninth *Eclogue* is much more complex. The poem itself features a piece of definitively bucolic space (9.7-9), thought by one of the dialogists (Lycidas) to have been saved by the songs of Menalcas (fragments of whose repertoire suggest that he is – as at the end of the fifth *Eclogue* – Virgil). However, while Lycidas has an exemplary Theocritean and pastoral name (see Theocr. *Id.* 7; [Bion] 2; Bion fr. 9, 10) and has also already appeared in the *Eclogues* at 7.67, and while he and Moeris seem about to begin a typical bucolic song exchange, this exchange never materialises.[45] Instead, the threat of land confiscations looms over the bucolic landscape, and the road Lycidas and Moeris are on – itself an unusual feature in the *Eclogues* – leads to the town (1 62, *urbem*), another ominous feature in Virgil's bucolic landscape. There is, in addition, the threat of night and rain (63), and the point that Lycidas and Moeris have reached has as its landmark one of the only two specifically identified tombs in the collection (59-60), Bianor's.[46] Moeris may himself contribute to these discords in the bucolic scene and setting, if we allow ourselves to be reminded of his role in the preceding poem[47] and in this context the lack of a pastoral background for his name may perhaps be a further subversive element.

The last human name to lack a pastoral background is that of *Bianor*, whose tomb marks the point on the road reached by Lycidas and Moeris at *Ecl.* 9.59, a place of dense foliage. The tomb itself is part of the correspondence between this poem and Theocritus' seventh *Idyll*, where again a tomb acts as a landmark. In the *Idyll* it is that of the otherwise unknown Brasilas, and 'Brasilas' tomb' is generally taken as a piece of Theocritean geographic realism (or pseudo-realism).[48] Virgil's use of the name Bianor, however, does not produce an effect of geographical realism. Bianor's tomb is not a place in Italy that Virgil's audience would recognise. On the other hand, the allusion to Theocritus is oblique: although it reminds us of Theocritus, Bianor's tomb is clearly not the same place as Brasilas' tomb. Moreover, the whole setting of the *Eclogue* is strongly coloured with Roman features and allusions: the Augustan land redistribution is in the air, Moeris quotes songs referring to Mantua and Cremona (27-8), and Lycidas and Moeris between

101

them mention three of Virgil's contemporaries, Varus (26), and the poets Varius and Cinna (35). We are looking through Virgilian layers.

Servius (at 9.60) believed that *Bianor* was the same as Ocnus, the legendary founder of Mantua (whose predicament appears in this poem at 27-8). Commentators tend not to accept this and cite with a little more favour the Bianor lamented by his mother in a funerary epigram by Diotimus (*Anth. Pal.* 7.261), or the Trojan Bienor, first of Agamemnon's victims at *Iliad* 11.92 (and otherwise unmentioned).[49] Virgil's use of an unbucolic name here may suggest the universality of death, and a name which could be taken as that of a real historical personage – or any of several real persons[50] – could well suggest the universality of death in the world of actual experience. Neither Diotimus' epigram – of all verse genres epigram is the most receptive to unimportant but real persons – nor the Homeric Bienor would do anything but enhance that suggestion. By contrast, it might well seem that a standard bucolic name would not maximise this sense of universality and – with the Daphnis of the fifth *Eclogue* in mind – would perhaps also open the door too much to ideas of post-mortem regeneration.

Two other names require consideration here, *Lycisca* (3.18) and *Hylax* (8.107),[51] both names of dogs. The former is a sheep dog, the latter a house guard-dog. Dogs in general are not animals characteristic of the *Eclogues* – apart from these two places, they only appear anonymously, once at 8.28, in figured speech in the plural (i.e. as linguistic entities rather than animals), and once, again anonymously and in the plural, as part of the hunting apparatus Gallus imagines in his eccentric version of the Arcadian myth at 10.57. Even Hylax the guard-dog (8.107) is something of a suspect feature in Arcadia. The dog-owner's house is not in the *urbs* (where she is afraid that her lover Daphnis has been detained), but it is clearly not far from it, and the house-dog seems a somewhat urban feature. The context derives from one of Theocritus' urban rather than his pastoral poems (*Id.* 2) and barking dogs feature there; they are not the girl's own guard-dog, but (we infer) they are town dogs, the guard-dogs of other houses in the neighbourhood (*Id.* 2.30).[52] The other Virgilian dog, Lycisca (3.18), also has a stereotypical dog-name (cf. Ov. *Met.* 3.220)[53] which also appears as a common personal name for low class humans[54] and hence a stereotypical name for literary female objects of erotic interest in the more urban genres (Juv. 6.123; cf. also Lyce, Hor. *Odes* 3.10, 4.13). However, despite its non-bucolic name, this dog serves a suitable bucolic purpose as sheepdog.

Apart from the mythological and Roman names (for the latter of which see below), most of the natives of Arcadia have names which come from Theocritean or other pastoral, from other Theocritean poetry, or, while not actually attested in extant pastoral, are formed so as to resemble typical pastoral names. Virgil treats Theocritean names as having their own autonomy from the Theocritean situations in which they originated. They resemble fancy-dress clothes in an old chest and can be donned by the *dramatis personae* of an eclogue more or less at random. Over and above these names, there is, however, a substantial group of names which do not appear to have a pastoral or Theocritean background at all – including some which clearly have identifiable sources in other genres (e.g. Lycoris, Alexis). Sometimes such names are an index of a degree of otherness in the bucolic context, but this is not always so. Sometimes a name may seem to be naturalised by appearing in an archetypical bucolic role, or by re-peated appearance in the *Eclogues.* However, there remain cases which are unexplained.

Special figures (i) Virgil, Daphnis, and Polyphemus and Galatea

We have seen how some names recur in the course of the *Eclogues*, and how in such cases it is by no means clear that we are meant to interpret these as references to the same persisting character. We have also seen that when Virgil uses a Theocritean situation, he may replace the original Theocritean names with names from other parts of the Theocritean corpus (cf. *Ecl.* 3.1ff.). There is yet another phenomenon which contributes to the evasiveness of the names of Eclogue-land, viz. the persistence of certain roles under different names.

One such case is the role of 'Virgil'. We understand that it is his voice which speaks in the introductions to the even-numbered poems, that his is the first person voice appearing in the openings of *Eclogues* 4, 6, 8, and 10, implied in the close of *Eclogue* 10, and that he is the 'poet' referred to at 10.70. However, Virgil appears also as Menalcas in the fifth *Eclogue* (at the very least at its end) and arguably in the ninth, and also as Tityrus in (at least) the sixth.

However, one cannot perform a simple mapping of Virgil on to these figures: both Tityrus and Menalcas appear in other poems in which the identification seems in various degrees less certain.[55] A conspicuously Theocritean Tityrus (cf. Theocr. *Id.* 3.3-5), for example, appears off-stage at *Eclogue* 9.23 – a poem in which Menalcas already seems to represent Virgil.[56] Perhaps the reference to 'Tityrus' here is part of Menalcas' song as recalled by Lycidas, and to the extent that Menalcas is closely aligned with Virgil, Tityrus' name is like a *sphragis*-feature, or programmatic seal of authenticity (as it is in the later *Georgics* at 4.566): we come close to having Virgil wrapping his poetic and bucolic identities inside each other like Russian dolls.[57] One could, however, take the song as simply a variant of other 'Tityrus-songs' (cf. *Ecl.* 3.96-7) or as the singer Menalcas' dramatisation of himself sloping off to visit Lycidas' beloved Amaryllis (22) and leaving Tityrus to do his work (just as a Theocritean singer visits an Amaryllis and leaves a Tityrus to watch the goats at *Idylls* 3.1-5). The amount of Virgil that one sees in the figure here depends partly on the particular emphasis one lays on the lines, and no definitive quantification is available. One might say that 'Virgil' is neither present nor absent here, but that sometimes the reader thinks he can see him and sometimes not.

Menalcas and Tityrus are linked also at 5.12, where Menalcas keeps Tityrus occupied and out of the way (cf. 9.23) while he and Mopsus get on with singing. This Menalcas becomes closely identified with Virgil by the end of the poem (5.86-7), and here it is less tempting to connect Virgil and Tityrus. However, there may be an effect derived from even a failed attempt on the reader's part to make an identification. What if we imagine that Menalcas (?Virgil) invites Mopsus to sing and says that Tityrus (?Virgil) will look after the goats? Could we see this even for a moment or two as a humorously humble third person self-reference, or a case of one of the bucolic charade players momentarily confused about which mask he is wearing? Let us say that we reject these possibilities; we can, nonetheless, enjoy teasing out the possibilities and seeing what they are like.

Tityrus also appears in the first *Eclogue* where not all would make the identification with Virgil.[58] Servius did, however (at *Ecl.* 1.1), and it is perhaps only a narrowly sequential reading that prevents us doing so too. If we think of the book as one which has been read, one, therefore, in which the temporal and spatial organisation is partially synchronised, this pressure is removed. In this case, we can see the picture of Tityrus and Meliboeus in the opening lines of the poetry book as symbolising interaction of the poet and the 'reader', the poet rehearsing his poetry and the reader – subject to the whims of real life – pondering what the poetry means to anyone other than the poet who is separated from the real world. Here Meliboeus plays the role of the audience (burdened with its own problems, perhaps) and Tityrus corresponds to that of poet.[59] This reading might be seen as reinforced by the setting, the situation, and the iconic *fagus* tree of the opening lines, all of which combine to suggest a picture which is programmatic and emblematic.[60] Tityrus can suggest something of the Virgil role in this case, and the fact that Tityrus has arguably lost something of his pure bucolic identity by going to Rome may add something interestingly suggestive to the idea:[61] Virgil as bucolic poet is not exactly the same as a bucolic native.

The other reference to Tityrus is in Damon's song of the madness caused by unrequited love in the eighth *Eclogue*: let everything turn upside down, 'let Tityrus be an Orpheus' (8.55). If we think of Tityrus as Virgil here we gain an amusing touch of Virgilian modesty (like that of Lycidas at 9.35), and nothing prevents us from seeing this as an extra layer of reference.

Menalcas, equally, is not a simple case. He is definitely and closely aligned with Virgil by the quotations of previous *Eclogues* (*Ecl.* 2 and 3) at 5.86-7. The Menalcas of the ninth *Eclogue* too is quite convincingly aligned with Virgil by the character of his song repertoire as recalled there. If we read this back into the third *Eclogue*, what happens? Here there is a Menalcas who admires the poetry of Virgil's friend, Pollio (86). Moreover, perhaps we can retrospectively construe – since the fifth *Eclogue* tells us so – Menalcas as in some sense the composer of the third (not to mention the second, whose opening line is also quoted), a poem in which a Menalcas is himself one of the contestants in the singing contest presented there! Finally, in the tenth *Eclogue* – where Virgil is present himself, unnamed but in his own person, in the voice of the introduction and in the close of the poem (10.70-7), a Menalcas is also brought on within the poem (10.15) quite emphatically, as though standing for bucolic poetry – i.e. Virgilian bucolic poetry.

As regards the Virgil role, Virgil sometimes enters an eclogue in his own right (though anonymously), sometimes he enters in the part of Menalcas (even in a case where he is already present in his own person), and at least once he enters in the guise of another role, as Tityrus.[62] But it is not easy to exclude other references to Tityrus from being Virgilian masks, even when Menalcas has that role elsewhere in the same poem. The masks change in a way in which may defy the observer's full analysis, but seems at the same time to invite the attempt.

Daphnis is another role which can be taken up by different named parts. The dying Daphnis is at the heart of the fifth *Eclogue*, but Gallus also takes on the role (though not the name) in the tenth *Eclogue*. Impersonation is evident in a more straightforward sense in the eighth *Eclogue*, as Damon (perhaps) and Alphesiboeus (certainly) assume roles in the songs they exchange with each other. However, the major case of fluid superimposition of identity on different names is that of Polyphemus and Galatea.

Polyphemus and Galatea appear twice in Theocritus, most famously in *Idyll* 11, but also in the sixth.[63] The 'I' in the third, although his beloved is Amaryllis, also has Polyphemus-trappings. In the *Eclogues* the situation is somewhat more complex.

In the second *Eclogue* Corydon pines unrequitedly for Alexis. The poem is modelled on and takes a good deal of detail from Theocritus' eleventh *Idyll*. It is clear that Corydon takes on the role of Polyphemus and casts Alexis as Galatea. The relationship of the bucolic to the idyllic characters is analogous to the relationship between Gallus and Daphnis in the tenth *Eclogue*. Humans assume mythological roles.

It is very striking that in the seventh *Eclogue*, in the song competition remembered by Meliboeus, Corydon, who was a 'Polyphemus' in *Eclogue* 2, appears again and in one of his quatrains addresses the sea nymph Galatea; he also invites her to come to him in lines reminiscent of Theocritus' eleventh *Idyll*. Corydon assumes the Polyphemus-role as though it were a standard bucolic act (he retains his own name in this performance; 7.40).

The feeling that 'Polyphemus and Galatea' is a standard act – perhaps already hinted at in Theocritus' third *Idyll* – is reinforced in the ninth *Eclogue*. One of the songs half-remembered by Moeris is another call to Galatea (9.39-43). Here the situation even more explicitly recalls the Theocritean context, as the singer invites Galatea to leave the water and come to him on land (where there is a Theocritean-Homeric cave). The voice here is anonymous, unlike Corydon's in the seventh *Eclogue*, and as this fragment is for the Roman audience all there ever can be of the poem, it looks like a fragment of an imaginary poem, a Latin version of the eleventh *Idyll*. Since the other fragments which Moeris recalls suggest a distinctly Virgilian repertoire, the impression emerges that Virgil alludes to a lost Virgilian recension of the Polyphemus role.

Finally, there is a passage from the eighth *Eclogue*. Here the speaker, suffering from unrequited love, remembers his first sight of his beloved in lines that for the reader recall a passage from Theocritus' Polyphemus-*Idyll* (*Ecl.* 8.37-41 cf. Theocr. *Id.* 11.25-30). The speaker ends by promising to throw himself into the sea in a twist on the Homeric Cyclops' well-known inability to swim.[64] The 'Galatea' here, however, – and unlike the Galatea in the seventh and tenth *Eclogues* – has her own name, Nysa. As to the 'Polyphemus', Damon plays the role, but in a song exchange: he does not name 'himself' in the song and can therefore easily be construed either as indulging in autobiographical lament, or as performing as a semi-humanised Polyphemus.

Polyphemus and Galatea are clearly archetypal figures in the world of the bucolic natives.[65] The inhabitants of Virgilian Arcadia know the parts, and readily assume them in performance. Perhaps we can see a parodic allusion to this in Horace, when the rough freedman Sarmentus invites Messius to do the dance of the herdsman (*pastorem*) Cyclops in the abuse-exchange at Cocceius villa, overlooking Caudium, on the journey to Brundisium (Hor. *Sat.* 1.5. 63). The non-urban location, the antiphonal format, and the low status of the participants are all compatible with this possibility. Be that as it may, the roles of Polyphemus and Galatea seem to be standard repertoire among the herdsmen of the *Eclogues*. In addition, these herdsmen's own love stories seem sometimes to fall into the same shape, and their identity wavers. Here, as in other features of the collection, the Eclogues-book is criss-crossed with allusions to itself and to Theocritus, but the allusions do not fit exactly on top of each other. Rather they build up a palimpsest of variations on underlying patterns and themes, a palimpsest probably given extra laminations by the figuration of Polyphemus and Galatea in contemporary mural painting (see below).

7. Named People

Special figures (ii) Roman figures

There is a special category of non-pastoral figures in the *Eclogues*, namely more or less contemporary Romans. These fall into two groups, poets and others.

Romans appearing in the *Eclogues* who are primarily public figures other than poets are Caesar (9.47), Pollio (3.84, 86, 88, 4.12) – though he is a poet too – Varus (6.7, 10, 12, 9.26ff.), and the anonymous young man in the opening poem (1.42). There is also a dynastic, but as yet unborn, child in the fourth (4.8, 60ff.).

The anonymous young man is a profoundly significant figure in the first *Eclogue*. Rome and the city throw shadows into the happy life of Arcadia throughout the collection, but outside influence is not solely menacing, for the young man saves Tityrus from the disturbance of the land which threatens Eclogue-land both here and in the ninth *Eclogue*. The reader understands that Octavian is ultimately responsible for Tityrus' rescue (and the possibility of rescue in the real world too), and commentators point to other examples of Octavian being referred to as *iuvenis*. However, we have no reason to suppose that in the fiction of the poem Tityrus actually saw Octavian. He is a naïve countryman, awed by the city, and is as likely as not to have seen a minor functionary – not even, perhaps, Octavius Musa, the boundary commissioner – and thought him to be the great man. In any case, Tityrus (and those with him; *Ecl.* 1.45) is reprieved, and the poem thus suggests a less than wholly implacable process in regard to the land redistribution.

Caesar (Julius) appears – or rather his posthumous and reborn star appears – in one of the fragments of Menalcas' songs recalled in the ninth *Eclogue* (9.46-50). The general tenor of the fragment is one of regeneration (reinforced by the address to Daphnis, the regenerative figure of the fifth *Eclogue*), though the surrounding context is ominous. Also hopeful in its import is the unidentified figure of the dynastic child in the fourth *Eclogue*.

Varus appears in two of the *Eclogues*, the sixth and ninth. In the sixth he is the military figure who prompts Virgil's Callimachean *recusatio*, like Agrippa in Horace's *Odes* (1.6). As always in the *recusatio* two kinds of poetry are set against each other, epic and the poet's own current (and apparently slighter) genre. Here – as is always suggested in the figure – the wars are harsh (*tristia*, 6.7) and the alternative genre provides a more congenial refuge or ideal. That is not to say that love and song are always necessarily part, and signs, of an ideological opposition to war. Nevertheless, the hope that resides in the young man, Caesar's star, and the unborn child is not at all so strongly visible in the figure of Varus in this poem. The reference to Varus in the ninth *Eclogue* (27-9) is clearly implicated in some kind of political discourse. Varus will be praised if Mantua is saved – as Cremona wasn't. However,

107

the song by Menalcas (Virgil) of which this is a fragment was never completed (26), and Virgil indicates that the hope was thwarted before the song was finished.

Although the young man (*Ecl.* 1) can be reached by Tityrus, he and the other non-poetic Roman figures, who nevertheless influence life in Eclogue-land, are remote. Pollio is a partially different case. He is known as a poet by some of the Arcadians (see below). In his public capacity, however, he, like the non-poet Romans, remains outside the bucolic world. In the fourth *Eclogue* he figures in the extra-bucolic frame as the consul in whose year the transformation will begin (11-12), and in the eighth he is the prospective subject of Virgil's future praise. This is an inversion of the Callimachean *recusatio,* and suggests the complexity of the world outside the *Eclogues* (the boundary point is marked with explicitly geographical references here, 6-7).

There is a very strong contrast with the position these figures have in the *Eclogues* and that accorded to Roman poets, for the latter have a much more integral presence in the world of the bucolic natives.

Pollio, Gallus, Varius, and Cinna all appear in the *Eclogues*. Virgil himself appears as well, as we have seen, as himself (or 'himself', if we prefer), but anonymously, in the openings of *Eclogues* 2, 4, 8, and 10, and the close of 10. In the remaining even-numbered poem, *Eclogue* 6, he appears in the opening, but in a Callimachean epiphany Apollo addresses him there as Tityrus (within the collection as a whole, the connection between Tityrus and Virgil is variable). Menalcas clearly overlaps with Virgil in the fifth *Eclogue*, quoting *Eclogues* 2 and 3 as part of his repertoire, and, it seems, in the ninth, where his repertoire is Virgilian in character without actually quoting other passages of the *Eclogues*.

If Virgil sometimes assumes a bucolic name in order to make his appearance in the bucolic world, he contrasts signally with Gallus in this. Gallus is referred to under his own name in Silenus' song (*Ecl.* 6), although he does not figure actually in the bucolic landscape in that poem, nor interact with bucolic natives. On the other hand, he does appear in the bucolic landscape, and under his own name again, in the tenth *Eclogue*, where he plays out the role of the dying Daphnis. Even so, he is not fully assimilated, although he knows some of the bucolic inhabitants' names, whereas Virgil portrays himself anonymously as pursuing the bucolic task of weaving a basket with hibiscus (10.71), and may also lurk in the figure of Menalcas earlier in the poem (10.20). This contrast must have poetic-ideological connotations about elegy and bucolic, and the degree to which different kinds of poetry are compatible with what Arcadia stands for.

Other poets too, however, have some kind of showing. In *Eclogue* 9 Lycidas knows by repute the Roman poets Cinna and Varius (9.35). In the third *Eclogue*, both Damoetas and Menalcas know of Pollio.[66] Although Pollio shows no sign of actually appearing in the bucolic land-scape here, Damoetas implies some sort of interaction when he sings that Pollio loves his (Damoetas') poetry (3.84). Moreover, Menalcas (who has a shadowy connection with Virgil here, as the 'author' of *Eclogue* 3, according to 5.87) is aware of Pollio as a maker of new poems (*nova carmina*, 3.86). Just as Pollio himself hovers on the threshold between the bucolic and the Roman worlds here, so the aesthetic values implied in the judgement-word 'new' has a reality both inside and outside Arcadia.[67] Menalcas also (3.90) knows of the bad poetry of Bavius and Mevius (perhaps the same figure as at Hor. *Epod.* 10.2).[68]

Codrus is known as a quality poet (by Corydon and Thyrsis, 7.21-8); we do not know a Roman poet of the name, but some lines of Valgius survive in which he is praised as one who sings as Cinna used to, and uses the same metres as he did – a post-neoteric, in other words.[69]

Varius does not appear by name, but a line of his *de morte Caesaris* is quoted at *Eclogue* 8.88 (see Macrobius 6.2.20). Alphesiboeus is actu-ally the singer here, and we may perhaps be inclined to take this as a piece of Virgilian texture rather than a learned allusion by the bucolic native.[70]

Through poetry the natives of Eclogue-land have a purchase on a broader world (we could also note Menalcas' knowledge of Conon in 3.37ff. here). The Roman poets referred to seem almost to have entry visas, or to be allowed in as guests; they are not Arcadian icons as the archetypal poets Linus, Orpheus, and Hesiod are, but they are poets and that is the only class of Roman to achieve such a clear welcome in Eclogue-land. Virgil himself, as a bucolic poet, has dual nationality and two identity cards with Arcadian names on. However, it is not a simple matter, for though Gallus tries to enter he is hampered by his poetic (elegiac) sensibility. His poetic identity leaves him in winter, hunting, and being a feeble imitation of the bucolic ideal. He must, then, be somehow different from Varius, Cinna, and Pollio, and that difference is likely to be connected with the generic issue of elegy and its attitude to love.[71]

Bucolic charades

Corydon plays the part of Polyphemus in the second *Eclogue*; analo-gously, Gallus that of the dying Daphnis in the tenth and (after the *Eclogues*) Propertius takes the role of Penelope (with Cynthia as his Odysseus) in *Elegies* 4.8.[72] In the forgoing pages various identifications between Virgilian bucolic figures and real Roman contemporaries have been suggested or reported.[73] I gather them here for convenience, and as a preparation for a point to be made further below.

Menalcas aligns himself very strongly with Virgil at the end of the

fifth *Eclogue* by quoting Virgilian bucolic lines. He is strongly aligned
with Virgil in the ninth by his role and by the character of the songs
attributed to him. Apollo addresses Virgil as Tityrus in the opening of
Eclogue 6. Tityrus' situation in the first *Eclogue* has allowed some to
make a Virgilian connection, and this goes as far back as Servius.
Servius explicitly points out, however, that not every Tityrus in the
Eclogues need be Virgil. Meliboeus can be seen as given a Virgilian
colouring by retrospective allusions later in the Eclogue-book,[74] and
Mnasyllus is read as Virgil by Servius (*Ecl.* 6.13).

As to others, Servius took Silenus to represent Siro in the sixth
Eclogue, and recently Harrison (2007: 47-8) has argued for Silenus
representing Parthenius. In the same poem, Chromis represents (for
Servius; 6.13) Varus. Servius records suggestions that Stimichon in the
fifth *Eclogue* represents Maecenas, and I have suggested (above) Pollio
as an alternative.

Starr (1995) argues that once the principle of identifying bucolic
characters as Romans is accepted, the game is open for readers to
indulge a degree of subjectivity in playing it, especially if Virgil allows
himself to enter the role of Menalcas here and Tityrus there. Starr cites
Asinius Gallus (DServ at *Ecl.* 4.11) and Remmius Palaemon (Suet.
Gramm. 23) as – for different reasons – reading themselves into, respec-
tively, the child prophesied in the fourth *Eclogue* and the song-judge in
the third. I would suggest that at some level, the Eclogue-book encour-
ages readers both to indulge in such speculation,[75] and also to read
themselves into its bucolic space (rather as someone claimed to be
Corinna, or so Ovid claims at *Am.* 2.17.29-30).

Pollio provides another way in which a reader might read himself
into the bucolic space of the poems. The reader is made aware in the
third *Eclogue* that Pollio is known by name to the bucolic natives. As
Henderson suggests, Virgil lets us glimpse through the bucolic texture
Pollio's role in the *recitatio* salons of Rome.[76] The Roman poetry audi-
ence could imagine itself trailing along with him in the Arcadian
penumbra like the extra guests at a Roman dinner (cf. Hor. *Sat.* 2.8).
Indeed, given that Virgil builds up an impression that the ten poems in
the book are only part of a continuum of bucolic song (of which the songs
of Menalcas referred to in the ninth *Eclogue* are just a hint), the reader
is permitted to imagine bucolic songs in which he too is known by name
to the inhabitants.

There is yet another way again in which the reader can enter a
Virgilian bucolic space. Poetry does not exist only while we read it or
listen to it. In the outside world the poetry-reading individual can create
and see echoes between experience and prior reading.[77] Thus, we must
be struck by a picture of Maecenas (composed after his death) in which
various bucolic elements appear in juxtaposition:

maluit umbrosam quercum lymphasque cadentes
  paucaque pomosi iugera certa soli:
Pieridas Phoebumque colens in mollibus hortis
  sederat argutas garrulus inter avis

Elegiae in Maecenatem 1.33-6

He preferred the shady oak and falling waters, and a few sure acres of fruit-producing earth: cultivating the Muses and Apollo in luxurious gardens, he sat babbling among the clear-voiced birds.

We are not actually told that there was an occasion on which Maecenas sat under a shady tree producing verse, nor that it was his custom so to do. The collocation of images, however, gives us a strong impression of him indulging in a typical bucolic posture. We are not told that the verse was bucolic verse, but the assemblage of images fits strikingly with the iconography of the Eclogue-book. The author seems to invite us to see Maecenas as playing the role of Tityrus at the opening of the first, or Daphnis at the opening of the seventh *Eclogue*.[78]

The various elements of charade in the Eclogue-book invite the reader into bucolic space in a way which, I shall suggest below, has analogies in Roman art and gardens.

Poetry and poets in Rome and Eclogue-land

The ability of some Roman poets to enter Arcadia gives a sense of qualified or potential parity between the class of Roman poets and that of Arcadian songsters. If Gallus fails to establish himself in Arcadia, some Arcadians are themselves imperfectly integrated in the bucolic world (the love-struck Corydon in the second *Eclogue*, for example) or are dislodged, or in danger of being dislodged, from it (Meliboeus in the first and the characters of the ninth *Eclogue*). In a symbolic sense, the one kind of poet stands for the other (in this context we might recall the use of the emblematic *fagus*-tree for recording bucolic song by Mopsus (5.13-14) and elegiac poetry by Gallus), and this makes it worth looking at how the sociology of poetry, so to speak, works in Arcadia. Apart from the fact that song in Arcadia resembles the recitation-scene in Rome in that it generally takes place in a formalised social context and is heard rather than read, there are two other interesting comparisons to be made.

There are two models of how the dynamics of the Arcadian poetry-scene works in the *Eclogues*: inheritance and competition.

First, as regards inheritance:[79] at *Eclogue* 2.37-8, the dying Damoetas hands over his pipe to Corydon, who is now second in line to be possessed by it ('*te nunc habet ista secundum*', 38).[80] Likewise, the senior (cf. 5.4) singer Menalcas will hand over to Mopsus his bucolic pipe (5.85-7). In the sixth *Eclogue* (67-71) something similar again happens.

111

The archetypal poet Linus (here a quasi-bucolic *pastor*, 67) hands over the Orphic Hesiod's symbolically bucolic reed pipes (*calami*, 69) to Gallus. In the cases of Damoetas and Corydon, and Menalcas and Mopsus, there is a clear continuity of the bucolic genre, so to speak (the recession into the past may not be deep, but this suits the shallow time-perspective of the bucolic native); in the case of Hesiod and Gallus (and perhaps, by implication, Linus and Orpheus too) the bucolic details of the presentation – however tendentiously – make the same point (and here the temporal perspective is much longer, and involves real-world poets). According to this picture, both within the *Eclogues* and in the real literary world of Rome, the poet carries on a line or school of a particular kind of poetry from illustrious predecessors.[81]

Of course, this is a somewhat artificial picture in both cases. *Eclogue* 5.10-11 may, perhaps playfully, be taken as dividing bucolic song into the proto-genres of love-song, praise-song, and blame, but even so the over-riding impression that we get from the collection is that the only song is bucolic song. In the context of Augustan poetry, on the other hand, the notion of 'schools' of poetry or poetic genres is part of a systematically tendentious self-representation by the poets. If we look in one way, the genres exist – elegy, bucolic, satire, lyric, iambic, epic, didactic, epigram –, and one poet follows the generic flagship of another in a line of inheritance. However, if we look another way, genres evanesce, sometimes almost immediately. Latin lyric is born with and dies with Horace's *Odes*; Gallo-Propertian elegy has importance only until Ovid's radical transformations in the *Ars* and *Remedia Amoris*, the exile poetry, and the *Fasti*; satire is resuscitated after long disuse by Horace and then disappears for about a century; Latin bucolic was born inside Lucretius' didactic poem, the *De Rerum Natura* (4.572-94; 5.1379-1411), and does not reappear after the *Eclogues* until the (probably) Neronian Calpurnius Siculus.[82] Nevertheless, the idea of inheritance as a major element in the literary scene is important in both Rome and Arcadia.

The other model, a synchronous one, concerns coevals; here the relationship is one in which respect is mixed with competitiveness, for the singing-contest is a recurrent and archetypal format in the bucolic setting, and in the real-world context there is rivalry both between co-workers in a genre, and between genres. Satire and elegy, for example, both set themselves against epic, and there is tension between Virgilian bucolic and Gallan elegy, and later between Horatian lyric and elegy.

8

Containing Reality; Realisms
and Realities

The names of people and places in the *Eclogues* are a mixture of
flagrantly literary and oddly real. It is a compound distinct from that of
other Roman genres.[1] The setting, too, with its elaborately constructed
landscape – rural and non-agricultural, but artificial too – provides a
space for and contributes to the mixture of natural and artificial. For
the modern reader, the *Eclogues* conspicuously are not realistic.
Realism, however, is a relatively modern concept; for the Romans,
each genre had its own mimetic and imaginative relationship with
the world of experience, and its own artistic validity.[2] Using the
evidence of art and literature from the early and middle Empire,
Coleman (2005) identifies among the Romans a tendency to blur the
distinctions between their experience of the contemporary world and
'a fictive realm', and observes that 'the precise chemical equation in
the coalescence is unique to each example: in some the fiction is
"weak"; in others, "strong" ' (Coleman 2005: 41). The *Eclogues'* com-
bination of natural and unnatural needs to be seen against this
background, and to be considered in terms of how the strength and
nature of its fictions draw attention to themselves in contrast with
surrounding genres. If we consider the collection in this light, the
issue of reality versus representation shows itself as a matter of core
importance in the *Eclogues*.

Rome and Romans are represented in the book, but obviously they
were also real-world entities outside the book. Referring to them in the
poems is a way of putting models, so to speak, of them inside a
fantastical representation. The Rome, the Pollio, the Caesar, the Gallus
in the poems are verbal constructs – in an obvious sense they are words
and not things –, but the fact that the bucolic natives talk or sing about
them means that for those natives – and they are to some extent our
eyes as we hear or read the poems – the respective entities have degrees
of reality. Looking from a different perspective, we might see the
representation of Rome, Pollio, and the rest as emanations or emissar-
ies from the real world infiltrating the literary space of the
Eclogue-book. By a logical short-cut, Rome (the place in the real world)
affects even the world of the imagination. Paradoxically, the audience's
sense that the influence of the real-world Rome on the imaginary

113

bucolic world is real gives the impression that the Rome which the bucolic natives talk about in the *Eclogues* is actually the real one too, and not just a literary picture. This is an illusion, but a powerful one. In this sense, the real inhabitants of Rome and the fictive ones of Arcadia share a common experience.

It does not follow from this that the *Eclogues* are somehow more impregnated with reality than poetry books in other genres. What is reflected, however, is the fact that literary works, as well as competing with their own generic antecedents and with other genres in their own literary field, all aim to have some kind of relationship with their audience's world of experience. This aim takes a competitive form, and perhaps especially so for Roman writers, since competition was so radically entrenched in Roman social values, especially in the late Republic. In the jostling of genres, individual authors try to get a more complete or suggestive grip on experience than others. This positioning as regards reality is often polemic as well as merely competitive. An author claims, often explicitly, that his genre is more real than others and he distils transformed elements of other genres into his own. Reality, of course, cannot be wholly subsumed into or contained in a literary artefact (any more than it can in speech or painting). Rather, an author tries to give an impression of a relationship with reality that is more vivid, say, or convincing, or meaningful than someone else's. This attempt is part of a complex game in which tradition and novelty hang in an unstable balance, and in which, explicitly or implicitly, different representational modes take antagonistic stances towards each other.[3] We see this, for example, in the claim made particularly by Roman satirists and epigrammatists that the dominant genre, epic,[4] does not correspond to real experience, we also see it embodied in Numitorius' parody of the opening of the third *Eclogue*,[5] and we see it in the portrayal of comedy as a 'mirror of life' (*speculum vitae*; Cicero ap. Euanthius *De Fabula* 5.1).

Although there is no Latin word for realism as such, various Roman concepts overlap with it and had currency in rhetorical theory – credibility, verisimilitude, vividness and so forth:[6] there was a multiplicity of ways in which the Roman could conceptualise the relation between literature and experience, and the variety of strongly demarcated genres in the literary field demonstrates in a pragmatic way a considerable interest in what we might call realisms and realities.

There are various ways in which the *Eclogues* show this concern for the issue of reality and its representation. In the discussion which follows I concern myself especially with self-referentiality and the representation of representation, illusionism and reality effect, and Roman conceptions of the natural and of landscape.

Self-referentiality and the depiction of depiction

Literature and life are different categories (cf. Catullus 16), but the one plays with the other and seems to want to represent it in some way. It is, however, something of a cliché to say that reality defies full representation. No literary depiction is equipollent with the realities it transcribes. Indeed, the more fully, accurately or suggestively one tries to describe reality, the more one tends to draw attention to the process of producing a cultural artefact. If we accept that part of the literary impulse is indeed concerned with reality, a range of possibilities emerges. Attempting to convey experience directly to the audience requires a degree of unselfconsciousness that is hardly credible in the adult world. Therefore, one might, as a writer, accept the challenge that a full embodiment of experience in text is not possible, and actually draw attention to the artistic process by making some sort of show of indeed attempting to make a full and detailed transcription of a real or fictive reality. Alternatively, one might make a show of casting aside all pretension to literariness and of using means which, though of course they remain literary, purport to be as direct and simple as is possible.[7] Again, one might try to mix different levels or modes of representation to draw attention to the hypothesis that there is something that could be deemed a reality behind the various modes.[8]

It would not be hard to suggest Roman writers who resemble each of these types to some extent (Seneca the tragedian for the first, perhaps, Lucilius, Horace in his satires, or Juvenal for the second, Catullus, Ovid, or Petronius for the third). The Romans, as suggested in the preceding section, were interested in these issues. Evidence from Roman art will also be adduced shortly; meanwhile one might point also to the element of playing with reality and representation in the mythological and historical charades that were part of both Roman theatrical and amphitheatrical experience.[9]

In a play in which actors really get killed, as far as the spectator is concerned, their deaths are to some extent 'in character' rather than the actors' own personal deaths. In a play which uses the 'play within a play' form, the actors impersonate actors who are in turn acting roles. Such roles can be seen as being acted simultaneously both by the members of the cast and by the *dramatis personae*. Insofar as what the actor is doing (acting) matches what the character is meant to be doing (acting), the distinction between reality and performance is blurred.[10] Again, we can see Classical examples of such a phenomenon. Euripides' *Bacchae* provides a particularly clear model in the scene in which Pentheus dresses up to play the part of a bacchant (787-861), but we can see the interest in different levels of 'reality' and 'narratedness' much more widely in a common feature in Roman literature, the form of included tales.[11]

There are two intersecting issues here, recursion and modelling. If we take literary artifacts – along with visual and sculptural art forms – as related to the production of scale-models, we can relate the whole range of phenomena to both the construction and use of children's toys. The toy is a simplified image of something in the real world which, in conjunction with the playing that it takes part in – has a role in the child's cognitive development. Likewise, the poem is simpler than the world of experience, but allows the reader to engage with experience in particular ways. If we think of the toy again, we can see it as miming part of the larger reality of which it is itself a part. The relationship between the part and the whole thus has the property of recursiveness. This relationship can itself be reproduced within literary and other artistic works, as when the painter or photographer appears within the painted or photographed image, or the actor within the play. The effect is sometimes referred to by the heraldic term *mise en abyme*.[12]

Given the wide distribution in time and space, it is not surprising that degrees of recursiveness, degrees of explicitness, and function vary immensely. The painter may be one of the figures in the scene depicted, involving a mild impossibility; alternatively, a mirror within the painted scene may reflect the painting artist who was outside the picture while it was being painted, thus making an issue of the absence of the painter when the work is seen by the viewer. The subject, with or without variation, may appear in a painting within the painting. At a more extreme level of recursiveness, we can cite Escher's image of a hand drawing itself. Relatedly, in everyday real experience, we may find ourselves on an escalator between wall-sized facing mirrors, infinitely multiplying our reflection. There is a degree of cultural specificity about forms, degrees, and media, but we need to see the whole range in a universal cognitive context.

Recursion is a fundamental cognitive pattern implicit not only in every act of model-making, but lying at the heart of the basic cognitive process of mental mapping and imaging. What we see is not like a picture; it is not a flat entity confined within a border and suspended in front of our eyes. Rather, we move about in it, changing its alignments as we do so, and at the same time as we move ourselves about within a mental model of our surroundings. Although we do not see the chair, we know that it is behind us as we sit down, because we have already looked from a different angle. This mental modelling is so basic to our ability to move around in the world that we barely distinguish the model from the reality it represents. However, when we externalise it – by drawing maps, making physical models, drawing pictures, giving instructions – we are more aware of the constructed nature of what we are doing and its separateness from the contextual reality.

Explicit and extreme forms of recursion thematise this relationship. In terms of literature and art the phenomenon is widely – but not uniformly – spread through time and place. It is prominent, for example, in Augustan poetry,[13] and a feature, particularly, of the programmatic language that is such a feature of Augustan poetry. Even in the purportedly rough and unliterary *Satires* of Horace we find a description of Horace's father in one of the poems which is presented as a model for Horace's own satiric programme and clearly replicates the approach taken by Horace in the *Satires* (*Sat.* 1.4.105ff.). The roughly contemporary *Eclogues* represent the opposite end of the spectrum in that they are flagrantly refined and literary. Amongst other examples of recursiveness in the collection, there is a very striking instance in the fifth *Eclogue*, analogous to the play-within-a-play in Euripides' *Bacchae* mentioned above, but more extreme.

> *Mopsus:*
> Quae tibi, quae tali reddam pro carmine dona?
> Nam neque me tantum uenientis sibilus Austri
> nec percussa iuuant fluctu tam litora, nec quae
> saxosas inter decurrunt flumina ualles.
> *Menalcas:*
> Hac te nos fragili donabimus ante cicuta:
> haec nos 'formosum Corydon ardebat Alexim',
> haec eadem docuit 'cuium pecus? an Meliboei?'
> *Mopsus:*
> At tu sume pedum, quod, me cum saepe rogaret,
> non tulit Antigenes (et erat tum dignus amari),
> formosum paribus nodis atque aere, Menalca.

Ecl. 5.81-90

> *Mopsus:* What, what present shall I give you for *your* song? For neither the hissing of the oncoming South wind, nor the shores struck by the waves, nor the rivers that run down through stony valleys please me so much.
> *Menalcas*: I will first present you with this delicate pipe: this taught me 'Corydon burned for lovely Alexis', this same pipe taught me 'Whose flock? Is it Meliboeus'?'
> *Mopsus*: But you take the crook which Antigenes, though he often asked me for it, did not get (and he was then worthy to be loved) – beautiful with even knots and brass, Menalcas.

When the second and third *Eclogues* appear inside the Eclogue-book as part of the repertoire of one of the imaginary bucolic songsters in the fifth *Eclogue*, there is a profound confusion of the boundaries between reality and representation. *Eclogues* 2 and 3 belong to the real world of Virgil's time; written on papyrus, they could be carried from place to place and recited to audiences by Virgil and his contemporaries. When they become part of the property of the fictive Menalcas, we have the sense that actual reality is infiltrating the literary artefact. Likewise, when we see how closely Menalcas' songs as recalled in the ninth

Eclogue resemble Virgilian bucolic, we are encouraged to infer that these are indeed parts of real Virgilian poems (even if only in an imaginary sense), and that bucolic poetry – and perhaps the bucolic landscape – has an existence wider than that confined to the Eclogue-book, that what we see of bucolic in the *Eclogues* is just the visible part of the bucolic spectrum. If I were to suggest that these Menalcan fragments should be entered in future *corpora* of fragmentary Latin poetry as the remains of lost Virgilian poems, it could not be a real suggestion, but it would be a justifiable way of trying to convey the shifting goalposts of literary reality.

Similar shifts also lurk within the representation of Gallus' poetry, especially in the tenth *Eclogue*, and in the presence of a representation of Conon (and the anonymous other) on the cups wagered by Menalcas in the third *Eclogue* (40-2). The permeability of the boundary between representation and reality is also visible in the way that Pollio and others are known to the bucolic natives, just as they were to the real contemporary audience. Even the sense that Menalcas and Tityrus might not always represent Virgil gives a sense that sometimes Virgil himself actually does step into the bucolic world as an actor to take on those costumes.[14] The Eclogue-book does not just reflect or imitate reality/experience, it reaches out into reality and draws something of reality into its circumference. The notion of inside/outside the book becomes important (and is reflected, as we have seen, in the use of geographical place-names to chart the rather permeable edges of Eclogue-land).

Illusionism and reality effect[15]

We can see the effects generated by the self-reflexivity of the *Eclogues* and its representation of representation as a form of *trompe l'oeil* device. This term is most familiar in the literature of Art History, and the phenomenon itself tends – rather carelessly – not to be thought of as a feature of the 'great' art of any period.[16] At any rate, we should not allow it to be too marginalised, for it has a quite strong profile in certain times and places, as for example in Dutch art of the 1650s and later. One readily thinks of van Hoegstraten's Peep-Show boxes, or his 'quodlibet' painting of a littered tray, or the work of Cornelius Gijsbrechts. *Trompe l'oeil* painting is too easily dismissed as not quite artistically respectable – a little like Halls of Mirrors. It is, however, currently a widespread phenomenon in public art, and there are artists and companies who specialise in commissioned work, and indeed programmes of training for *trompe l'oeil* mural work.[17] The interiors at the Amsterdam headquarters of Woningbouwvereniging Het Oosten by the Dutch artist Kenne Gregoire (born 1951) are striking examples of high quality. It is a mode of representation which continues to fascinate a rather wider audience than at first seems to be the case,[18] and has strong precedents in the Greek and Roman literature of art, and in the remains of Roman art itself (more below). Moreover, *trompe l'oeil* effects are not limited to the visual art of painting, for analogous devices are also found in literature.

In the second chapter of William Heinesen's novel *De fortabte spille-maend* ('The Lost Musicians', 1950), the narrating voice refers to a poem about one of the novel's characters by another of its characters, but one written subsequently to the action of the novel. The brief description of the poem vividly conjures up a scene involving the character it is about, a scene loosely related to the present time of the novel's action. This scene acquires a strong reality effect through being taken out of the novelistic framework and fitted out with a documentary one, which in turn contributes to the reality-effect of the novel as a whole. Here, as in visual works of art, the *trompe l'oeil* effect involves a blurring of real and illusory. In the Roman context, such effects are well established from early times in mural painting and stucco effects,[19] and continue to be found later in the sometimes very elaborate illusory painting of architectural extensions and in the painting of 'additional' sections of garden in gardens, and – with a different degree of realistic illusionism – in the representation of dinner-detritus on floor-mosaics.

In the context of Roman art (as elsewhere), there are, of course, different degrees of illusionism (mosaics, for instance, cannot present the same illusionistic surface that the image plane of a painted surface can), but we have, indeed, a number of ancient anecdotes which attest an interest in – and esteem for – successfully illusionistic visual art. Pliny (*NH* 35.155) records M. Varro as having known at Rome an artist, Possis, who made clay models (or so it seems) of fruit and grapes that were indistinguishable by sight from real ones. He provides anecdotal material about the rivalry between Zeuxis and Parrhasius (35.65); Zeuxis' painting of grapes deceived birds, and Parrhasius' painting of a curtain fooled Zeuxis into asking for the curtain to be opened so that the painting might be shown. Pliny has another story of fruit-painting by Zeuxis (35.66) and also relates that crows tried to land on 'roof-tiles' that were a painted part of stage scenery on the stage erected by Claudius Pulcher in 99 BC (35.23) as an indication of their noteworthily successful illusionism. The diffusion of such anecdotes attests a popular regard for illusionistic painting, and a popular belief that artists might reasonably be thought to share it. The verisimilitude of Roman still-life painting and the sometimes virtuoso application of linear perspective and regard for shadows in architectural illusionism around Virgil's time provide collateral evidence for a high regard for illusionistic realism.[20]

However, even when the success of *trompe l'oeil* effects depends on the degree of successful illusionism in the painted surface, the illusion is never complete. It usually only works fully – to the extent that it does work – from a particular viewpoint to which the viewer must proceed (and from which he must ultimately depart) with his eyes open.[21] In Pompeii, markings on floors sometimes indicate the optimum viewing point for certain illusions,[22] just as in Colin Wilbourn's 1997 anamorphic harbour-wall painting of a doorway (at Sand Point Road, Sunderland)[23] a seat and fixed eyehole perform the same function. At a certain point the illusion clicks into place and the viewer agrees to be pleased by the success of the trick. At this point, when the painted surface clicks into successful illusion, it gives the illusion not of a realistic representation, but of reality. The illusion remains precisely that, an illusion – the reality is not real –, but the viewer enjoys the fact that the illusion is at loggerheads with reality, and can enjoy swapping the one for the other at will.

The passage of the fifth *Eclogue* quoted in the preceding section (*Ecl.* 5.81-90) is very much this kind of device. The Roman audience knew that Virgil was the author of the second and third *Eclogues*, and that Menalcas and Virgil did not fit on top of each other with a perfect and absolute match, but the quotation of two of Virgil's *Eclogues* by Menalcas opens within the *Eclogues* a window from the fictional world onto the real world, thereby extending the former's compass, and also creates the spectre of an Eclogue-book inside the bucolic world of its fictive inhabitants. In an imaginary sense, *Eclogue* 5 contains an unlimited amount of bucolic poetry and/or song including the *Eclogues* themselves and all the songs in various genres composed by Mopsus (cf. 10-11). Nor is this passage a solitary phenomenon in the book. In various ways, the multiplicity of realities and illusions become superimposed on each other. The way that we can see the bucolic natives as producers of bucolic song which is recorded in Virgil's bucolic verse involves a play on senses of 'bucolic'; likewise, the way we can infer the existence of a non-existent Virgilian version of Theocritus *Idyll* 11 from Menalcas' songs opens another window onto an imaginary extension of the bucolic world, and one that tempts us to look at the other fragments of Menalcan song in the same light.

In *trompe l'oeil,* the depiction and the surface are at loggerheads. Different realities materialise and compete for the viewer's attention. Holbein's *Ambassadors* is an extreme case: the picture plane contains two images. When one is right (the ambassadors seen perpendicularly) the other (the skull, which must be viewed at an acute angle) is wrong, and vice versa. It is not possible to see both depicted realities properly at the same time. Although extreme this is not unparalleled. The renaissance 'perspective picture' on pleated paper showed different representations from different angles, and this becomes a metaphor for alternative subjective realities in Bushy's attempt to console Queen Isabel in Shakespeare's *Richard II* (2.2.14-26). In the *Eclogues*, Virgil both is and is not Menalcas (and not every Menalcas is a Virgil in the same degree). In addition, the relationship between Rome and Arcadia as depicted entities is also equivocal. We see the depiction of Rome and its world both in the *Eclogue* frames (*Ecl.* 4, 6, 8, 10) and also inside *Eclogues* (especially *Ecl.* 1 and 9). This Rome is depicted in the poems as outside Arcadia, though its influence reaches in. We also see, of course, the depiction of Arcadia in the *Eclogues*. The two depictions, although they have a dynamic and fluid boundary, exist in more than one plane, so to speak. From one angle, Arcadia is an idealised literary construct in a particular Greek tradition, whereas Rome and its world surrounds the audience both in other literary genres and in reality. However, the audience can look at the depictions of Rome and Arcadia from both the inside and the outside, and the equation between the ideals of Arcadia and the realities of Rome is neither straightforward nor necessarily static.

There are symptoms of such fluidity of interpretation elsewhere in Latin literature, in a handful of what might be seen as paradigmatic passages, and in the context of Roman declamation. When Diana has caused Actaeon's dogs to tear him (now in the form of a stag) to shreds, Ovid tells us, there were two opinions about her action, and both had their reasons (Ov. *Met.* 3. 253-5). Similarly, after Eumolpus' performance of the story of the widow of Ephesus, Petronius describes briefly the three quite different reactions of the various hearers (Petr. *Sat.* 113). Thirdly, in Juvenal's sixth satire, in a catalogue of types of women one would be foolish to marry, there is the woman who, enthusiastic about Virgil, takes Dido's side (Juv. 6.434-5). The personal leanings and circumstances of the readers or hearers in all these cases produce conflicts between different subjectivities. The poetry reading as a Roman social event[24] had built into it the space for discussion after the reading, and therefore allowed room for the airing of differing perspectives – and is likely to have encouraged a sense that such tensions were a contributing factor in the plurality of meanings that the audience took away with it. Indeed, a context in which poetry is primarily received through performance is likely to foster the proliferation of degrees of subjectivity.[25]

We have no record of the discussion following a poetry reading, but we have the Elder Seneca's records of comments about, and discussions of, declamatory performances (*Controversiae* and *Suasoriae*).[26] In the *controversiae*, the declaimer takes one or other side in an imaginary lawsuit arising from a set of circumstances given in brief narrative form. The discussions are naturally often concerned with alternative or antithetical motivations. In the *Suasoria*, the declaimer offers a speech of advice to a mythological or historical character, telling – for example – Agamemnon not to sacrifice Iphigenia (*Suas.* 3), or Cicero not to beg Antony's pardon (*Suas.* 6). The advice could run counter to the known facts of the story, and could involve an upside-down reading of standard evaluations.

Recursiveness and *trompe l'oeil* effects create alternative realities and question the nature of representation and its relationship with reality and between the alternative realities created. In the *Eclogues* this has both an aesthetic function, and a political dimension as well.

Landscape and painting

As regards the bucolic 'reality', obviously we cannot draw a map of Eclogue-land on the basis of what is in the poems. Nor can we see the poems of the collection as linear aural maps or travelogues in the way in which we could see Horace's travel satires (*Sat.* 1.5 and 1.9). We could certainly, however, draw a schematised outline plan of the bucolic interior surrounded by a dangerous exterior. We might put a sea-icon and some snowy mountains at the boundary between inside and outside.[27] This is still, however, a good way from visualising a landscape. If we wanted to draw or paint a scene in Eclogue-land we would be faced with a huge multiplicity of questions for which Virgil supplies no answers. Nevertheless, the *Eclogues* provide a generous distribution of features – plants and animals, streams, and so on – vivid (even if stereotypical) details, and passing references, all of which cumulatively conspire to give the reader the impression that he *can* visualise eclogic scenes:[28] the *Eclogues* seem more than any other Latin poems to represent a place or what we might think of as a cognitive landscape.[29] Descriptive writing does not have a very high profile in the Eclogue-book, but descriptive elements are distributed throughout, and by often beginning with the immediate foreground give the reader an entry into the wider imaginary space.[30]

However, what we see in this way in Eclogue-land is an artificial and stylised depiction. To start with, the bucolic natives, for example, are typically herdsmen, and the nature of the plant and animal life in the poems is geared towards that demography. As this bucolic world is so artificial we should ask how it might relate to the Roman conceptualisation of the world at large. It owes a lot to Theocritus, certainly, but to what extent are there concepts of physical space, landscape, nature, or the country to which it can also relate? It will emerge that the landscape of the *Eclogues* has its roots rather in the world of the garden and the garden painting than in any tradition of landscape painting, landscape literature (both of which are harder to find in the Roman context than is sometimes thought), and that there is only a partial connection with other concepts of space and landscape in the Roman mind.

The Roman perception of geographical space was largely conditioned by conquest and rule (Nicolet 1991: 2), and by trade and food. The Romans came increasingly to need and to acquire or produce maps, route descriptions and route-maps, navigational accounts and manuals (*periploi*), roads, geographical and ethnographical treatises, and the histories of Roman military experiences,[31] and to be aware of differential time zones.[32] To a large extent, the world was divided into Rome – or Italy – and a variegated 'not-Rome/Italy', or into centres (linked by routes) and 'betweens'. The distinction between the urban centre and the food-producing surroundings is itself coloured by political and logistic needs with the result that non-urban Italy is commonly presented as the home of the hardy small-holder of the Roman moralising tradition and agricultural literature (Cato, Varro, Virgil's *Georgics*, etc.), the citizen small-holder who is ready to become a Roman soldier when so called upon. This overlaps only in part with the visual and mental space presented in the *Eclogues*. However, the conceptualisation of space as structured on the lines of a defined inner and a relatively undefined outer region matches the fundamental structure of Eclogue-land and repeats itself at all levels in the material environmental sphere. This distinction is a powerful pre-verbal cognitive structure onto which is mapped, as the individual grows and matures from infancy, the centrality of the house,[33] the urban centre, Rome, Italy, the Roman world, and indeed the known world. In all cases, the outside reaches out into an undefined and potentially threatening shadowiness.[34]

Evocations of walking in the countryside are few, and tend to be limited, or incidental. Horace wanders in the woods (*Odes* 1.22; 3.4.9ff.; 3.13) and might enjoy a solitary trip to Tarentum (*Sat.* 1.6.104-6) and takes part in a group journey to Brundisium (Hor. *Sat.* 1.5), but his scenic effects are generally in low profile, and the pleasures usually poetic or social rather than visually aesthetic.[35] A passage like the following is rather exceptional:

ne perconteris fundus meus, optime Quincti,
arvo pascat erum an bacis opulentet olivae,
pomisne an pratis an amicta vitibus ulmo,
scribetur tibi forma loquaciter et situs agri.
continui montes, ni dissocientur opaca
valle, sed ut veniens dextrum latus aspiciat sol,
laevum discedens curru fugiente vaporet.
temperiem laudes. quid si rubicunda benigni
corna vepres et pruna ferant? si quercus et ilex
multa fruge pecus multa dominum iuvat umbra?
dicas adductum propius frondere Tarentum.
fons etiam rivo dare nomen idoneus, ut nec
frigidior Thracam nec purior ambiat Hebrus,
infirmo capiti fluit utilis, utilis alvo.
hae latebrae dulces, etiam, si credis, amoenae,
incolumem tibi me praestant Septembribus horis.

Hor. *Epp.* 1.16.1-16

My dear Quinctius, lest you ask whether my farm feeds its master from the field or enriches him with the fruits of the olive, or with apples, or meadows, or with the elm clothed in vines, I'll write to you chattily about the nature and disposition of the land. The mountains are continuous, except where they are broken by a shady valley, so that the sun looks on their right flank as it comes, and warms the left as it leaves in its hurrying chariot. You would praise the mild climate. And if the kindly bushes bear red cornels and plums, if the oak and ilex delight the herd with much produce and the master with much shade? You would say Tarentum was in leaf and had been brought nearby! A spring flows too, fit to give a name to the river – Hebrus does not wash Thrace more coolly or clearly – good for an invalid's head, good for his stomach. This sweet retreat – even (if you believe me) beautiful – keeps me whole for you in the September heat.

Indeed, as a rule, scenic effects are not a very high priority in Latin verse. Lucretius' visual field does not pick out the country as a special category as such, and the priority is virtually always that whatever is visible is the source of evidence of atoms, their behaviour, and the like. The moralising tradition mocks the aristocratic racing from town to country and back again, but without exploiting the scenic possibilities (Lucr. 3.1060-70; Hor. *Sat.* 2.7.28-9; *Epp.* 1.1.83-7; 1.8.12). Paradoxical visual effects (e.g. Romans building villas out into the sea)[36] have a special point and a different agenda. The country also has a place in the town-country contrast frequent in Roman moralising, but this is the country of that potent ideological symbol, the farming smallholder, and has comparatively little value in its own right.[37]

Elsewhere, the *locus amoenus* has a literary currency as a setting for Roman gentlemen to stage a drinking party, as does the Callimachean spring (for poetic inspiration), and the wilds of hunting myths (V. *Ecl.* 10; Prop. 1.1), but these are all contextually confined phenomena. There is nothing in Roman literature comparable to the poetry of Wordsworth, or to the use of landscape in the portraiture of the eighteenth and later centuries as a backdrop helping to suggest the sitter's enlightened harmony with nature or the sublime. Certainly, there is in Horace (esp. *Epp.* 1.18.103-11; cf. 1.16.1-16, cited above) a picture of country life – together with some descriptive detail – as a suitable locus for the philosophical/ethical life, but this is a rather special Horatian development (and later than the *Eclogues*), although there is some precedent in Tibullan elegy and indeed in the *Georgics*.[38]

A strong literary sense of countryside is lacking. If we look in the sphere of Roman art we see various types of painting that seem to be relevant in various ways and degrees to the visual field with which we are presented in the *Eclogues*, but again the bucolic-landscape connection turns out to be flimsier than we might have expected. However, there is, as we shall see, other valuable material.[39]

The evidence is patchy and there are issues of chronology, prove-

nance, and conceptualisation. Much of our knowledge of Roman paint-
ing of the second and first centuries BC comes from material preserved
by the eruption in AD 79 of Mount Vesuvius. However, there is some
material from Rome as well, and we know also that Romans frequented
the Campanian area, owned villas there, and visited each other.[40] As
regards conceptualisation, there is the matter of the term 'landscape'
itself. It is not infrequently used in the context of Roman art history,
but the extent to which what we actually see in Roman art corresponds
to what we might think of as landscape is problematic.

For us, the concept of landscape is a complex entity, and on inspection
more and more fragmentation sets in. If we think of landscape painting,
we are likely to be thinking of a tradition which assumes some impor-
tance from the Golden Age of Dutch painting and which at that time has
to be seen in the contexts of contemporary social values and other
genres of painting.[41] Subsequently, other values enter the picture and a
landscape painting in the eighteenth century or now may refer to the
tradition, but has other contexts to shape its relationship with its
audience. A landscape by Ruysdael is very different in composition,
technique and colour from a French impressionist landscape – with or
without accompanying social event – or David Hockney's recent and
immense landscapes. Attitudes to the ontological status of natural
phenomena change (in earlier landscape painting there is still a notion
that the viewer of natural phenomena is looking at evidence of the
existence of God), as do attitudes to the incorporation in landscapes of
humans, of architectural elements, of social events, and of signifiers of
social class and dynamics. The twentieth- and twenty-first-century use
of landscape in film is an additional complexity. Over and above this,
one might also think of landscape-gardening – another phenomenon
with a strong presence in seventeenth-century Holland (also, as we
shall see, in the Roman world). Here, the idea of landscape is not that
it is a representation of a particular type of visual field, nor even just
the construction of such a field, but the shaping of an area to provide an
aesthetic stage for human and social activity.

Various attitudes to nature wrestle with each other in all this mate-
rial. At one extreme, nature is a wild thing which evokes and reflects
the madder elements of the soul or surrounds the fragile centres of
humanity and civilisation; at the other, nature – and sometimes it needs
domesticating to be able to do it – has to do with a principle of harmony
with which humans may try to align themselves. However, another
picture again of what landscape is comes from the use of archaeological
evidence in the study of local economies and the interactions of man and
environment, urban and rural.[42] Here too the interest is anthropocentric
and emphasises elements of control, alteration, and domestication, but
not in the purposely aesthetic manner of the landscape-gardener. The
growth of ecological sensibilities has also coloured attitudes to non-

urban space, and from a quite different angle. The visual element of countryside has been important in endlessly ramifying ways in the last quarter of the second millennium. Often there is little or nothing in the Roman mindset to correspond to these ways,[43] but the element of shaping of nature and its representations for socio-aesthetic purposes is certainly present in the Roman mind.

In fact, landscape is not an exterior reality. It is not a location, or a particular kind of visual field; it is not a category of place, nor is it the same as any portion of the globe even if defined in terms of circles whose centres are individual or group viewers. Rather, it has to do with the viewer or viewer-group feeling able to explain or justify a sense of identity or difference, and to that extent it has a rhetorical force. An utterance such as 'I don't like the country; it smells of animals and there are not enough shops, restaurants, concert halls, there isn't enough glass or concrete there' is form of individual self-expression. At a more complex level, John of Gaunt's speech about England (*Richard II*, 2.1) as a 'fortress built by Nature', 'a precious stone set in the silver sea which serves it in the office of a wall, or as a moat defensive to a house' weaves 'landscape' and 'history' together in a rhetoric of fictive English-ness. Gaunt's internal image of England is a dynamic part of the configuration of his identity and could be expressed and re-expressed under whatever circumstances, in whatever location, and with what-ever colour he might feel the need so to do. Landscape is made of history and memory; it is a subjective thing, the bearer of meaning, a mode of representation, an internalised language of self-projection.[44] Landscape in art and literature is, then, a sort of meta-language, one whose vocabulary is culturally conditioned, a cultural product, but also one to which the cultural producers themselves – in the widest sense – contrib-ute.[45] In a period of social change, the language changes too, and in the emphasis on a coherently expressive quasi-natural space Virgil's bu-colic poetry is a symptom of, and collaborator in, a wider cultural shift.

In his *Natural History*, Pliny refers to an Augustan painter, Studius, who, he says, instituted the fashion of painting murals of villas, porti-coes and gardens, groves, woods, hills, fishponds, canals, rivers, and coasts, and containing people pursuing various appropriate activities (*NH* 35.116). Surviving paintings support the notion that this became an important element in the Augustan period (although it has antece-dents), but it is striking that in the passage from Pliny, and in the paintings too, architectural elements are strongly foregrounded, and human activity is an important element.[46] Pliny also refers to the element of humour or wit in some of the human figuration. We might well call such paintings villascapes, harbourscapes, and the like, rather than landscapes as such, and be aware that the comic aspect is another complicating variable. There is much in this overall picture that does not fit our ideas of landscape neatly, but equally does not correspond

altogether well with what we find in the *Eclogues*. There the aristo-
cratic carriages, fishponds, and dwellings, and the coastal cities, to
which Pliny refers, are all more or less absent, nor are the fishing,
fowling, and hunting typical bucolic pursuits. There is humour in
Virgil's portrayal of his herdsmen, but of a quite different kind from the
men slipping in the marshy approaches to villas after they have bar-
gained to carry women across.

If we ask what other kinds of Roman painting may be able to provide
enlightening resonances with the world of the *Eclogues*, in addition to
the *trompe l'oeil* effects of Roman architectural painting already re-
ferred to, four other areas seem to stand out. First, there are the scenes
called sacral-idyllic. These are set in the open air and typically involve
some human presence, some sheep or goats, some plantlife (a few trees,
perhaps), an element of architectural detail, a rock formation. Secondly,
there are paintings of gardens or garden-like visual fields. Thirdly,
there are paintings *in* gardens; often these are paintings of gardens,
garden extensions, or garden-like visual fields, but they are not always
so, and it is in any case important to recognise the category of paintings
in gardens as a distinct entity. Fourthly, there are mythological
scenes.[47] This category often involves landscape elements in the back-
ground, and more importantly includes scenes in which the characters
are set in a more or less pastoral setting, not unlike the settings of
sacral-idyllic scenes. Other types of painting – still life and architec-
tural – may also have a degree of importance which is not at first
obvious.

The four main categories listed above seem to provide obvious points
of contact with the Virgilian bucolic world. However, as well as the
potentially hazardous issues of chronology and provenance, there is also
the matter of the larger contexts in which these categories must be seen.
A necessarily very crude outline of the Roman art-scene will prepare the
way for a closer look at what is relevant to the *Eclogues*.

In Rome the formation of private art collections was a distinctive
phenomenon of the late republic,[48] stimulated by the vast quantities of
Greek art taken as loot in the third to the second centuries BC and later
supplemented by Greek artists migrating to Rome (cf. Pliny *NH* 35.155-
6 on Arcesilaus the sculptor and his prices).[49] The Greek distinction
between public and private art, already rather eroded in the 'private'
art patronised by Hellenistic monarchs, was further blurred by this, the
larger role of private patronage, and the appearance of public art
galleries.[50] In Rome (and other cities), a range of art forms was accessi-
ble to the poetry reading classes in their own and in each other's houses,
and in public (including murals at baths and other leisure facilities) to
a wider audience as well (cf. Cic. *Tusc.* 5.102),[51] and thought about art
was fed by collectors, the existence of collections and galleries, and the
dissemination of informal and popular ideas in a variety of writers.[52]

The status of artists and poets (or art and poetry) in Roman society is unequal.[53] We know of numbers of aristocratic amateur poets (including Cicero and Maecenas). Pliny, who himself indulged, gives an extensive list of predecessors going back to the republican period (*Ep.* 5.3). On the other hand, we know the names of some, but comparatively few, painters, and none of the aristocratic amateur type.[54] Verbal skills were part of the aristocratic education and power-system, and writing poetry was a way of demonstrating versatility. The painterly skills, by contrast, were too workmanlike for the aristocrat. That does not mean, however, that the values of art were unknown territory. Connoisseurship was a sufficient mastery for the aristocratic art-owner to demonstrate.[55] Thus, the field of aesthetic considerations was appropriated by the buying class. Moreover, even though the commissioning buyer of a work of art had control over content and even detail, the artist or presiding artist still had room for artistic choices in competition with his rivals,[56] just as Rembrandt or Hals were to have in their commissioned portraits of civic groups. Virgil himself, in however illusory a manner, gives us a picture of himself writing the *Eclogues* to order (*Ecl.* 8.11-12). All in all, visual art forms and their values were allowed enough prestige and recognition for them to have a degree of cultural equilibrium with poetry.[57] The famous passage in the *Aeneid* where Anchises tells Aeneas the future glories of Rome shows how admiration for art maintains a subtle balance with its citizen-viewer's superiority to its producers (it is rather striking that oratory, which was a perfectly respectable practice for the aristocrat, fares no better here than art does in comparison with the arts of ruling).[58]

> excudent alii spirantia mollius aera
> (credo equidem), vivos ducent de marmore vultus,
> orabunt causas melius, caelique meatus
> describent radio et surgentia sidera dicent:
> tu regere imperio populos, Romane, memento
> (hae tibi erunt artes), pacique imponere morem,
> parcere subiectis et debellare superbos.

V. *Aen.* 6. 847-53

Others shall shape with more suppleness breathing bronzes[59] (yes, I am sure), and mould living faces from marble, others shall better plead cases, and mark out with a pointer the journeyings of the sky and say the rising stars: you, Roman, remember to rule nations with authority (these will be your arts), to impose usage upon peace, to spare the beaten and war down the proud.

We know of a variety of media and genres. We know of public statuary and relief work (and here one might also include coins), much of it to do with divine figures, military events, major public figures, and much of it celebratory or memorial, and involving major personages in

128

quasi- or semi-mythological guises, although the Romans increasingly also represented actual events and persons (in general the Romans were more interested than the Greeks in representation of specific historical events and portraiture). In the late Republic, victorious generals sometimes showed commemorative paintings (sometimes incorporating map-like elements and bird's-eye views).[60] We also know of private works, a development deriving to a large extent from the Hellenistic courts. Here we can add domestic ornament, tableware and table-statuary, house and garden murals, paintings on panels,[61] mosaics etc., and the buying of copies of famous originals for home and garden ornament. We know also of portraiture, especially in the context of the family images (*imagines*) in the home's hall, and of theatrical scenery painting. In the case of the latter, it is important to think of the scene painting as incomplete without the presence of the actors on the stage, and in this regard scenery painting shows in a more explicit way a feature of a much broader range of Roman art.

In terms of the themes of Roman art, we know of public and monumental celebrations, mythological scenes and narratives,[62] gardenscapes, villascapes,[63] harbour scenes, a range of erotic scenes, sacral-idyllic scenes, gladiatorial scenes, still lifes. Crudely these types can be seen as part of a generic system analogous to that visible in the literary sphere.[64] Indeed, the relationship between the literary sphere and the visual arts is more than one of analogy. Poets allude to or play with the conventions of art (notably, but by no means only, in the *ecphrasis*), and painters and sculptors annex the material of the poets.

Public art differs from private art (with the qualifications mentioned above) and in domestic art there is a tendency to match image to the typology of the room in which it is located.[65] As with literary genres, one sees – perhaps in a fragmentary way – links between art and social history. For example, the development of naturalistic portraiture suggests a growth of interest in individual identity, and may connect with the competitive individualism of Roman politics and literature from the late Republic, and with the thematisation of the public-private polarity in Augustan literature.[66] The growth of domestic themes, likewise, may be seen as reflecting a growing consciousness of the domestic sphere as deserving evaluation. Mythological scenes generally have a special connection with epic, the cultural cherry on the literary generic cake, and assert (as knowing the poetic repertoire itself also does) socio-cultural prestige.[67] Some evidence (below) points towards the growth also of a deheroicised para-mythology akin to phenomena in the poets of the late Republic and Augustan times. In the second half-century BC, in the House of Livia (Palatine, *c.* 30 BC) – along with a monochrome landscape with figures and buildings and, in another room, a rustic shrine with trees and offerings – there are the remains of a Polyphemus and Galatea wall painting.[68] In the Villa of Agrippa Postumus (Boscotrecase, two miles from Pompeii, *c.* 11 BC), along with sacral-idyllic scenes and landscapes, there are mythological landscapes, including another Polyphemus and Galatea (now in the Metropolitan Museum of Art, New York), complete with the bucolic trappings of sheep and a herdsman's crook.[69] In the light of the importance of Polyphemus and Galatea in the *Eclogues* these are – problems of chronology notwithstanding – perhaps particularly interesting.

Uncertainties of chronology are a problem, but not necessarily too much of one as far as we are concerned here. They certainly complicate the apparent simplicity of the four-style analysis of Pompeian art (which stems from a passage of Vitruvius: 7.5.1-3).[70] In addition, different houses are constructed and decorated and redecorated at different times. The Roman guest on a social circuit sees not only modern, but also older art. Moreover, at any point in the larger time frame there are both modernising and conservative eddies[71] (as indeed we see very clearly in the literature of the late republic and Augustan period). Individual tastes are complex and varied: old masters were indeed prized at the same time as new works were commissioned. There were, of course, analogous tendencies in the literary sphere, as we see from Horace's (*Epp.* 2.1) complaints about the archaizing taste of some of the poetry-reading audience.

Nevertheless, if we step back from the four-style analysis we can see that a number of important elements are spread – albeit unevenly – throughout the whole continuum. For example, we find a varying use of illusionistic optical tricks in architectural painting – sometimes very elaborate around the period of the *Eclogues*.[72] Elements in such painting evoke a grander style of building than that of the houses in which it was displayed. This is true not only of aristocratic houses, but also of the small houses and shops in which mural art is also often found. According to Stewart,[73] it was evidently important 'for Romans of greater or lesser financial means to surround themselves with complicated, imaginative paintings that conjured up the impression of an even more elaborate environment'. Of course, the domestic display of wealth *was* important,[74] but these painted illusions (cf. Vitruvius 6.2.2 for the idea of deceit) – as Stewart also notes – remain palpably illusions; the viewer is not really fooled at all (hence Petronius' fun at the expense of the simple Encolpius who is, indeed, tricked by a painted dog: *Sat.* 29). *Trompe l'oeil* effects often depend on a particular viewpoint, and no-one in a house, guest or inmate, remains standing in one fixed place.[75] Even if one were to remain static for some time (sitting at a poetry reading, say) the trick could not be operative for long.[76] This is particularly the case with 'illusory' architectural vistas and false 'extra rooms', such as were becoming fashionable in the second style period (within which the *Eclogues* fall). In the case of the first-style imitation of, for example, marble panels, in which the illusion is aided by some architectural features being modelled in relief (in *stucco*), the illusion is less subject to the angle from which one looks, but even here the illusionistic convincingness is to be enjoyed rather than fraudulent.

Wallace-Hadrill[77] thinks all such decoration makes an *allusion* to wealth and manages to avoid the criticism of luxury and excess, because it is recognisably only an allusion, and not real, and writes that this allusiveness is a more important function than 'visual games'. However, aristocratic Romans were genuinely competitive in luxury and in architecture, and it is very doubtful that only partially illusive allusions would be enough to satisfy this; it is much more plausible that this kind of decoration expresses and satisfies a taste for games with illusionism both for their own sake and as part of social activity, and this is a major point of contact with the poetry of the Augustan period, with its interest in mixing and contrasting different modes of representation. These architecturally illusive murals may indeed have satisfied a competitive spirit as well, but we should look for this – as with poetry – in terms of the elaboration and craftsmanship of the art displayed, and in the taste and cultivation of the owner.[78]

It is only later that one finds much domestic evidence of theatrical scenes and paintings of theatrical sets with actors in mythological roles,[79] and garden paintings; nevertheless, their tendency to turn the living viewers into actors in a scene to which the depicted element is a backdrop is already anticipated in domestic architectural murals, and here too we will find analogous effects in the *Eclogues* (see below).[80]

Garden paintings,[81] in fact, expand on ideas already long implicit in gardens themselves, and any question of chronology is therefore of reduced impact in any case. It is worth considering one very striking example here. In the Villa of Livia (Prima Porta, nine miles north of Rome) there is an underground room, known as the Garden Room because the walls are decorated with a mural painting – continuing round the four walls and unbroken except by a single door – of realistic trees, plants, and birds (largely identifiable), and provided with (in the painting) an awning and parapet.[82] The room measures nearly 12 x 6 m. This is said to be the earliest surviving garden painting, although there are antecedents in the form of murals showing an architectural screen (pillars or arched openings in a colonnade) through which remoter trees, buildings, and gardens, or ivy-wreathed grottoes, fountains, and vine-pergolas may be seen, as at the villa of P. Fannius Synistor at Boscoreale, near Pompeii (*c.* 40s BC).[83] The overall effect of a mural like that in Livia's garden room is that the owner or guest in the room can see himself as looking out from a canopied pergola into a garden. The owner of such a room becomes the owner of the imaginary prospect. The owner and guests are, while they are there, part of the 'landscape' in a sense analogous to that in which the Roman reader can imagine himself into Virgilian bucolic space. Although Livia's garden room is later than the *Eclogues* (built and painted around 20 BC), it manifests and embodies the tensions and ambiguities between inside and outside which we see in the poems, in less advanced form in Synistor's villa, and, as we shall see below, in public gardens surrounded by the openings between pillars in colonnades or in the painting of trees 'glimpsed between arched openings and a fictive colonnade' decorating part of the House of Menander at Pompeii (Ling 1991: 150). In Livia's garden room, the guest is inside a room, but the painting puts him in an open-walled (but terraced), thatch-roofed summer house in a garden,[84] a garden which itself is contained by a wall of leafage in the painting's background (and behind that, one might infer, a garden wall). There is here an immensely sophisticated and dexterous game with real, represented, and imaginary boundaries which is distinctly reminiscent of the Eclogue-book.

There are other points of resemblance to the *Eclogues*, too. Strikingly, in Livia's painted garden, 'everything is in bloom simultaneously. The periwinkles, wild laurel, iris, roses, poppies, and daisies of spring burst forth at the same time as the oleanders of July, the chrysanthemums of September, and the quinces and pomegranates of late autumn' (Kellum 1994: 221).[85] This transcendence of the natural seasons is like that seen in the assemblage of flora in Corydon's imaginary collection of offerings (*Ecl.* 2.45-50). In a broader sense, the same sort of transcendence can also be seen in the Eclogue-book as a whole, combining as it does – but without setting them in a chronological frame or sequence – poems set at different times of year.[86]

One should also notice the sheer multiplicity of plantlife in this and other such garden paintings. There is a density and variety which is certainly not matched in uncultivated nature. It might exceed the variety shown in a real garden too, but that is because it is a distillation rather than a transcript of what might be seen in a real garden. Again, Corydon's floral assemblage in the second *Eclogue*, various individual *Eclogues*, and the collection as a whole provide analogues.

Another aspect of Roman art which is relevant to the bucolic world is the interplay of different levels of reality and representation implied in garden statuary and in portraiture in the guise of divine figures. In the case of the former, statues in a garden create a scene in which the garden-ambulant is an actor. In the latter, there is an analogous element of imaginary role-playing with which we may compare (for example) the literary divine presentation of Emperors (cf. Stat. *Silvae* and Hellenistic antecedents). At a lower social level (and found closer to the time of the *Eclogues* too) we have Horace acting out epical scenes in his divine rescue in *Sat.* 1.9, and more overtly mythological-poetic in *Odes* 2.7 (where he is rescued from the battle at Philippi by Mercury). At another and more mixed social level, we have also the mythological charades in the arena.[87] If we think of this business of role-playing in

various art and semi-dramatic forms, of the caricature of the phenome-
non in Petronius' fictional account of the vulgar freedman Trimalchio's
dinner, and of the way in which painting and sculpture sometimes cast
the audience in the role of actors, we can think of the fanciful interpene-
tration of art, the mythological story-pool, and life as a major feature of
Roman culture. In turn, this may allow us to see the presence of Pollio,
Gallus, and company in the *Eclogues* as implying that we too (in our
capacity as representatives of the Roman audience) might be part of an
extended Arcadia – a game that some Romans seem to have played
themselves.[88] The interest in mythological scenes which is sustained
through most of late republic and Augustan period, is both a corollary
and a constant reinforcement to self-mythologising tendencies we see
here.

Thinking in terms of garden paintings, paintings in gardens, and the
interplay of levels of representation and reality, we could speculate
profitably about the typical spaces in which the *Eclogues* might be
recited: they could not always, by any means, have been recited in
surroundings of mythological paintings, sacral-idyllic scenes, or gar-
den/park scenes, nor always in gardens[89] with faunal or other statues,
but many recitations might have been in such appropriate surround-
ings, and the audience which knew the *Eclogues* would also have been
aware of such surroundings. Such surroundings could easily make some
Romans think of the *Eclogues*,[90] and in turn some hearers of the
Eclogues might remember such surroundings. Indeed it is possible that
any of the possible contexts for a recital might contribute to the disso-
lution of the boundaries between art and reality implicit in the
collection itself. The absorption of art into literature is also built into
the set-piece descriptive format of the *ecphrasis,* where the description
is itself like a work of art, and is a backdrop or stage for the literary
action to be played out against. In the case of the wall paintings the
human audience itself provides this action by being there and engaging
in social activity. In the *Eclogues*, the bucolic natives and Roman guests
provide some of the 'narrative' action, but the audience too can imagine
itself as being part of the scene as well.

Finally, there are the landscapes and sacral-idyllic scenes. The inter-
est in 'landscape' and natural-world elements is also a sustained
substrate from the Augustan period onwards. At around the mid-first
century BC, water-birds, plants, and fantastic creatures begin to adorn
the architectural features of mural painting. In the last third of the
same century, landscapes and sacral-idyllic scenes appear in friezes
and in the central band of the wall.[91] The landscapes are, first, anthro-
pocentric in that they often contain human figures or architectural
features (and the same is true for theatrical scene painting, not least
because of the presence on stage of the actors in their roles). The
landscape element does not convey an interest in what might be called

unmediated nature. In the Garden of Livia painting, analogously, the painting contains a representation of a parapet, and in addition the viewers themselves become, as it were, part of the picture like actors in a scene.[92] Secondly, landscape elements are subject to various degrees of stylisation – in mythological scenes there are, for example, unnaturally steep and expressionistic rock formations; in garden pictures there is a concentration, selectivity, or density of depicted items compared with anything in real visual fields. The tendency of Latin poetry to concentrate scenic description and detail in the ecphrasis reflects the localised concentration of landscape elements in painting. (Moreover, in both painting and the ecphrasis the scenic effects are analogous to the theatrical backgrounds to human activity in stage-painting.)

As regards the sacral-idyllic images,[93] unmediated nature (again) is not of prime interest in this genre. With regard to the landscape element in these scenes, it is true that we do not find the concentrated variety of faunal and floral types which can be seen in garden paintings. Instead, the basic artistic unit of the landscape elements is the overall profile produced by a small menu of individual elements working as a collective, rather than the variety shown within each of the categories of elements. The trees, for example, are disposed so as collectively to generate a unitary outline. The images are anthropocentric; even if the human figures occupy a fairly small percentage of the picture plane, their presence is a core feature. Pompeian examples show herdsmen and goats arranged elegantly about stylised settings with landscape features including a selection of: trees, rocks, architectural elements (shrines).[94] How do these compare with what we see in the *Eclogues*?

There are striking similarities between these scenes and both the visual fields of 'Lucretian bucolic' and the *Eclogues*.[95] The foregrounded presentation of a quite small number of individual humans in the sacral-idyllic images makes the resemblance between them and the *Eclogues*, in which generally two or three herdsmen come upon each other, particularly striking.[96] There are, nonetheless, different emphases. In the murals there is a significantly higher presence accorded to architecture (and no vineyards, orchards, or fields), whereas in the *Eclogues* the element of singing (perhaps hard to thematise effectively in painting) is more evident. The goats which are so evidently programmatic in the *Eclogues* are perhaps more consistently foregrounded presences in the murals than in the poems, whereas love is more obvious a feature in the poems. There is, of course, nothing in the murals which brings the land distribution issue to mind. The fauns which appear in Lucretius' version of bucolic and appear along with satyrs and nymphs in statue form in Roman gardens are treated by Virgil as though they are standard generic features, but in an intertextual sense rather than as part of the general action or visual fields of the poems.

There is a similar kind of likeness to the world of the *Eclogues* in quasi-bucolic mythological scenes. The early first century Polyphemus and Galatea from the Villa of Agrippa Postumus (see pp. 129-30) has bucolic-type features (rocks and goats) which remind us of the importance of this pair of characters in the Theocriteo-Virgilian tradition. The villa also contains sacral-idyllic scenes,[97] landscapes, and mythological landscapes, evidencing a sort of generic relatedness. Although the date is later than we might like, there are antecedents in the House of Livia in the other Polyphemus and Galatea mentioned earlier, and in the landscapes. One presumes that such remains are surviving representatives of more widespread examples.

In conclusion, there is evidence of various types of painting which are thematically related to the world of the *Eclogues* – paintings in which natural features (trees etc.) are important, or in which deheroised mythical figures play unepic roles, or in which there seem to be bucolic elements. We have signs of a cultural phenomenon, viz. bucolic-style and related representations, which, on the one hand, take us little or no further towards a concept of landscape as such, but do allow us to recognise in principle some degree of intertextuality between visual art and a Graeco-Latin verse genre.[98] In this case, we should picture the Roman audience of the *Eclogues* as experiencing Arcadia as a synchronically continuous substrate into which poetic and artistic windows – as in the architectural illusionism we can see in Pompeian visual art – can be opened (cf. above on *Eclogues* as only the visible spectrum part of Arcadia).[99] As well as this, we have to recognise that, irrespective of thematic content or subject matter, there are features of Roman art which play with the boundaries between reality and representation in ways which seem to resemble representational oddities in various Roman genres, but perhaps especially Virgilian bucolic.

Nature, art, and artifice; the Garden

Looking at Roman art provides us with suggestive perspectives for reading the Eclogue-book, but does not take us very far in considering how those elements that seem to involve what we might call landscape work in the collection. However, progress may be possible in other directions. We start by considering the various ways in which the Romans conceptualised their place in the physical world.

Rather than thinking in terms of countryside or landscape, for the Romans the world is more appropriately considered as the city surrounded by the Other – a tract whose outer boundary is obscure and whose inner regions are variously farmland, mountain, sea, etc. and traversed by *routes* (trade routes, military routes, provincial government routes, and, for those so minded, epic journey-routes), for within this space are destinations with various relationships to the city.

135

There are also generalised Roman concepts of nature.[100] These (like their somewhat flimsy concept of landscape) have a different agenda from our own, but neither are they uniformly embedded in the world of the *Eclogues*. Such Roman ideas as that of nature as opposed to (or supporting) reason (as for Horace in his hexameter works, or for the Stoics), or nature as the way humans or the cosmos operate, do not explicitly present themselves in the bucolic world with any force. When Cicero writes about nature as the highest good (Cic. *De Leg.* 1.21.56) and looks at the sky, earth, sea, and the nature of all things (Cic. *De Leg.* 1.23.61), his cosmic-philosophical interest is again different from the emphases of the *Eclogues*. Even the personified idea of Nature as a generative principle which we find in Lucretius is only implicitly felt in Virgil's assemblage of plants, animals, seasons etc.[101] On the other hand, the iconography of the Golden Age – that time when man needed to do no work and food supplied itself spontaneously, nor were artefacts like ships known – is surely immanent in the *Eclogues* (and not just in *Eclogue* 4). Likewise, the moralising and agriculturally oriented town and country contrast[102] whereby the town stands for luxury and the country stands for the values of simplicity, hard work, manliness and so forth, makes itself felt in their atmosphere. These notions, however, are not obtrusive presences in the texture of the book.

However, if the Romans lacked a fully fledged notion of landscape, countryside, or nature as represented by, or embodied in, the extra-urban environment, there is important physical material relevant to the representation of Eclogue-land, both within and outside the *urbs,* in the world of gardens, parks, and estates. There is a very large range of phenomena here, even without taking into account parallels and analogues in cultures contemporary with the Romans, or the various precedents.[103] Gardens, parks, and estates are referred to in a broad range of Roman literature, but, in addition to this, they were part of the reality surrounding the Roman wherever he or she went in Italy. We should see Rome as ringed and sprinkled with gardens, parks, villa gardens, estates, palatial roof gardens, gardens in restaurants and inns and at baths,[104] tomb gardens, and sacred groves.[105] Investigation of the cities and farms buried by the eruption of Vesuvius (79 AD) shows that 'almost all private houses had at least one garden. It could dominate the house and occupy a surface area larger than the rooms used for sleeping, dining, and socialising. Even if space was limited in a very small house, a corner of the courtyard was set aside for a modest planted area. For those who lived in blocks of flats, window boxes could provide space for growing plants'.[106] In a passage usually taken as referring to window boxes, though possibly referring to painted scenes, Pliny (19.59) comments on the urban lower classes affording their eyes a daily view of country scenes by means of 'images of gardens' (*imagine hortorum*) in their windows.[107] The miniature garden of the window box allows the imagination to play on natural countryside, but, strikingly, Pliny sees the window box itself as an imaginary garden. It follows that the urban domestic garden in general is a medium for imagining the country, or for mediating between ideals associated with rural nature and the urban attractions of civilisation (Purcell 1987: 203).

Given this broad socio-cultural background, an analogy between the enclosed and poetically ordered visual fields of the Eclogue-book and the enclosed and artificially ordered visual fields of garden and parks is extremely tempting.[108] It is true that smallholdings also present nature in an artificially contrived form, and the inhabitants of the *Eclogues* are in some sense presented as smallholders; nevertheless, the apparently leisurely level of work and the large importance of social activity for the bucolic natives tends to suggest that the analogy of gardens is at least as important as, and perhaps more so than, that of farms, and the seclusion of the bucolic world reinforces this feeling very strongly (see below).

In the Roman period, the forms of garden, parks and estate are prolific in variety. Lying behind this variety, the small *hortus* as vegetable or kitchen garden, the original sense of the word,[109] continued as a reality as well as figuring in literature. It figures in the tenth book of Columella, which in its hexametrical format gives a kind of appendix to Virgil's *Georgics*.[110] Kitchen plots might be part of urban gardens or smallholdings, or villa estates.[111] There is extensive archaeological evidence for varied productive gardening within the town walls of Pompeii (especially viticulture, vegetable patches, and orchards), and the same garden may contain elements geared to pleasure and elements geared to production.[112] The kitchen garden is clearly evocative for Horace and his audience (*Sat.* 2.6 init.). Market gardens and orchards came in various sizes and locations and figure repeatedly in, for example, the *Priapea*, that form of epigram in which an animated statue of Priapus exacts sexual penalties from fruit stealers. The garden of Alcinous (Hom. *Od.* 7.114ff.) and the garden of the Hesperides where the Golden Apples grew add a mythological lustre to the idea of the orchard.

However, such more or less utilitarian gardens are by Virgil's time only a small part of the whole picture, and the values and attitudes surrounding the range of phenomena are complex. Whatever its size, a garden is not *only* a garden. It expresses attitudes, predilections, social status and aspirations, intellectual and literary tastes and affiliations, the owner's personality, and his idea of his place in a larger context, and it does so in a way that contributes to and follows fashions.[113] The garden is yet another stage on which the owner can impersonate himself.[114]

The garden of the Greek philosopher Epicurus – which appears in the same context in the Elder Pliny (*NH* 19.49-51) as the gardens of Alcinous and the Hesperides, and the Hanging Gardens of Babylon, along with the kitchen gardens, public gardens, and luxury gardens that they saw around them – had for the Romans become part of the garden of the imagination.[115] Cicero's Tusculan garden, adorned with Greek works of art and a statue of Plato (*Ad Att.* 1.4; 1.6; 1.8-11), draws on this philosophical connection;[116] so too does his account of a walk to the walks and groves of the Academy in Athens (with M. Piso, Atticus, and his brother Quintus), passing the garden of Epicurus on the way (Cic. *De Finibus* 5.1.1-3). Somewhat similarly, Horace's Sabine farm, which figures in the *Odes, Satires,* and *Epistles,* comes to embody a philosophical-ethical way of life (cf. *Sat.* 2.6.32-4; *Ep.* 1.19), and becomes a core location in Horace's poetic thought, irrespective of genre. The Romans who took part in the equestrian exercises in the Campus Martius were enacting the performance of being Roman because that activity is enshrined in the *Aeneid* as one that can be traced back to the proto-Roman time of King Latinus (*Aen.* 7.160-5). Another way of looking at this would be to say that both the exercisers and the poet were taking part in affirming their ancient group identity. They become one with and celebrate their ancestral images. One might also mention that Virgil's Elysian Fields (*Aen.* 6) are imagined with garden like attributes. The garden, public and private, was a place designed for, amongst other things, the play of the imagination; it was, as von Stackelberg puts it (2009: 2), 'not just a place, it was an idea of a place, experienced on both a societal and an individual level'.[117]

Associations could be attached to individual trees as well as to green spaces, their ornaments, and the activities associated with them. This might be in the general sense in which the oak is sacred to Jupiter, the myrtle to Venus, the laurel to Apollo and so on (cf. Helen's plane-tree at Theocr. 18.42-8),[118] or in which a particular tree figures in one of the stories of metamorphosis which appear in Greek and Latin poetry; or the significance might be more specific, as with the sacred oak under which Romulus founded the Temple of Jupiter Feretrius (Livy 1.10).[119] Augustus used trees variously in his own iconography.[120] For example, he had a palm tree which grew in the pavement crevices in front of his house transplanted to the nearby Temple of Apollo (Suet. *Aug.* 92.1-2) and he placed in front of his door a pair of laurel trees when the Senate gave him the name Augustus in 27 BC (Dio 53.16.4). The laurel – which has a degree of prominence in the *Eclogues,* both as tree and in the person of Daphnis (*Ecl.* 5) – came to carry various Augustan resonances, not only triumphal, but also to do with notions of peace and healing.[121] Over and above this, there were various reportedly very old trees about Rome (Pliny *NH* 16.235-7), with stories attached to them remembering Rome's antiquity, or figures from Roman history. Hartswick points out that districts on the Quirinal were sometimes known by names such as *ad malum Punicum* ('at the pomegranate'), presumably indicating the presence or even prominence of individual trees in particular loca-tions.[122] At a more individual level, trees could increase the value of the house where they were found (Hor. *Epodes* 1.10.22; Stat. *Silvae* 1.3.59; Pliny *NH* 17.1-5). All in all, the significance of trees and various kinds of groups and arrangements of trees in Rome is pervasive and complex.

The suburban palace-gardens of Roman aristocrats exhibit the same kind of complex semiology, but on a larger scale.[123] They too were called *horti*, preserving the kitchen garden as a shape in the imagination (cf. Pliny *NH* 19.50-1). These large gardens were bought, sold, and inherited, there was prestige in their acquisition, and they were named after their owners.[124] Horace tells that Damasippus lost his fortune selling pleasure gardens (*Sat.* 2.3.24). Owners of such gardens favoured the artificial reshaping of the ground, the use of slopes, scenic views, sculpture, and architectural features: galleries are often sited in gardens.[125] Natural features such as springs, streams, caves, woods – features more or less familiar from sacral-idyllic scene-painting, and from the *Eclogues* – were improved or created, fountains added. Topiary was known and valued, its invention attributed to an equestrian friend of Augustus, C. Matius, by Pliny the Elder (*NH* 12.13).[126] Flowers were prized (though more limited in garden-use and season than they are now).[127] They need much more frequent watering than trees, and therefore their extensive use needs a more complex and costly infrastructure (water supply, manpower).[128] Statues, as in other gardens, were a general feature, but such gardens could also accommodate public art displays (see Dio 54.29 on the gardens of Agrippa). In addition, there was always the potential for the evocation of literary landscapes, as in Hadrian's villa at Tibur (cf. SHA, *Hadrian* 26.5).[129] The specialist art of gardening, in line with the concept of shaping a place (*topos* in Greek), was called *ars topiaria*, and the *topiarius* (gardener) is attested from the late republic (Cic. *ad Quintum fratrem* 3.1.5 in 54 BC).[130] The ideas implicit in this level of gardening-as-art were spread widely over the Roman world. The artificiality, benignity, order and anthropocentricity of such areas, the importance of woods and streams, and the literary allusiveness all recall the landscape of the *Eclogues*.[131]

These palace-gardens overlap with a range of public green spaces: covered colonnades with groves and gardens, porticoes (roofed and colonnaded walkways surrounding on all four sides a planted public space),[132] and the public gardens themselves,[133] sometimes constructed on a very grand scale, such as Maecenas' *Campus Esquilinus* at Rome (new in Horace *Sat.* 1.8; cf. *Odes* 3.29.10; *Epod.* 9.3) and the *Horti Sallustiani* (originally laid out at the end of the first century BC).[134] Together with the gardens of Pompey in the *Campus Martius* (whimsically celebrated in Catullus 55.6-14),[135] these gardens lay at the east, north, and west of the ancient city,[136] but there were many others forming a necklace around the city, some, like the earliest large pleasure garden, the famous *Horti Luculliani* (c. 60 BC)[137] and the Gardens of Caesar (Hor. *Sat.* 1.9.18), antedating the *Eclogues*, others, like the

Augustan *horti Lolliani*, postdating them. Augustus himself was well aware of the value of public garden space – along with festivals, temple renovation, building, and poetry – for self-projection. As von Stackelberg points out (2009: 78) his garden on the Palatine, the *Horti Pompeiani*, his mausoleum groves, the shrine and grove of his grandsons, Lucius and Gaius, 'were either available to the public or public property (Suet. *Aug.* 50-51; Dio 54.27.3, 54.29.4). ... His transformation of *Horti* into public parks was an act of euergetism that confirmed his position as sole head of the social and political system.'[138]

In the context of the *Eclogues*, various points of resemblance emerge. The *Campus Esquilinus* contained as a legacy from its former use *magna sepulchra*[139] which remind us of the Eclogue-land tombs of Daphnis and Bianor.[140] Monumental tombs on villa estates were, indeed, already characteristic features by the second century BC, and ancient custom reserved the right for patrician families to have such tombs on their property even within the city.[141] In the light of the social activities of Virgil's bucolic natives, one should remember also Horace's account of his daily routine in *Satire* 1.6, which includes a ball game in the *Campus Martius* (1.6.126). Another reference (involving Horace and Maecenas; 2.6.49) reinforces the impression of the kind of social activity that went on in public green space. One should also think of the presentation of Maecenas as indulging in what seems to be a bucolic posture in a garden setting (*Elegiae in Maecenatem* 1.33-6, discussed above). The enclosedness of public gardens with their massive niched and buttressed walls[142] also recalls the sense of the bucolic landscape as sealed off from an outside by mountains and differentiated place names, not to mention the violently steep rock formations in sacral-idyllic paintings, and mythological paintings such as the Polyphemus and Galatea already referred to.

Contrariwise, we can look at Virgil's composition of the Eclogue-book as miming, on a literary level, the construction of a public garden. The performance of a poem superimposes upon the space in which it is performed another space conjured up by its own content. The opening of Juvenal's first *Satire*, for example, conjures up a poetry reading. The real and imaginary spaces almost coincide, but in the imaginary recitation space Juvenal creates an arena in which the generic voices of Roman literature jostle until they are driven aside by Juvenal's satiric voice. In the rest of the satire the performance superimposes on the recitation space another setting, the street in which malefactors pass as the satirist stands at the corner transcribing everything on to his writing tablets.[143] In satire, the genre which claims over and again to have a direct non-literary purchase on reality, the distance between the real and the superimposed spaces is different from that in Virgil's bucolic. In the Eclogue-book, the poetic voice conjures up for its audience a green space with trees, shade, water, sheep, a space in which the

140

friends and contemporaries of the poet and his audience have fleeting presences. If the bucolic natives know about Pollio's poetry, and indeed the *Eclogues* themselves, by a simple extension, the barriers between these natives and the members of Virgil's audience are eroded, just as the public garden allows classes to mix with a degree of apparent freedom.

As well as such public gardens, there were very numerous courtyard gardens (peristyles)[144] located within the walls of the urban home. This was a more frequent location for gardens belonging to either homes or public buildings than at the rear of the building, and the home generally has an inward orientation.[145] The size-range of these gardens is large, and some houses might have three or four large gardens,[146] but in all cases the courtyard garden is an extra room for social activity. Many masonry dining couches are known from Pompeian gardens.[147] In literate social levels poetry readings might be held here, providing a sort of real-world analogy to the bucolic song-exchange.[148] However, as well as being the site of social activity, the courtyard garden is also private, and walled-off from that which is outside the house – indeed it is more intimate than the rooms of the house itself,[149] many of which had various (and in varying degrees) public functions such as the reception of morning visitors and the display of the images of the family ancestors.[150] In it we have statuary[151] and simulation of scenic effects, where a statue of a sleeping nymph might be seen as quasi-epiphanic, and the viewer can for a moment become, say, Jupiter, or Bacchus, or Actaeon. 'The principal function of sculpture was to set an associative mood for the garden' (von Stackelberg, 2009: 27) and Silenus, prominent in *Eclogue* 6, frequently appeared as a garden statue emanating a sense of cheerful pleasures. Cicero writes of the Greek statues in one of his brother's villas, that they seem to be landscape gardeners themselves offering their ivy for sale (Cic. *Q.Fr.* 3.1.5), creating another sort of imaginary self-drama.[152] If we consider the stereotypical portrayal of woods and streams as archetypal places of poetic inspiration,[153] we can see how easily the landscape of the garden can become poeticised. Pools and fountains were essential water-supplying devices for those who could afford them, but were much more than functional in their embellishment and decoration,[154] and could readily suggest the nymphs of the Graeco-Roman reservoir of mythological stories, or – for those who felt inclined to see it – Callimachean water imagery. In this way, the garden – and this is not limited to the courtyard garden – becomes in part an assemblage of a whole range of literary allusions. The frequent presence, moreover, of shrines and altars in courtyard gardens[155] provides a sounding board for echoes in the offerings made by Virgil's bucolic natives (*Ecl.* 1.43; 3.62-3, 68-9, 77; 7.29-30, 33-4). The prospective recipients of these offerings are the anonymous young man of the first

Eclogue, Apollo, Venus, Delia, and Priapus, of whom Venus and Priapus were particularly associated with gardens.

However, as important again is another level of significance, and that is the courtyard garden's particular kind of embodiment of the tension between inside and outside. Outside the house – and the sheltered and literary enclosure of the garden is (subject to qualification) the innermost part of the house[156] – is the world of politics, banking, commerce, military affairs and all that counts as *negotium* rather than *otium*.[157] There is here too a point of contact with the *Eclogues*. The combination of the walling-in of an area of artificially arranged nature,[158] its human occupancy and social function, the separation from a strongly differentiated 'dangerous' outside, and the scope for literary allusion, combine to provide a very powerful connection between the garden and Virgil's Arcadia. Moreover, in both the garden and the book, the boundaries are permeable. The garden owner must sooner or later go into the outside world and the choppy seas of public life, and guests from that outside world will be invited into the house and the garden, just as Tityrus goes to Rome and Gallus enters Arcadia.[159] If we allow for some degree of relaxation of normal social restrictions in the garden,[160] we can see an analogy for the apparent low profile of social distinction in the interior world of the *Eclogues*. This includes the rareness of indications of status among the herdsmen, but also the way bucolic herdsmen can seem familiar with Romans of various social level – Pollio, Gallus, and (under the names of Tityrus and Menalcas) Virgil himself.

There is another point of contact worth observing, too, namely that the garden boundary is – like the edge of Arcadia – only one of a set of boundaries nesting inside each other. The two-way movement into and out of the garden is made among a nexus of rooms, each of which is more or less interior or exterior than other rooms, until the *vestibulum* abuts onto the street.[161] After that the confines of Rome, Italy, and the empire mark successive boundaries, like Russian dolls.[162] The physical structure of the house is organically entwined with its domestic and social structures, its hierarchies of privateness and so forth, and deeply embedded in the mind of the dweller from infancy. The pattern of garden and surrounding house is further reinforced by the multisensory nature of the subject's contact with it,[163] so that it becomes part of a powerful pre-verbal cognitive structure which provides the infrastructure for other such patterns, and hence becomes part of a general model of multiple boundaries. The child's learning of the house's geography and rules becomes a model for its mental mapping of larger, and indeed quite other, systems.[164] It is no coincidence that Quintilian uses the structure of the house as the basis of a mnemonic technique for memorising speeches (11.2.20-4; cf. *Ad Herrenium* 3.29).[165] Just as the garden wall is only one of a set of concentric boundaries, so in the *Eclogues* the core of the bucolic homeland is marked off not only by distance from an outer region which includes Rome, but also by mountains from a dangerous and remoter outer world. Another, though more complex, boundary is marked by the use of Greek, Roman, and barbarian place-names, and the presence of Pollio in both the *Eclogues* and in the Rome of Virgil's audience signposts a boundary between the real world and the world of the poems. And there are other (also permeable) boundaries, which have relationships with these, such as those between bucolic, elegy, and epic, and between the bucolic song of Virgil's characters and the poet's own bucolic verse.

The inner-outer tensions that are embodied in the garden resemble those of the Eclogue-book also in the matter of orientation. The Eclogue-book points both inwards and outwards. Similarly, while the courtyard garden is inside the house, physically and emotionally, it is also outside in the sense of being unroofed and in the open air. It is not irrelevant that the word for roof (*tectum*) is used for the buildings in which people live in both Latin verse and prose. The garden's area of more or less natural greenery is thus *outside* the residence, just as the country's more or less natural greenery is outside the city's conglomeration of residences. In that sense the garden-house complex is a simulacrum of the town-country relationship. Since the house with its garden is located within the town-country context which it replicates, it demonstrates a recursive property: we can call it a form of *mise en abyme*.[166] In this way it reflects the recursive properties both of the Eclogue-book's self-reflexiveness, the way it includes within itself small-scale images of itself, and of its status as scale-model within the world that it transforms and reproduces. Paradoxically, the courtyard garden also inverts the relationship between image and subject, because in the larger sphere the country surrounds the city, whereas in the smaller the house surrounds the garden. This too can be applied to the *Eclogues*, since the core in which the bucolic natives live is surrounded by a partially urban outside world, and by the urban world of the book's audience.

To return briefly to the child for a moment, before passing on to villa gardens, it is worth observing that for the developing house-dwelling identity the experience of the garden gradually becomes a lens through which the home landscape between the urban house and the villa is perceived and constructed (so too, for the literate adult, the *Eclogues* themselves), and against which it is measured. Moreover, since external nature is reflected in the garden (and *Eclogues*), there is a process of circular reinforcement. By various degrees of extension, Italian farmland, Germanic forests, and Libyan sands (each with their stereotypical populations) are all variously like or unlike the preformed internal landscape behind which the house-garden dyad lies.

Villa gardens mix the roles of garden, informal park and productive estate.[167] In villa gardens we find orchards, vineyards together with terraces (*xysti*) with flowers (Pliny *Ep*. 2.17.17; 5.6.16), rooms with

views, colonnades, *ambulationes,* designed walks which take advantage
of or create scenic values (cf. Pliny *Ep.* 5.6.17; *CIL* 6.29774-5), *gestatio-
nes* (shaded avenues for riding or being carried in a litter; cf. Pliny *Ep.*
2.17.14).[168] Augustus favoured colonnades and landscape gardening at
his villas, and incorporated the display of rarities such as immense
skeletons of beasts (called 'the bones of the giants') and the weapons of
heroes at Capreae (Suet. *Aug.* 72.3).[169] This polar tension between
usefulness and pleasure is in fact a broadly attested feature of Roman
thought, and one which appears strongly in the context of literature –
Horace discussing his *Satires*, for example, claims the need to mix the
two (Hor. *AP* 333-4; 343-4).[170] Thinking of the *Eclogues*, one could indeed
visualise the villa-owner and his guests in one of the pleasure buildings
or on one of the benches in the garden or parkland looking over at the
work in progress in the productive area and fancifully imagining the
slaves to be bucolic natives wrapped in their own lives and unaware of
the proximity of their master (cf. Pliny *Ep.* 2.17.24; 5.6.9).

Looking at the *Eclogues* from different angles, we can see resem-
blances to both the useful world of the farm or smallholding, and the
more pleasure-oriented world of the garden or park. Indeed, the notion
of the productive villa estate can itself be transformed into a pleasantry.
Zanker draws attention to a 'rural idyll inside the city' created by the
owner's attempt to make an aristocratic rural villa inside the city
bounds at Pompeii (cf. Pliny *NH* 19.50-1, writing of his own day, but also
referring back to Epicurus).[171]

Nor can we separate the matter of villa gardens from Roman paint-
ing. The villa was surrounded by prospects, and was itself perforated
with windows which find an echo in 'framed' paintings (as opposed to
whole-wall paintings).[172] In addition the garden is – as we have seen – a
frequent subject depicted in Roman painting.[173] One of Pliny's letters
describes the gardens at his Tuscan villa: there is a suite of rooms set
back from a colonnade and containing a court with four plane trees and
a fountain. 'There is another bedroom, green and shady from the
nearest plane tree, which has walls decorated with marble up to the
ceiling and a fresco of birds perched on the branches of trees' (Pliny *Ep.*
5.6.20-2). Likewise, the garden painting in Livia's Villa at Prima Porta
puts the guest in an imaginary garden, and at a much lower social level,
we find indoor restaurants at Pompeii which simulate garden settings
in emulation of garden-restaurants.[174] Nature and artifice, reality and
representation, and boundaries and the notion of boundaries are sys-
tematically thematised (as they are in the Eclogue-book).

The profile of trees and flowers (and birds and insects) in paintings
of gardens seems to agree reasonably well with that of real gardens -
and also of the *Eclogues* (and Horace's *loci amoeni*) – though there is a
more extreme concentration of variety in the paintings.[175] There are,
however, additional and more important considerations. The blending

144

of natural and artificial is deeply embedded in all gardens, but this is part of a wider cultural background. It is also visible in the aesthetics of literature, architecture, art, and the mythological charades of execution-shows. If the fanciful literary and mythological presentation of food in Petronius' account of Trimalchio's banquet is comic in its exaggeration, its confusions of detail, and in its attribution to a less than aristocratic setting, the same can not be said for the republican aristocrat Hortensius' parkland dinner with a slave dressed as Orpheus summoning various animals by horn.[176]

> Nam silva erat, ut dicebat, supra quinquaginta iugerum maceria saepta, quod non leporarium, sed therotrophium appellabat. Ibi erat locus excelsus, ubi triclinio posito cenabamus, quo Orphea vocari iussit. Qui cum eo venisset cum stola et cithara cantare esset iussus, bucina inflavit, ut tanta circumfluxerit nos cervorum aprorum et ceterarum quadripedum multitudo, ut non minus formosum mihi visum sit spectaculum, quam in Circo Maximo aedilium sine Africanis bestiis cum fiunt venationes.
>
> Varro *RR* 3.13.1-3

> For there was a forest, as he said, covering more than fifty iugera, enclosed with a wall; he called it, not a warren, but a game-preserve. In it was a high spot where a table was spread and we dined. He ordered Orpheus be called to it, and when he appeared with his robe and harp, and was ordered to sing, he blew a horn; whereupon such a crowd of stags, boars, and other animals poured around us that it seemed to me no less attractive a sight than when the hunts of the aediles take place in the Circus Maximus without the African beasts.

Hortensius and his guests here become participants in a piece of mythological role-playing as Orpheus, whose singing is standardly represented by poets as causing animals to follow him, leads edible animals to the diners. It would have been impractical for these same animals to have been cooked and served on the same occasion, but the enjoyable illusion that this was so may well have been present.

In the context of gardens and the blending of natural and artificial, we should also pay attention to trees serving as columns, and vines entwining ' "real" columns that appeared to be trunks of trees – a conceit shown clearly in landscape paintings' (Hartswick 2004: 12). Hartswick goes on to observe how 'arbor-trellises formed ceilings, and owners raised tapestries (with architectural designs) between rows of trees that acted like walls'.[177] As well as that seen in such *trompe l'oeil* effects,[178] we should remind ourselves of another transcendence of the natural: in the transcendence of the natural seasons shown in the assemblages of trees and plants in murals there is both an extension of the artificial cultivation and arrangement of flowers, bushes, plants, and trees (including imports)[179] in real gardens,[180] which represents in another form the same sort of game of reality and illusion.

Trompe l'oeil effects depend on the movement of the viewer for the trick manifestly to come into operation (see above), but the concept of the walk – movement from place to place – is an integral part of the notion of a garden in any case. Gardens regularly feature porticoes and colonnades, and these are a feature of paintings of villas. Pliny's description of his Tuscan villa and gardens (*Ep.* 2.17) is structured as a guided walk. Just as it is of the essence of the park or garden that one walk in it and look at it, so one can apply this to the aesthetics of a collection of poems which is so profoundly imitative of the concept of garden-space. In the garden the movement is directed by pathways whose determinant is leisure rather than goal, the reader's tour of the *Eclogues* is non-linear in the sense that cross references cut across a straight-through reading, and also in the sense that the direction is not governed by chronological or geographical progression. We have rather a succession of prospects or vignettes which together show a 'shifting set of centres of gravity that reflect the position of the reader at any given moment' (Saunders 2008: 6). Saunders goes on to say that 'a poem such as *Eclogue* 7, that is, is not simply one more staging post along the road from *Eclogue* 1 to *Eclogue* 10, but rather, for as long as it is the poem currently being read, it establishes the very shape and delineation of the universe within which all the other eclogues are, for the moment at least, to be placed and perceived'.

In addition to this, there is the playing with concepts of inside and outside. Just as the Eclogue-book creates a bucolic space surrounded by mountains and other dangers, so the house-owner arranges a garden with trees, flowers, visiting birds, statues, fountains, altars, and *triclinia* (dining couches) for social activity,[181] outside which – beyond the garden wall – is the world of real life and all its complexities. But in addition to this, members of Virgil's audience might have been able to see gardens upon whose walls were painted an imaginary outside world of untamed potential dangers among 'lakes or streams in a mountainous setting full of wild animals' (Jashemski 2002: 18). Here the garden is surrounded by the potentially dangerous outside constituted by urban real life, and the imaginary and exotically dangerous outside constituted by the representation of non-urban wildness. In the mind, the two interfere with each other. The one adds glamour and excitement to the other, as well as enhancing the tranquil retreat of the enclosure within.

Looking at the range of gardens we see competition and self-aggrandisement in the establishment of public gardens, but also the concept of the garden as a space for social activity within and sheltered from the public world.[182] We see too the idea of the garden as self-expression.[183] We can think of Cicero's garden filled with philosophical statuary as an Arcadia into which famous dead philosophers could go, or among which Cicero and his guests could themselves be part of the succession of philophers,[184] somewhat as the presence of Pollio and the poets in Virgil's Eclogue-land allows the audience to join with them in their imagination. The garden is a place in the architecture of the house, but it is also a place in the imagination where nymphs, deities, etc. may come, and in which the owner and his guests can be actors in a semi-imaginary world of their own devising. We can also see Roman ideas about usefulness and pleasure implicated in the continuum of phenomena which includes smallholdings, market gardens, courtyard gardens, public walks, groves, and gardens, villa estates, and luxury gardens. In many respects, we can see the Eclogue-book as a metagarden in which the reader can play safely with ideals and realities and alternative points of view. If, then, the *Eclogues* is a garden, what entity or entities in the real world correspond to the home that implicitly must surround and define the metaphorical garden? We might see this variously as the urban context of the city of Rome, or the house from whose rooms the guests the garden, or as the audience itself, coming out of their socio-architectural context in order to enter the metaphorical garden of the poems.

Structure; montage and complexity

Content, structure, and surround conspire to define bucolic space in the Eclogue-book. If we picture the *Eclogues* as a fictive landscape with strong resemblances to a garden or park, and bear in mind their tendency to timelessness and synchronicity, we may see how the book's multiple structures[185] are compatible with the image of a space within which the viewer may wander at will. Of course a performance or reading has its own chronological seriality, but the reader's mental model of the totality of the textual artefact is not limited in this way. Thus, for example, we can see the shape of the collection as a set of rings (1-9, the confiscation poems; 2-8, lovelorn monologues; 3-7, Theocritean song exchanges; 4-6, Roman and anomalous). Looking this way, we might see *Eclogue* 5 as centrepiece[186] and 10 as a portal. Then we might try looking at 10 as a way into Eclogue-land (one which Gallus fails to negotiate), or as a way out into reality, or on to the *Georgics* and *Aeneid* (hence *surgamus*, 'Let us arise', at 10.75?) We might also wonder whether the fact that the two poems on the outside of the main block, the first and ninth, are darker than those in the core because they are more exposed in that position to the harshness of the real world context. Alternatively – or additionally – we can see the collection as two blocks, 1-5, and 6-10, a configuration in which Gallus and the contemporary literary scene seem to have an emphasised prominence. Yet again, we may see the collection as two interlocking components, 1, 3, 5, 7, 9 – the dialogue poems in which the bucolic world stands up in its own right – and 2, 4, 6, 8, 10 – in which the complex relationship with contemporary realities is brought forward (although they are already included in the confiscation material in 1 and 9) by the Virgilian introductions.[187]

Looking in these various ways will generate different emphases, but nothing in the Eclogue-book allows itself to be pinned down completely. Menalcas is Virgil or not, as the case may be. Rome is inside and outside the book; the country is an ideal, but not necessarily a perfect one – reality may have factors that have to take priority in the real world. The collection is not *about* the land confiscations, any more than it is about poeticised herdsmen (what personal relevance would the latter have to the aristocratic and learned audience?); the collection is not a wrapper for a certain number of meanings. Rather, it uses patterns and themes to produce a satisfying construction in which meanings are but a contributory element.

The structures of the *Eclogues* are not unlike a photomontage – layers are superimposed on layers without wholly removing them from sight. In an analogous way there are other laminations too: Virgil's bucolic vision is laid on a bed of Theocritean poetry, Italy on Arcadia, Virgil on Menalcas and Tityrus, Alexis on Polyphemus, and so on. However, the complexities of the Eclogue-book are wrapped in a semblance of simplicity – whimsical songs by and about stylised herdsmen in a stylised poetical setting. One could put that the other way around: behind a semblance of simplicity, everything turns out to be complicated. Indeed, it is this double perspective that makes the book an intriguing combination of the immediately attractive and the sustainedly absorbing.

Complexity is, of course, a problematic thing to measure. In music what may sound a quite simple rhythm or melody may require highly complex notation, but in the performance the rhythm or melody may still be perceived as a simple. Likewise, a complex assemblage of notes can be simplified in the listener's perception as 'texture' or 'passage-work'.[188] What makes perceptible increase in complexity is the combination not simply of more elements, but of more *systems*. A journey involving a train and a bus is more complicated than one involving two trains because of the different kinds of infrastructure that support the two transport systems. The purchasing of train and bus tickets is a different *kind* of operation; the disposition of bus stops and train stations is different; luggage facilities and ease of exit are different, and so on. The involvement of different systems within a larger system gives a degree of quantifiability to the notion of complexity.[189] In terms of the *Eclogues*, the overlaying of Virgilian and Theocritean roles, the interaction within the text between different genres, the superimposition upon each other of different patterns, and the inclusion within the book of small-scale images of the book are among the major indices, making complexity a major part of Virgil's smallest book.

148

9

Conclusion

In the course of this study I have joined together a number of propositions (not all new, by any means) which are encapsulated below. Chiefly, I draw attention to the complex relationships between inner and outer perspectives in the construction of a bucolic space.

(1) Virgil locates the *Eclogues* as bucolic poetry in the literary field as representing a particular genre among other genres.

(2) Inside the Eclogue-book, the contents reinforce its bucolic identity i.a. by an unusually high level of self-referentiality or reflexiveness. In this respect, there are numerous mutually reinforcing signifiers: flora, fauna, geographical features, internal culture, nomenclature, typifying passages, collections of programmatic words, references to Theocritus and Sicily, and the nature of the inhabitants' songs.

(3) The homogeneity of these elements reinforces a feeling of a hermetically sealed world, with the city and various real-world places at its fringes marking the border (although in another sense Rome is part of the contents of the book).

(4) The self-referentiality of the book points both outwards and inwards. It defines bucolic space and also sets it in the context of other genres, particularly epic and above all elegy.

(5) The Eclogue-world is permeable in both directions. Song allows the shepherds to have a purchase on the world outside the *Eclogues*, and Roman poets from the outside world (Pollio, Cinna, Varius, Gallus) have some degree of entry into the world of the *Eclogues*. Virgil plays a bucolic role under different names, and it is possible that other Roman figures do also. In this respect the *Eclogues* are like that element of Roman visual arts and gardens which provides a quasi-theatrical background for the viewer to 'act' in. The readers themselves are thus invited to join in an imaginary charade and see themselves in the eclogic context.

(6) In varying degrees, the collection has points of resemblance with smallholdings and the whole range of garden-types (and their representations in art). The semiotics of these phenomena interact with those of the book. Moreover, the Eclogue-book gains a garden- or park-like quasi-spatial structure, and this pushes the reader towards a certain kind of reading in which the bucolic world itself is a space within which the reader can move around to gain varying perspectives. The

reprise of *Ecl.* 2 and 3 at the end of *Ecl.* 5 is a strong support for such a non-linear view.

(7) The real or outside world, especially represented by the city, can damage or threaten bucolic space (space as described inside the *Eclogues*). However, we should not naively accept the proposition 'Arcadia good, Rome bad', for there are two 'realities' pertaining to the poems – that of the internal residents and that of the Roman audience. Depending on which perspective is taken, the view changes: the Roman reader can see both Rome and himself as either inside or outside the boundary.

(8) The bucolic space of the Eclogue-book represents the complex intersection both of inner and outer literary spaces, of literary space and the real world. The boundaries are multiple and reflect the multiple boundaries of the Roman house and Roman world. The superimposing and blurring of boundaries in the Eclogue-book has analogies in the fluid cognitive structures of the Roman house-garden complex, and has attention drawn to it also by recursive or *trompe l'oeil* effects analogous to those in Roman visual art.

Notes

Preface

1. The first appearance of the *Eclogues* may have been piecemeal, starting around 42 BC (Virgil's twenty-ninth year figures in ancient testimonia), and the whole collection assembled by about 39 BC (a three-year period for the composition is attested by Donatus' *Vita Vergili* 89-90); see Coleman (1977), 14-15. Clausen (1972) has 35 BC for the date of *Ecl.* 1, six years after the start of the Augustan land-redistribution which figures in *Ecl.* 1.

2. See Posch (1969); Garson (1971).

3. See Leach (1974, 1988). In defence of the use of the term 'art' see Stewart (2008), 2-3.

4. See, briefly, Skoie (2006). Giesecke (2007), 127 calls the *Eclogues*, the *Georgics*, and the *Aeneid* 'three gardens' on the *Eclogues* see 152-5; the application of the term to the latter two poems seems to me to weaken its force in connection with the *Eclogues* themselves. Spencer (2006) uses the term 'Garden' metaphorically, 'as shorthand for the human(e) and highly artificial, mimetic and fantastic landscapes that saturate Horace's conceptual topographies.' See also, very briefly, Berg (1974), 5-6.

1. The Generic Landscape and Bucolic Space

1. On the text as space, see Barthes (1977), 146: 'A text is ... a multi-dimensional space in which a variety of writings, none of them original, blend and clash. The text is a tissue of quotations drawn from the innumerable centres of culture.' Theories of space are also important in geography and archaeology (see Nicolet 1991; Laurence 1994, 1997; Laurence and Wallace-Hadrill 1997) and these too will become relevant below in the context of the natural and human geography of the *Eclogues*, and in the relationship with them of real-world boundaries (see Chapter 8 below). On treating physical space as discourse and the resulting interpenetration of physical and linguistic space, see Spencer (2010), 48-61.

2. The tradition is, to some extent, a fiction created by Virgil in the *Eclogues*.

3. For this as an important linguistic concept see Brown and Yule (1983), esp. 235-70.

4. In this regard, at least, the same point could be made of Theocritus.

5. Roman poets certainly have a way of referring to particular kinds of poetry as intimately connected with particular places. Bucolic is Syracusan verse (V. *Ecl.* 6.1), didactic – or perhaps one kind of didactic – is Ascraean song (V. *Georg.* 2.176), lyric is Lesbian in Horace's opening ode (1.1.34), and iambic is Parian (Hor. *Epp.* 1.19.23). Although the division is different, one of Horace's odes (*Odes* 1.7) suggests a duality between his own kind of poetry and different subdivisions of epic, each based in its own locale. The occupation of different parts of a landscape by different kinds of poetry, poetic material, or poetic

inspiration is also implicit in the untrodden ways Callimachean poets need to follow; cf. Lucretius' claim to traverse the trackless places of poetry and pluck poetic flowers from where the Muses have previously garlanded no-one (1.926-30; here the generic field is not wholly labelled, but contains unexplored tracts for poetic innovators). In Juvenal, the image of himself as choosing one particular battlefield to drive his poetic chariot over (Juv. 1.19-20) is very striking: *hoc campo* emphatically rejects others, as though each genre has its own field of operation (cf. also Prop. 3.3).

6. Of course there are still other ways of cutting the cake, as with 'love/erotic poetry'. When Juvenal pairs Lesbia and Cynthia (6.7-8) as representative of the spirit of the age, he conjures up a picture of a particular kind of poetry, identifiable by its own salient characteristics, and one which redefines standard generic boundaries. Love/erotic poetry, irrespective of narrowly defined genre, is also at point at Prop. 2.34.81-94, Ov. *Am.* 3.9.59-66, *AA* 3.321ff., *Tr.* 2.427ff., Pliny *Ep.* 5.3.

7. For similar generically arranged lists see Hor. *AP* 73-85, Ov. *RA* 373ff., Quint. 10.1.85ff., Mart. 12.94; cf. also Hor. *Epp.* 1.19.21-34, Ov. *Am.* 1.15.9-30. On cross-generic lists, see Jones 2007, 28-9. On Graeco-Roman generic thought cf. Harrison (2007), 2-10.

8. It is also true that Lucretius' *De Rerum Natura* weaves into the didactic texture passages with other generic affiliations (including bucolic! – see below) marked out for their difference.

9. In fact, the Augustan poets tend to give two not wholly compatible impressions of the literary field. In one, it was laid out like an eternally existing grid within which the poet chose this or that genre to practice. In the other, the Latin literary field is a more open, dynamic place, chiefly characterised by new annexations from Greek literary territory. On the poets' claims to primacy, see Hinds (1998), 52-83.

10. On the *Eclogues* as the earliest arena for the playing out of generic dramas against the background of 'expectations generated by both Roman political circumstances and Greek literary models', see Harrison (2007), 33.

11. On genre, and the possibility of alternative ways of cutting the cake, see Jones (2007). This is a rather different picture from Genette's (1987) account of genre as a palimpsest upon which the new writer encrypts his version. Alpers (1982) regards the view that Theocritean and Virgilian pastoral are different genres as a *reductio ad absurdum*, but the absurdity is not as conclusively self-evident as he claims. His account of the labile retrospective definitions of pastoral points strongly to a considerable element of self-invention by successive poets claiming the notion of 'bucolic' as a justifying myth. Halperin (1983) defines Theocritus' *Idylls* generically as a Hellenistic form, a kind of ironic miniature para-epic rather than as 'bucolic'; from this perspective it is easy to regard Virgil's casting of Theocritus as his generic model as retrospectively turning the *Idylls* into bucolic.

12. Cf. also the apostrophe to Arethusa at *Ecl.* 10.1 and cf. Harrison (2007), 60-1. Kennedy (1987: 48-9) reads Arethusa as representing Gallus' partially bucolic version of elegy, on which cf. Ross (1975), 85-107. See on the use of generic figureheads Harrison (2007), 28-30.

13. The modern arrangement of the *Idylls* is due to Stephanus in his *Poetae Graeci* (1566); the manuscript tradition is messy. There are at least three different selections and arrangements and various hybrids. See Gow (1952), xxx-lxix. On Theocritus' supposed bucolic book see Lawall (1967); Halperin (1983), 136; Hunter (1999), 27-8.

14. For a convenient overview see Harrison (2007), 34-6.

15. See Nauta (1990) for the possibility that there was a pre-Virgilian collection of Theocritean bucolic. Martindale (Martindale, 1997: 108) asks suggestively whether the supposed selector of such a collection might be called the inventor of the bucolic genre. Fantuzzi (2006) uses the post-Theocritean reader similarly to locate a 'strongly coherent bucolic Theocritus, in some cases more coherent than Theocritus himself might ever have tried to be' (p. 261). For Theocritus' followers see Bernsdorff (2006); Reed (2006); see also Sens (2006) on post-Theocritean epigrams with bucolic features. The Hellenistic poet Philetas may have written bucolic poetry (see Bowie 1985: 74-6).

16. On the role of real or imaginary anthologies in genre definition see Jones (2007), 30, 38, 43, 173.

17. The fictiveness of Virgil's implicit equation of Theocritean and bucolic poetry is intensified if one argues on the grounds of metre (hexameter) and Homeric intertextuality that Theocritus designed the *Idylls* as a modernist version of epic (Halperin, 1983; Martindale in Martindale, 1997, 107-8).

18. On Virgil's use of Lucretius see Lipka (2001), 66-80. Although the Eclogue-book is a new thing in Latin poetry, Virgil was not the first to notice the tradition. Note that Virgil refers to some kind of commission from Pollio (*Ecl.* 8.11-12), which is supported by an explicit statement (if not wholly unambiguous) in Servius' *Vita Vergili* 24-5: *tunc ei proposuit Pollio ut Carmen bucolicum scriberet, quod eum constat triennio scripsisse et emendasse* ('Then Pollio proposed that he write bucolic poetry/a bucolic poem, which, it is agreed, he wrote and emended in three years'). If Messalla wrote bucolic (*Catalepton* 9.13-19, cf. Pliny *Ep.* 5.3), it seems to have been in Greek.

19. Also relevant is Lucretius' account of primeval mankind (Lucr. 5.925-1010). Here we find people who did not have to work, but fed on the arbutus and the acorn (939-42), and on woodland animals that they hunted (966-9), had no fire, clothing, law, or marriage slept cn the ground and feared wild beasts. Here the Golden Age, which the world of Virgil's bucolic natives resembles, is given an alternative colouring.

20. On dominant genres see Jones (2007), 28, 68, 71-3, 95, 131-2, citing Opacki (2000).

21. Cf. Hinds (2000). This absorption has a Hellenistic model in the treatment of Medea in Apollonius' *Argonautica*. See also Cairns' (1989) reading of Dido as a figure of elegy.

22. On competitive inclusiveness, see Jones (2007), 34-6.

23. See Harrison (2007: 38-9) for regarding the Sibylline oracular material which influences the fourth *Eclogue* as a recognisable hexametrical genre in itself (on this material see also Nisbet (2008)). Harrison (2007: 39-40) brings epithalamial poetry (and Catullus 64) into the picture as well.

24. Gallus is unlikely to have written pastoral elegy himself: see Whitaker (1988).

25. Cf. Paschalis (2001) for the contents of Silenus' song.

26. Harrison (2007: 47-8) argues that Silenus represents Parthenius, and that the source of Silenus' song was Parthenius' no longer extant *Metamorphoses*.

27. Getting information from Proteus is in the *Odyssey* (4.363ff.).

28. *Chalcidico versu, Ecl.* 10.50, may allude to Theocles, the originator, it is said, of elegy, from near Chalcis. Otherwise the reference could be to Gallus' mythological poetry in hexameters after the manner of Euphorion of Chalcis,

or his Chalcidic verse, i.e. elegy and mythological hexameters. See Coleman (1977). Quintilian (10.1.56) believed the reference was to Euphorion.

29. See Harrison (2007: 71-3) on the basket, the complex incompatibility of elegy and bucolic, and the host-guest relationship. See Jones (2007: 34-6) on competitive inclusiveness.

30. Breed reports some sensible cautions about this alternation (2006), 6-7. Nevertheless, there are clearly greater centrifugal forces in Theocritus, where there is considerable generic variety and where (even in the more or less pastoral poems) there is a mixture of dialogues, poems with narrative introductions, and poems in a sustained 'I' form (*Id.* 2; 3; 7; 12; 13).

31. Jonathan Bate (2000) writing on 'ecocriticism' and in relation to poets like Wordsworth, talks of experiencing a book in the way we experience a garden or a cathedral. We can, indeed, wander around our memories of a book that we have read. The dynamic and flexible structures that evolve and supplant each other in Ovid's *Metamorphoses* suggest that there is something programmatic about his picture of the labyrinth through which Theseus must go, and which has been made by the archetypal craftsman Daedalus (*Met.* 8.159-68).

32. Jenkyns (1989) argues (not convincingly, I believe) against referring to the landscape of the *Eclogues* as a place which can be called Arcadia; see also Kennedy (1987). On the history of Arcadia as a bucolic symbol see Schmidt (2008).

33. One could perhaps, however, talk of a thematically Italian landscape in the foundational *Aeneid*.

34. One should note, however, that the narrative also refers to *gelidi ... saxa Lycaei* ('The rocks of frozen Lycaeus') at *Ecl.* 10.15.

35. For rain, wind, night, mountains, and sea, see Chapter 5 below.

36. Wolves are generally only in figures of speech, but in *Ecl.* 8 a love crazed Arcadian woman (in a song) has seen an Arcadian with magic powers (i.e. outside the norm) becoming a wolf (8.97), and the proverbial *lupus in fibula* is connected with the silencing of poetry at 9.54.

37. A snake (*Ecl.* 3.93) figures in a song in a singing contest; at 4.24 it is to be absent in the coming age, at 8.71 it is in a figure of speech; lions, lynxes, gryphons, sea monsters, fish and horses appear in figures of speech.

38. Hunting is, however, a motif in love poetry (cf. Prop. 2.19.17ff.; [Tib.] 3.9; Parthenius 10.1; cf. Ov. *RA* 199f. for hunting as a cure for love).

39. Poison plants appear in a figured prophecy (*Ecl.* 4.24), and in the crazed love-lorn woman's song (*Ecl.* 8.95). The useless plants *lolium, carduus,* and *paliurus* (*Ecl.* 5.37, 39) in a figure of speech only.

40. *Amomum* appears in figures of speech at *Ecl.* 3.89 and 4.25.

41. Birds might be kept in enclosures on estates for market or pleasure; Hartswick (2004), 14. See also Varro's description of his bird-garden at Casinum (*RR* 3.5.9-17). In the *Eclogues*, doves and swans are associated with poetry and love. A crow gives a warning omen in the unusually dark ninth *Eclogue* (9.15). Owls (8.55), the goose (9.36), and the eagle (9.13) only in figures of speech. See Chapter 3 for more details.

42. More detail in Chapter 3.

43. For the individualism of horses in the *Georgics* see esp. 3.73-113.

44. Horses: 8.27. The pig is implied by the pigmen (*subulci*) at 10.19; boars appear, but often in connection with hunting as an unbucolic marker: 2.59; 3.75; 5.76; 7.29; 10.56.

45. Dogs: a sheep dog at *Ecl.* 3.18, a guard dog at 8.107; in figurative language at 8.28; significantly different are Gallus' generically alien hunting dogs at 10.57.

46. See p. 157 n. 3 below.

47. *Horti*: 7.34, 65, 68; *nemora*: 6.11, 56, 72; 7.59; 8.22, 86; 9.43; 10.9; *arbusta*: 1.39; 2.13; 3.10; 4.2; 5.64. See also *lucus*: 6.73; 8.86; 10.58. It may be noted that *nemus* is over twice as common as *lucus* in the *Eclogues*: outside verse it is possible that the range of meaning of *nemus* includes artificial divine grove, whereas *lucus* connotes natural divine grove. See Scheid (1993) and Coarelli (1993).

48. Cornfields: 1.71; 5.33; 9.48.

49. *Silvae*: 1.5; 2.5; 3.46, 57; 4.3; 5.28, 43; 6.2, 39; 8.58, 97; 10.8, 52, 63; cf. *silvestris* 1.2; 3.71; 5.7.

50. Programmatic *silvae*; 1.2; 4.3; 6.2; cf. 8.58; 10.63; *silvae* as nearly a title at 4.3; cf. 6.2. On *silvae* and Lucretius cf. Lipka (2001), 30-1, 67. This is part of a very pervasive recurrence of 'bucolic' vocabulary; see Rumpf (2008), 66-73.

51. *Pastores*: 1.21; 2.1; 5.41, 59; 6.4, 67; 7.25; 8.1, 23; 9.34; 10.51.

52. *Casia* (2.49) is probably a spring-flowering trailer (see Coleman) rather than cinnamon (cf. V. *Georg.* 4.30); *calta* (2.50), the marigold, flowers in July; *mala* (2.51) may be quinces or apples and autumnal; chestnuts (2.52) are autumnal, but not available together with quinces (if that is what they are at 2.51) or plums (2.53).

53. There is a comparable unnatural synchronicity about the flora depicted in the garden mural in a large underground room in the Villa of Livia at Prima Porta (on which see further below); see Kellum (1994), 221. In the garden too (on Roman gardens see Chapter 8 below) there can be an element of the extension of the natural seasons.

2. Flora

1. Maggiulli (1995) provides a detailed catalogue of all the plant names in the *Eclogues, Georgics*, and *Aeneid*. See also Sargeaunt (1920); D'Herouville (1930). See von Stackelberg (2009), 42-8 for the trees, shrubs, and flowers of Roman gardens.

2. Lipka (2002); Morgan (2000), 76-7.

3. Tityrus at Theocr. *Id.* 3.2-4; 7.72. He recurs in the *Eclogues* at 3.20, 96; 5.12; 6.4; 8.55; 9.23. On Tityrus = *calamus* and other programmatic hints see Cairns (1999); see also Lipka 2001, 155, 182-3. For Amaryllis see Theocr. 4.36ff. She recurs in the *Eclogues* at 2.14; 3.81; 8.77; 9.22. In Longus' Daphnis and Chloe Philetas appears as a pastoral songster with a garden, and as onetime lover of an Amaryllis, whose name echoed in his song (2.3-7). Longus' use of the name Philetas may be intended to recall the Hellenistic poet of the same name (see Bowie 1985: 72-3), and we certainly seem to have an archetypal bucolic setting and characters. For the influence of Philetas in the *Eclogues* and in Propertius see Bowie (1985), 80-6.

4. The allusion to Lucretius in *silvestrem musam* (1.2; cf. Lucr. 4.589; note also *agrestis musa* at Lucr. 5.1398 and V. *Ecl.* 6.8), for the context of which see above, may also draw attention to the Theocritean tradition. Note also the Alexandrian terminology of *tenui* (2, cf. *ludere*, 10) see Cairns (1999); Lipka (2001), 66.

5. Here it provides a typically bucolic shade. According to Athenaeus (2.523),

Philemon described it as an 'ornament of Pan', and Pan is the presiding deity of Eclogue-land (cf. 4.58f., and *Pan deus Arcadiae* at 10.26), and patron of rustic music.

6. Smith (1970) shows that there is an analogous treatment of the bucolic *avena*. Throughout the *Eclogues*, Virgil uses a range of words (*avena, calami* etc.) as virtually interchangeable terms for the instrument of bucolic song; in fact, outside bucolic verse a range of different instruments is signified by these terms. Similarly again, we shall observe (below) the blurring of the boundaries between the names Menalcas, Tityrus, Meliboeus, and the unnamed figure of the poet himself.

7. Coleman (1977) suggests that the bucolic native would not strip bark, so the text must be carved on a tree, as are, later in the book (*Ecl.* 10.53-4), Gallus' *amores*. That, however, is an elegiac motif (cf. Callim. *Aet.* fr. 73 Pf, *Anth. Pal.* 9.341.3-4; Prop. 1.18.22) and may indicate Gallus' imperfect assimilation to bucolic ways.

8. For Octavian's settlement of veteran soldiers on land confiscated in Italy see p. 53.

9. Hence, perhaps, *veteres* ('old'), although the beeches are also so at *Ecl.* 3.12.

10. Menalcas: 2.15; [Theocr.] *Id.* 8 and 9, in tales of unhappy love (cf. Athen. 14.619c, *schol. ad Id.* 9 *argum.*).

11. It is possible that the songs at *Ecl.* 9.39-43 and 46-50 are Moeris' own rather than Menalcas', but that quoted by Moeris at *Ecl.* 9.27-9 is definitely Menalcas' (as indicated by the third person verb, *canebat*, at 9.26), and it would be very hard to read that at 23-5 as anyone other than Menalcas'.

12. *Ecl.* 9.23-5 are very close to Theocr. *Id.* 3.3-5, and we may therefore see the programmatic shadow of yet another bucolic Tityrus here.

13. Menalcas' songs also refer to Varus as Virgil does in *Eclogue* 6, and the land confiscations as Virgil does in *Eclogue* 1. They refer too to the archetypal bucolic figure of Daphnis (and his bucolic activity) and Caesar' star. Menalcas' songs also include what must have been, if it had really existed, a version of Theocritus' version of Polyphemus and Galatea (*Id.* 11) – which Virgil himself plays on, under other names, in *Eclogue* 2.

14. *In urbem* (V. *Ecl.* 9.1) also recalls (and inverts) the journey of Theocritus' seventh *Idyll* (where see 7.2, *ek polios*).

15. The cups are poetic in another way too. The passage is based on Theocritus 1.26-60 where an unnamed goatherd promises Thyrsis an elaborately (and programmatically) adorned cup (of unspecified material) for a song like that of his contest with Chromis (Thyrsis goes on to sing again his lament for the archetypal bucolic figure, Daphnis). Although *Eclogue* 3 does not have a single specific Theocritean model, it can be seen as iconically Theocritean in a sense which the first two *Eclogues* are not. The first lacks a Theocritean model and Rome figures in it in a quite unTheocritean way; the second is based on *Idylls* 11, but that poem with its mythological characters is rather peripheral to the central features of Theocritus' pastoral poems; by contrast, *Eclogue* 3 is based on the core-format of the singing contest and alludes to a range of Theocritean bucolic. Virgil may have thought of *Idylls* 1 as the opening of the Theocritean corpus (cf. Barchiesi in Depew and Obbink (2000), 171-3 on first poems in Hellenistic collections) and it may be legitimate therefore to expect the programmatic function of the cup in that poem to resonate in the cups at *Ecl.* 3.36-48. On the metapoetic significance of the Virgilian passage see also Wray (2003), 234-7; Saunders (2008), 10-21.

16. The foliage of the yew is poisonous for cattle, and it would be inappropriate for this tree to be frequent in the *Eclogues*.

17. We could see Meliboeus in 1.73 as alluding to, and ironising, the Menalcas song at 9.50 in advance.

18. A markedly distinct usage is found at V. *Ecl.* 4.38, where *pinus* is used in the epic sense of ship in that *Eclogue* which has strongly epic colourings. Cf. Catull. 64.1.

19. At V. *Ecl.* 8.13 the reference is to the victor's garland on Pollio's brow; at 8.82-3 it is used in magic in a magical play on Daphnis' name.

20. Jashemski, Meyer, and Ricciardi (2002) for the evidence in these paragraphs.

21. The olive, one of the most valuable crops of ancient Italy, is seldom pictured.

22. *Pirus* and *poma* are found at V. *Georg.* 4.142-5 in the garden section.

23. Pliny (*NH* 17.240) and Virgil (*Georg.* 2.299) say not to plant near vines, though growers now plant various trees including the hazelnut near the edge of vineyards and at intervals throughout the vineyard.

24. On plane trees as the background for philosophical discussion and Roman appropriation of Greek thought, see Spencer (2010), 65. Pliny describes the plane-tree as an alien import, but his subsequent account indicates that it was long naturalised (*NH* 126-13).

25. For references, see p. 155 nn. 49 & 50 above.

26. Cf. Jashemski (1979), 54. On the flower industry at Pompeii see Jashemski (1979), 267-88.

27. Jashemski, Meyer, and Ricciardi (2002); flowers evidenced in gardens or garden painting, but not in the *Eclogues* include: chrysanthemum, carnation (*dianthus*), iris, water iris, water lily.

28. For poetry as garlands see *Anth. Pal.* 4; 5.147; 6.345; 7.20; 12.257; cf. also Sappho fr. 55.

29. The 'authorship' of the fragments is not undisputed; cf. Segal (1981), 290-1.

30. Children also pick flowers at 3.92 and they surround the cradle of the forthcoming child at 4.23.

31. As well as the places cited above, see *Ecl.* 8.54 where its programmatic function is questionable.

3. Fauna

1. *Oves* are found at 1.21; 2.33, 42; 3.3, 5, 94; 6.5; 6.85; 7.3; 8.52; 10.16, 18, 68; *agni/ae* at 1.8; 2.21; 3.6, 103; 4.45; 7.15.

2. *Capellae* at 1.12, 74, 77; 2.63-4; 3.96; 4.21; 7.3; 8.33; 9.23; 10.7, 77; *capri* at 3.17, 22-3; 7.7, 9; 9.25; *capreoli* at 2.41; *haedi* at 1.22; 2.30; 3.34, 82; 5.12; 7.9; 9.6, 62; *hirci* at 3.8, 91.

3. *Boves,* 1.9, 45; 5.25; 6.58; *tauri,* 1.45; 3.86, 100; 4.42; 5.33; 7.39; *vitula,* 3.29, 77, 85; *vacca,* 6.60; 9.31; *bucula,* 8.86; *iuvencus,* 8.85; *iuvenca,* 8.2. The *pecus* at the beginning of the third *Eclogue* bears a closer look. It is a flock of sheep, but those who remember the Theocritean passage (*Id.* 4.1-3) upon which Virgil's is based will know that in that place there was a herd of cattle. Perhaps Virgil's flock has something of the ambiguity of the *fagus-phegos* at the beginning of the Eclogue-book.

4. Bees at 1.54; 5.77; 7.13; 9.30; 10.30; bee-products (wax/honey) at 2.32; 3.25; 8.80.

5. Bacchus is an odd figure in pastoral, but see Coleman (1977) ad loc.

6. On the individualism of horses see V. *Georgics* 3.73ff.

7. *greges*; 2.30; 3.32; 5.33; 6.55; 7.2, 7, 36; *armenta*; 2.23; 4.22; 6.45, 59; *pecudes*; 1.74; 2.8; 3.1, 6, 20, 34, 101; 6.49; *pecora*; 1.50; 2.20; 5.44, 60; 7.47; 8.15; 10.17; *examina*; 7.13; 9.30.

8. For the herdsman as bucolic poet cf. *Lament for Bion* 11 (*boukolos*).

9. *Dicere* ('say/speak') is quite often used in the sense of *canere* ('sing') both here and in Horace's *Odes* there are quite frequent examples of this usage (V. *Ecl.* 3.55, 59; 4.55; 5.2, 51; 6.5; 9.35; 10.3, 6, 34; Hor. *Odes* 1.6.5; 1.21.1, 2; 1.32.3; 3.4.1; 3.11.7; 3.13.14; 3.38.15; 4.2.19 (parallel with *canit*, 13); 4.9.21; 4.12.9 (in a poem addressed to Virgil and here alluding to the *Eclogues*); *Carmen Saeculare* 8, 76; see also Catullus 61.39; 62.4, 18 (cf. Ennius *Annales* 451 Sk.); in both authors more prosaic usages are also found. Given the slimmed down song of Callimachean aesthetics to which Virgil here refers, 'say' rather than 'sing' may be both possible and appropriate, and even pointed in connection with the next word, *carmen*.

10. In Gallus' picture of Ethiopian sheep (10.68), their ethnicity and epic resonance, are marks of elegy's inability to assume the bucolic role.

11. Cf. Cairns (1999).

12. The bee, that 'most discussed, observed, respected, and admired' (Jashemski, Meyer, and Ricciardi, 2002) insect in antiquity, which features widely in poetry, including Virgil's *Georgics,* like its hive is not a significant feature in wall art.

13. Bee-production of honey is implicit rather than explicit in the *Eclogues*: at 4.30 in the new Golden Age, oaks will drip honey.

14. *Palumbes*, 1.57; 3.69; *columbae*, 9.13; *turtur*, 1.58; *ululae*, 8.55 (cf. Theocr. *Id.* 1.135); *cycni*, 7.38; 8.55; 9.29; *olores*, 9.36; *cornix*, 9.15; *aquila*, 9.13; *anser*, 9.36; *cicada*, 2.13; 5.77. Although the cicada is not a bird, it was famed for singing (it was the favourite of the Muses; Plato, *Phaedrus* 259c) and appears programmatically in Theocritus (1.148; cf. 7.138). Corydon's apparently low value judgement (*raucis*, 2.12) on the sound it makes may, then, indicate the alienation induced in him by his unrequited love. On the bird house and the Roman villa, see Spencer (2010), 79, 80-2.

15. Heraclitus' 'nightingales' (Callimachus at *Anth. Pal.* 7.80.5) are his poems, or a book of his poems (to which *Ecl.* 9.52 may allude).

16. Virgil's list of birds is also much smaller than, and not significantly in overlap with, birds known from the dining table.

17. Lizards are not infrequent in Pompeian wall-painting, usually in association with birds, and often threatened by them (Jashemski, Meyer, and Ricciardi, 2002). There is also 'a marble garden statuette (0.32 m high) of "a bird with a lizard in its mouth"' in the House of Julia Felix (Jashemski, Meyer, and Ricciardi, 2002, 334).

18. *Incondita* plays with the idea that Corydon's lines should be taken as speech and not song (cf. 2.4-5); Servius – half-paradoxically – glosses *incondita* as *agrestia* (along with *incomposita*, and *subito dicta*). See Helck (1932); Putnam (1970), 85-6; Breed (2006b), 31. On Virgil's use of Theocritus in this *Eclogue* see DuQuesnay (1979); Hubbard (1998), 54-68.

19. On guard dogs see Chapter 6 under 'dwellings' below.

20. The *calamos* here (3.13) are perhaps not ambiguous, but we cannot help remembering the usual, musical, sense of the word in the *Eclogues*.

21. The doe (*dammae*) appears in figured speech at *Ecl.* 8.28.

22. Later, in *Aeneid* 7 the shooting of Silvia's pet stag is an intrusion on a bucolic world which leads to war.

23. *Murice* (*Ecl.* 4.44) plays on shellfish, but actually just refers to the colour here. It is the absence of the shellfish-dyed material (a luxury) that is at point.

24. The word is rare in poetry (once in *Georgics*, three times in *Aeneid*), and probably here has a Lucretian flavour (cf. Lucr. *DRN* 2.727, 927).

25. The plant-setting for Pasiphae's story is bucolic; for the hyacinth (*Ecl.* 6.53) cf. 3.63 (Menalcas' offerings for Apollo, the god of song; note also the story of Hyacinth and Apollo; see 3.106-7), and in Theocritus (*Id.* 3.64,71; 10.26-9).

26. Looking at this the other way round, we could say that the bucolic animals both help the non-bucolic material fit into the Eclogue-book and help point up the difference between original source and new context. Cf. Harrison (2007), 50-3. In this context Harrison also draws attention to the Theocritean precedent for Hylas (*Id.* 13; V. *Ecl.* 6.43-4), and the bucolic colour given to Saturn's reign (6.41) in Tibullus.

27. The passage is shaped like an epyllion with one story inside another.

28. The 'marine dogs' (6.77) are a vile transmutation of the other dogs in the *Eclogues*.

4. Places in and out of Eclogue-land

1. For a different approach to geography and place names in the *Eclogues* see Saunders (2008), 59-72.

2. The riddles at *Ecl.* 3.104-5 and 106-7 imply some notion of other places.

3. See, e.g., for other places and/or geographical mobility, Theocr. *Idylls* 1.59; 4.6, 29, 33ff.; 5.2, 72-3; 7.12, 48, 52, 71ff., 111ff., 130.

4. Perhaps one might think it in character that the somewhat thoughtless Tityrus should use such vocabulary to Meliboeus, since the latter is on his way to analogous parts, which are, indeed, mentioned by name in the following lines.

5. Cf. also *murice* (*Ecl.* 4.44) for purple. Gallus' Parthian bow at 10.59 is somewhat similarly decorative, though rather more pointed as an index of the elegist's badness of fit with Eclogue-land.

6. There is some Theocritean precedent for this at *Id.* 7.111, but the passage there is extra-pastoral.

7. Damoetas: *Ecl.* 2.37, 39, 3.1, 58, Theocr. *Id.* 6; Aegon: *Ecl.* 3.2, Theocr. *Id.* 4.2; Alphesiboeus: *Ecl.* 8.1, 5, 62.

8. Near to Lyctus was Mount Aegaeon, which may produce an extra resonance with Aegon.

9. Cf. Ariusian and Lyctian at *Ecl.* 5.71-2; Hybla at 7.37, Sardinian at 7.41, Cyrnean 9.30.

10. On *pastor, pastores,* see p. 155 n. 51 above.

11. Cf. Callimachus *Hymns* 3.81 (whence perhaps taken by Gallus: see Courtney (1993: 270 and addendum in 2003 edition, p. 519); Hor. *Odes* 4.9.17-18; for Cretan archery cf. V. *Aen.* 4.69-72.

12. *Dictaeae* (*Ecl.* 6.56) and *Gortynia* (*Ecl.* 6.60) both signify Cretan in Pasiphae's neoteric speech in Silenus' song, but here there is a degree of alienness aided by the other non-bucolic features in the local context.

13. See Coleman (1977) ad loc.

14. See also, but differently, Rhodope (*Ecl.* 8.44) as harsh Amor's birthplace.

15. Orpheus is associated with Bion in a bucolic context at *Lament for Bion* 14-18.

16. The tenth *Eclogue* is clearly set in Arcadia (13-15; 31-3), and the bucolic natives are called Arcadians at 7.4, despite being set by the Mantuan river, Mincio (7.13). Arcadia is referred to at 4.58, 7.4, 26, 8.21 (*Maenalios*) etc.; 10.13-15, 31-3 and the last in particular may suggest that Arcadia is retrospectively being presented as the name of the bucolic setting of the *Eclogues* as a whole in a poetic rather than a geographical sense. See below for this and Jenkyns' (1989) counter-view. Cf. also Kennedy (1987).

17. Most of the figures mentioned in passing in the second *Eclogue* have names which we might consider typically 'Arcadian' – names that are found dispersed through the rest of the *Eclogues* (and drawn from Theocritean bucolic): Amaryllis, Menalcas, Daphnis, Pan, Amyntas, Damoetas, and Thestylis.

18. The audience will see Theocritus' comic Polyphemus (*Id.* 11.34) behind Corydon here.

19. Alexis stands out in name and characterisation as belonging to erotic epigram rather than bucolic (see further under 'names' below); similarly Alexis' rather unbucolic master, Iollas, has a name not in Theocritus, and only once elsewhere in the *Eclogues* (3.76). One could also take the reference to sheep in the Sicilian mountains as Virgil's comic portrayal of the besotted Corydon's love-inspired delusions: he momentarily presents him as like a Roman aristocrat with remote estates (Lucilius, for one, had property on Sicily); cf. Garson (1971) below for Corydon's dementia.

20. Gallus' Arcadia is dominated by Maenalus, Lycaeus, Parthenius – but the latter could pun on Parthenius the poet too (Lipka (2001), 106).

21. In particular, we note that one of Menalcas' songs alludes to the first *Eclogue*: *insere ... piros* ('graft pears'; 9.50) picks up the same phrase at 1.73, where Meliboeus uses it – or perhaps we could say that Meliboeus alludes to the song of which we will hear a fragment in *Ecl.* 9.

22. Pollio himself is only partially placed inside Eclogue-land. As a poet and lover of the shepherds' bucolic poetry (here called *rustica* (3.84) rather than *agrestis* (6.8) or *silvestris* (1.2)), he is known to Damoetas and Menalcas in *Eclogue* 3, but he does not appear in the bucolic landscape or talk to the inhabitants. In the fourth as well as the eighth *Eclogue* he is addressed outside the framework of the bucolic contents.

23. See Harrison (2007: 34 n. 2) and Volk (2008: 9) for the question of whether *Eclogue* 8 refers to Caesar/Augustus' Illyrian campaigns of 36-5 or those of Pollio in 39.

24. Compare the use of *superare* (*Aen.* 1.244) and *superas* (*Ecl.* 8.6).

25. The association of Antenor and the Timavus also appears in Lucan (*Bellum Civile* 7.192-5) and Silius Italicus (*Punica* 12.213-21). It is associated with the voyage of the Argo by Martial (4.25), though Pliny (*NH* 3.128) is uncertain of the river's identity.

26. Likewise 'the city' (*urbs*): in Theocritus' *Idylls*, by contrast, civilised urban contexts are glimpsed or heard of from time to time even in the pastoral poems, and the urban mimes present a prominent benign picture of the city.

27. Skoie (2006: 299-300) writes that in the *Eclogues* the countryside 'never seems very far from the city', but 'near' and 'far' are subjective concepts. From the point of view of the bucolic natives Rome seems definitely to be far.

28. Alexis does not appear in Theocritus (nor Iollas, his quasi-elegiac *dives amator* at *Ecl.* 2.57), but the name is found at Plato *Anth. Pal.* 7.100; Meleager *Anth. Pal.* 12.127. The Corydon in *Eclogue* 7 mentions Alexis (55) in his song

competition with Thyrsis. On possible appropriate etymologies of the name see DuQuesnay (1979), 44; Van Sickle (1979), 125; O'Hara (1996) 245-6. On elegiac elements in the Eclogues see Kenney (1983).

29. Nysa (*Ecl.* 8.18, 26) is found nowhere else in pastoral. However, Damon too is not in earlier pastoral (though he is perhaps naturalised by his presence in *Ecl.* 3.17, 23). Mopsus, likewise, Nysa's new husband (26, 29f., 32) is not in extant Greek pastoral, though he is one of the two singers in *Ecl.* 5.

30. For Damon as husband, see *coniugis* (*Ecl.* 8.18). In the same *Eclogue*, Alphesiboeus clearly assumes a character (a woman) for his song, but Damon (male) is not so clearly distinct from the (male) part he sings (see Breed 2006, 12).

31. In this part of the eighth *Eclogue*, Virgil uses Theocritus' second *Idyll* – a poem with an urban setting which is not in itself threatening.

32. The travellers in Theocr. *Id.* 7 (which lies behind the ninth *Eclogue*) are coming *from* the *polis,* and – in contradistinction to what we see in the *Eclogues* – there seems nothing questionable about the *polis* in *Id.* 7, as elsewhere in the *Idylls.*

33. In the *Eclogues via* occurs only at 9.1, 23, 59, 64. Of these, one (1, 59, 64) leads to the *urbs*, the other (23) across some of Eclogue-land. Cf. also *triviis* at 3.26.

34. The tomb of Daphnis (5.42), the tomb of Bianor (9.60; see Brenk, 1981). The tombs at 8.98 are hearsay only. The source of Bianor's tomb in Virgil, the tomb of Brasilas (Theocr. 7.10), is not itself sinister, but reflected the memorials and votive shrines that were a feature of the Greek landscape. (There is another tomb at Theocr. 1.125, and a grave at 5.121.)

35. The first *Eclogue* is rather exceptional in its architectural content: Pompeian sacral-idyllic painting (although rather later, and in a different city) quite often contains quasi-architectural stonework, whereas the Virgilian bucolic landscape tends strongly not so to do. In this poem, however, there is a reference to Meliboeus' cottage (*tuguri*, 1.68) and perhaps to distant Roman aristocratic villas (82).

36. A trace is also implicit in the 'consular dating' at *Ecl.* 4.11. Here the influence is in the reverse direction as the quasi-bucolic golden age reaches out into Rome and its world.

37. Skoie describes introducing politics in to the pastoral landscape as 'an urban invasion', but seeks also to reduce the impact of the threat (2006: 303-8).

38. Cf. Rosenmeyer (1969), 208, and on the interrelationship of city and country in the late Republic and in the *Eclogues*, Leach (1974), 72; Skoie (2006). If the ninth *Eclogue* is darker than the first *Eclogue*, it does not necessarily mean that its darkness is authorially emphasised and given the greater authority. We see such patterns often, and the final darkness may be part of an aesthetic pattern of contrast rather than summatively climactic as such; cf. the outer ends of Lucretius' *De Rerum Natura* and of Hor. *Odes* 3.1-6. For variations in scholarly attitudes to the question of Virgil's 'Augustanism' in general see Volk (2008), 4-5; with regard to evidence in Servius of perceptions of anti-Augustanism in Virgil, Thomas (2001), 93-121; with regard to the *Eclogues*, see Volk (2008), 7-8; with regard to the *Georgics*, the *Aeneid* and Ovid, see Galinksy (1996), 93-100; Griffin (2005) tracks the trajectory of Augustanism in Roman verse against the consolidation of Octavian/Augustus' power.

39. The herdsmen's hexameters, indeed, are conspicuously refined in comparison with those of Virgil's contemporaries and predecessors. Ennius' epic

(*Annales*), Lucilian (and Horatian) satire, Lucretius' didactic (*De Rerum Natura*), Cicero's *Aratea*, and even (in some respects) the Catullus of *Carm.* 64 all contrast in varying degrees. Virgil's own later works in other genres, the *Georgics* and the *Aeneid*, resemble each other in metrical behaviour, and are markedly different from the *Eclogues*. See further, Jones (2006).

40. See Keppie (1983); Eck (2003), 18-19.

41. The poems of Horace's second book of *Satires* date from around 33-30 BC, but Ofellus is remembered as a figure from the past (cf. *Sat.* 2.2.112-13). Having been a landowner, in the course of the redistribution Ofellus became a tenant farmer on the same property (114-15, 126-35). The confiscations are probably also noticed by Horace at *Epp.* 2.2.50-1. If these lines are to be interpreted as meaning that Horace lost his father's farm in the confiscations, they are matter-of-fact rather than complaining in tone.

42. The Britons were stereotypical of the remotest barbarism in Latin verse: Cat. 11.11-12; Hor. *Odes* 1.35.29-30; 4.14.47. The Oaxes has been a problem for commentators since Servius (who thought it was either a Mesopotamian or a Scythian river), because the name is not otherwise known. It is generally taken that Virgil was thinking of one of the two rivers called Oxus, and that he may have conflated the name with that of the Araxes. However, it may be that the name is meant to be recognised as an unreal conflation of names, in keeping with Meliboeus' exaggeration.

43. Both veteran soldiers – impatient to benefit from settlements – and threatened occupants were a source of trouble in 41 BC. Bands marched on Rome to ask for compensation and a fair distribution of the burden (Appian *BC* 5.2.12-13; Dio 48.6-12). Lucius Antonius, Mark Antony's brother, riding on the discontent, gathered a coalition against Octavian. He and his supporters were besieged by Octavian at Perusia which surrendered to Octavian in 40 BC. Lucius was spared, but the Perusians were killed (the bloodshed was still remembered bitterly by Propertius in around 30 BC; 1.21, 22).

44. Horace was born in 65 BC. The calibration of this memory against his boyhood (*Sat.* 2.2.112) is not precise, but gives a perhaps tendentiously heightened sense of the remoteness of the events.

45. For various perspectives on the town-country dichotomy and its complexities in Greek and Roman culture see Rosen and Sluiter (2006). On 'city and country' in Roman Satire see Braund (1989).

46. On the Golden Age in the *Georgics* see also Johnston (1980); in Augustan culture, Galinsky (1996), 91-120; in Augustan ideology, Wallace-Hadrill (1982).

47. On the bucolic theme in *Aeneid* 7 and 8 see Anderson (1968); Wimmel (1973); Hardie (1998), 60-1. On the *Aeneid*'s inclusion of other genres (including bucolic) see Harrison (2007), 207-40. On the spatial aspect of Evander's presentation of 'Rome' to Aeneas see Spencer (2010), 50-4.

48. For Rome before Augustus see Cornell (2000); for the Augustus' urban transformation see Favro (1996); Favro (2005). Although much of the transformation is realised from roughly 29 BC onwards, there were signs much earlier: at the battle of Philippi in 42 BC Octavian, the future Augustus, pledged a temple to Mars (finally dedicated in 2 BC), and in 36 BC he vowed a temple to Apollo (the temple was dedicated in 28 BC). Despite the traditionalising rhetoric of the programme, the scale and multi-layered nature of the transformation (going hand in hand with social changes) suggests that the perception of modernity is an issue worth pursuing, as it has been for more modern cities, such as Second Empire Paris (where, too, much of the massive architectural

development was carried out in an idiom that looked to the past). Cf., for example, Bergman (1983); Ferguson (1994); Harvey (2003). Given the temporal charting of urban life (Laurence: 1994, 122-9), the calendar reform of Julius Caesar (46 BC (Censorinus 20.8; Macrobius *Sat.*1.14.3)), still recent when the *Eclogues* appeared, would have contributed to the sense of pervasive change, as awareness of temporal progression was reinforced by the daily publication of the *Acta Diurna* (see p. 165 n. 6). The festivals revived by Augustus (see further, Beacham (2005)), some of which are 'foreshadowed' in the story of Aeneas as told in the *Aeneid* would later also contribute to altering the subjection perception of annual time.

49. The height of the buildings and the size of the population would contribute, despite the labyrinthine and chaotic streets, the beggars, dirt, and animals (see Holleran, forthcoming). Cf. Edwards and Woolf in Edwards and Woolf (2003), 1-20.

50. Horace *Odes* 1-3 were issued together (but see now Hutchinson (2002) for arguments against this), probably in 23 BC; the *Aeneid* was being composed from 26 BC onwards. The similarity of the two passages may indicate a common source in the proem to book 16 of Ennius' *Annales* (see Skutsch's commentary, pp. 568ff.). The Capitol complex embodied a nexus of ancient Roman religious and mythic associations. Its central feature, the temple of Jupiter Optimus Maximus, Juno, and Minerva, destroyed by fire in 83 BC, was rebuilt on the same foundations, but to a greater height. The work was initiated by Sulla and completed in 69 BC by Lutatius Catulus (Tac. *Hist.* 3.72; Cic. *Verr.* 4.69). The roof was at this point gilded, though Pliny writes that Catulus' contemporaries did not view this with universal approval (Pliny *NH* 33.57). This is the form in which the audience of the *Eclogues* would have known it. While Augustus made further renovations in 26 and 9 BC, and added a new temple (to Jupiter Tonans; Suet. *Aug.* 29; Dio Cassius 54.4), he also transferred a number of the Capitoline Hill's functions elsewhere, especially raising the importance of the Palatine (Favro 2002: 200-3).

51. Suetonius (*Divi Augusti Vita* 28), suggests that Augustus' transformation of Rome was motivated by a sense of disparity between the appearance of the city and its role in the world.

52. I take *extulit* as preterite, reflecting the moment when the astonished Tityrus saw the city.

53. *Ecl.* 1.20, 24, 34; 8.68; 9.1, 62; Cities appear as *oppida* in a quasi-mythological form at 4.32-3.

54. I do not mean to exclude the possibility of elite audiences elsewhere in Italy.

55. The odd numbered eclogues are dialogues in form; of the even each has a narrative or Virgilian introduction. In the seventh the distinction is somewhat reduced, since in a fairly literal sense only Meliboeus speaks, and the exchange between Corydon and Thyrsis is recalled by him.

56. We are told nothing else about where Meliboeus is (or whom he addresses) at the dramatic date, so to speak, of the *Eclogue* itself.

57. Somewhat similarly there are the Cyrnean yews that Lycidas hopes Moeris' bees will avoid (*Ecl.* 9.30); the adjective may merely connote the bitterness of Corsican honey, just as Phoenician (5.17; 7.32) sometimes means hardly more than 'red'.

58. See especially 4.1, 6.1, 10.1, 4, 51; cf. Hybla at 1.54 and (here) 7.37. See also (?another) Corydon's connection with Sicily at *Ecl.* 2.21.

59. See V. *Ecl.* 2.26; 3.12; 5.20ff.; 7.1; 8.68ff.; 9.46; Theocr. *Id.* 1.64-145; 5.20; 6; 7.73-7; post Theocritean *Id.* 8, 9, 27; 'Unlike other pastoral characters Daphnis belongs to earlier mythology; see Parth. *Erot.* 29, Aelian *VH* 10.18' (Coleman 1977).

60. Theocr. *Id.* 4; *Id.* 5.6; V. *Ecl.* 2; 5.86; 7.

61. Thyrsis is only in this *Eclogue* (7) in Virgil, but is the singer of the Daphnis-dirge in the opening *Idyll* of Theocritus: *Id.* 1.64ff.

62. Cf. Erucius *Anth.Pal.* 6.96 for Glaucon and Corydon, 'Arcadians both', as they sacrifice to Pan, 'presumably as fellow-countrymen of the god rather than as inhabitants of an idyllic Arcady' (Coleman 1977, ad loc.).

63. Jenkyns argues weakly that if Virgil calls the shepherds Arcadians they must be somewhere other than Arcadia (32).

64. Cf. *Ecl.* 1.1f.; 9.7-9, 40; cf. also archetypal characters (Daphnis, Tityrus, etc.) and programmatic words as listed above.

65. As well as *Ecl.* 7.4 and 26 see 4.58, 59 where it is associated with Pan; at 10.26 *Pan deus Arcadiae* comes to visit Gallus in his dying Daphnis act. Later in the poem Gallus' song refers to a number of Arcadian locations (see below) and addresses the *Eclogue*-natives as *Arcades* (10.31, 33). At 8.17ff. Damon's song's refrain refers to his song as Maenalian verses.

66. See above, Chapter 4 under 'Arcadia i'.

67. See also Breed (2006b), 117-35; Saunders (2008), 65-72.

68. But with Arcadian connections: the nymph Arethusa was turned into a river in Arcadia, which flowed undersea and emerged as a spring on Ortygia, an island off Syracuse (cf. Ov. *Met.* 5.572-641). The version at *Aen.* 3.694-6 (cf. Pindar Nemean 1.1-4) is different in detail, but maintains the aquatic Arcadian-Ortygian connection.

69. We may think of the way in which Horace begins *Odes* 1.9 among the winter trees of a mountain outside Rome, and seamlessly shifts to an urban scene in spring.

70. We infer that Gallus presents himself as dying of love in his poetry, and we may further think of the motif of the inadequacy of poetry in the face of pain, especially that of love; cf. the incurability of *Amor* at Prop. 2.1.

71. Cf. V. *Ecl.* 4.2; 6.10; 8.54; 10.13; cf. Theocr. *Id.* 1.12.

72. At 8.21 sqq Maenalus is the Arcadian mountain, the musical mountain of talking pines which hears the love of herdsmen (*pastorum*) and Pan (himself inventor of the bucolic *calami*, at 8.22-4), and is the imprimatur of bucolic song in Damon's refrain.

73. See Conte (1986), 100-29; Harrison (2007), 59-74.

74. Some qualification is needed here because of the odd vocabulary and the reference to pigs implied in *subulci*; see under 'occupation' below.

75. Laurels and Apollo in *Eclogues* 4 and 6 make Apollo a bucolic superintendent.

76. Similarly Tibullus was to imagine a rural (quasi-bucolic) retreat with Delia present, and visited by Messalla (Tib. 1.5).

77. It is perhaps implied by Servius on *Ecl.* 10 (*amorum suorum ... libros quattuor*, 'four books of his loves / his *Amores*') that *Amores* was a Gallan title.

78. So Servius on *Ecl.* 10.46-9; cf. Ross (1975), 85-6; Harrison (2007) 67.

79. On these lines see Ross (1975: 40-2) and Harrison (2007: 68-71).

80. Dryads are also at *Ecl.* 5.59, hamadryads only here. Nymphs are found not infrequently in Horatian lyric, and much more spasmodically in elegy, chiefly – as with other more or less mythological apparatus – in Propertius (e.g. Prop. 1.20).

81. As Harrison (2007: 71) points out, 'just as the pastoral *silvae* must retreat before elegy (63 *concedite silvae*), so Gallus as poet must yield to the poetics of Love (69 *et nos cedamus amori*)'. The *silvae* stand for bucolic, and Amor for elegy.

82. The notion of 'Ethiopian sheep' is a fine culminating conflation of epic (cf. *Iliad* 1.423 for Ethiopians) and bucolic (sheep).

83. Virgil's basket (10.71) can be seen as a symbol for *Ecl.* 10 which is itself a container for a scale-model of Gallan elegy. Cf. Harrison (2007), 72.

5. Climate, Time, Geology, Geography

1. For a different approach cf. Saunders (2008), 73-101.

2. Broadly, the setting of *Eclogue* 2 is harvest time (2.10), of 3 is spring (3.56ff.); the fourth *Eclogue* is set in the great cycle of time. *Frigus* appears fleetingly and decoratively at *Ecl.* 2.22, but winter is only strongly present in a Gallan context (see *Ecl.* 10.20, 47f., 65-6).

3. *Pluvia* is only at 9.63 (along with night; see below) and marks the darkness of this poem; *imbres* are only at 3.80 in figured language in Damoetas' song, in the cosmogonic section of Silenus' song (6.38), in figured language in Thyrsis' song (7.60), and, be it noted, as a pleasant phenomenon contrasted to parching. Dew is pleasant at 8.15 and 37. Wind: 2.58; 3.81; 5.82; 9.58. Breezes (*zephyri*): 5.5.

4. *Hiberna*: 10.20; *hiems*: 10.66; *nives*: 10.23, 47, 66; *frigora*: 10.47, 48, 57, 65 (only elsewhere in figured speech at 7.51); *glacies*: 10.49; *Boreas* is absent at 7.51.

5. Palaemon refers to the year now (*nunc*) being at its loveliest at 3.57.

6. See Laurence (1994), 122-32. The perception of the chartedness of time was reinforced by the daily publication since 59 BC (Suet. *Iul.* 20) of the *Acta Diurna*, recording social and political news and read in Rome and the provinces (Tac. *Ann.* 16.22). Patterns of time usage for the Roman noble may have been different in the country and in cities and towns other than Rome, but it was still patterned on the basis of the system associated with urban culture (Laurence 1994: 129-32).

7. The *Eclogues* are not entirely 'Golden' since (among other reasons) agriculture is post-Golden (V. *Ecl.* 4. 40-1; *Georg.* 1.125), and cornfields are part of the typical scenery of the bucolic setting. Husbandry is post-Golden in Hesiod (*Op.* 117-18), but remains very leisurely in the *Eclogues*. Hardie (2006) makes a case for the *Eclogues* alluding to cultural and historical narrative timeframes via Lucretius.

8. The corresponding cup in Theocr. *Id.* 127ff., by contrast, is newly made. The pipes at 5.85ff. are those that taught Menalcas his repertoire, the crook that Mopsus offers Menalcas (= Virgil) is one that Antigenes (a friend of Theocritus; see *Id.* 7.4 and Prefaces to the Scholia) did not manage to get.

9. Ovid's simple meal seems to have owed much to Callimachus' now fragmentary *Hecale*.

10. Temporal indications are not infrequent in the fragments of Lucilius.

11. Night references are most prominent in the ninth *Eclogue* (9.44, 63), and only elsewhere at: 8.14, 88.

12. If *surgamus* (10.75, 'Let us rise') and *nocent et frugibus umbrae* (10.76, 'Shadows also harm fruit') look forward to the *Georgics*, we may see the Virgil putting the Eclogue-book in literary-autobiographical time, somewhat as the

Virgil of the *Georgics* alludes to the opening line of the *Eclogues* in his construction of his poetic career at *Georgics* 4.565-6. For 'textual time' see also Breed (2006a).

13. Cf. Hardie (2006: 286) on the diffusion of *pueri* ('boys') throughout the *Eclogues*. Hardie connects this and the teacherly presences (the old Tityrus in *Eclogue* 1, Palaemon in *Eclogue* 3, Silenus in *Eclogue* 6, Moeris in *Eclogue* 9) with a Lucretian educational time structure.

14. Casual mentions of death appear in Theocritus at *Id.* 2.70 and 4.39-40.

15. This remains true even if we see *Ecl.* 9 as undercutting the qualified optimism offered in *Ecl.* 1.

16. The genre most resembling Virgilian bucolic in this respect is – perhaps paradoxically – the urban genre of satire, what was said above notwithstanding.

17. There are also some instances of mountains in figured language (*Ecl.* 5.76; 7.66).

18. For hunting as also not Golden Age activity see V. *Georg.* 1.140.

19. Cf. Berg (1974), 116-20.

20. Virgil's is the earliest example of the Greek loan-word *antron* in Latin (Coleman 1977). On the other hand, *spelaeum* is another Greek loan-word, and earlier examples are inscriptional/technical religious.

21. On Polyphemus and Galatea as a core element in the Eclogue-book see Chapter 7, 'special figures i' below).

22. On grottoes in Roman gardens see Grimal (1943), 17, 322-5, 427-8; Lavagne (1988); von Stackelberg (2009), 37; cf. also the grotto with grape-arbor in a wall-painting at the House of P. Fannius Synistor at Boscoreale, illustrated in Fowler (1989: 30) and Ling (1991: 31). Calypso's cave is certainly gardenlike and may sometimes be remembered by the designers and/or viewers of Roman garden-grottoes.

23. Hartswick (2004), 1.

24. Priapus also figures in Theocritus (*Id.* 1.21, 81), but in Latin Priapus is more conspicuously a figure of priapic epigram (and Horace's unbucolic garden poem, *Satires* 1.8, which resembles an expanded priapic epigram).

25. Garson (1971: 189-9) takes the reference to the sea as Corydon's fanciful exaggeration of a rock pool, and sees other comic exaggerations and oddities in Corydon's lament. Cf. p. 160 n. 19 above (citing Garson 1971) on Corydon's reference to sheep on Sicily.

26. In fact, although *Idyll* 3 has a pastoral frame, it is really a relocated version of an urban *paraklausithyron* with touches of a Polyphemus-song.

27. The change of the refrain in Damon's song from *incipe Maenalios mecum, mea tibia, versus* ('begin Maenalian verses with me, my flute') to *desine Maenalios, iam desine, tibia, versus* ('end Maenalian verses, flute, end them now') at this point (8. 61) indeed marks the end of Damon's song, but might also mark his departure from bucolic limits in an emotional sense as well.

6. Human Geography

1. Fruit of various kinds, or unspecified: *Ecl.* 1.37; 1.73; 2.51, 53; 3.64, 71, 81, 82, 92; 7.46; 8.37, 53; 9.50; vines at 1.73; 2.70; 3.10, 38-9; 4.40; 5.7; 5.31; 7.48, 58, 61.

2. On farming see White (1967; 1970); Frayn (1979, 1984).

3. See Jashemski (1979), 201-42, 251-88; cf. also Zanker (1998), 142ff.; Purcell (1987).

4. In Virgil's time Sicily, be it noted, was extensively farmed in *latifundia*.

5. Citizenship is more at home in Theocritus, even pastoral Theocritus (*Id.* 5.8).

6. Note also *lites* in a different context at *Ecl.* 3.108 – that of the bucolic song-contest.

7. Spencer (2010), 37 cites Cic. *De Leg.* 2.5 and draws attention to the Roman citzen as having 'two homelands: the city of Rome itself and their place of birth', which may be part of the background to the double perspective of the *Eclogues*.

8. On the greater profile of clothing in Theocritus than in Virgil see p. 173 n. 28 below.

9. On Roman aristocratic fishponds see Spencer (2010), 84-5.

10. Pliny *NH* 15.98-9; 23.151; Dioscorides 1.175; Columella *RR* 7.9.6; 8.17.13. According to Virgil bees also fed on the arbutus, *Georg.* 4.181.

11. Cf. Jashemski, Meyer, Ricciardi (2002), 91.

12. Jashemski, Meyer, Ricciardi (2002), 89-90.

13. The acorn (which figures at *Ecl.* 10.20) has a pre-urban suggestion about it; cf. in addition Lucr. 5.1416 (and cf. 5.14-17); V. *Georg.* 1.148-9.

14. Jashemski, Meyer, and Ricciardi (2002), 101-2, 122.

15. See further Wiseman (1970).

16. *Finibus* at 1.61 is in figured language, but the context is still of displacement. Of course the bucolic world is itself bounded from a remote and dangerous outside (cf. also the difference between the people of the neighbourhood (*finitimi*) and the Roman visitors in Lucretius' bucolic world (Lucr. *DRN* 4.581).

17. On genre and failure to live up to genre see Jones (2007), 8, 73.

18. Cf. Paschalis (2001), 216-18.

19. See Coleman (1977) at *Ecl.* 7.21 for Libethridan maidens as muses in Euphorion.

7. Named People

1. For names as a generic indicator see Jones (2007), 48-75; (2006).

2. Lipka (2001), 177. For 'bucolic names' in the *Eclogues*, see also Rumpf (2008).

3. Damoetas and Menalcas have a singing competition – cf. Damoetas in Theocr. *Id.* 6, Menalcas in [Th.] *Id.* 8 and 9; but they also correspond to the dialogists Battus and Corydon in Theocr. *Id.* 4 (see 1-3).

4. The only other appearance of the name in the *Eclogues* is at 5.86. As this is a virtual quotation of *Ecl.* 2.1 (serving as the name of one of the songs in Menalcas' repertoire along with *Ecl.* 3, whose first line is similarly treated), no additional character is added to the register of Corydons in the book.

5. See Chapter 4 'Arcadia i' for Tityrus as Virgil in *Ecl.* 1, even if the reader has not reached *Ecl.* 6.4.

6. Or perhaps Moeris. Either Lycidas is still apostophising Menalcas, or he returns (without marking this) to addressing Moeris again. Cf. Segal (1981), 290-1.

7. When Menalcas' songs address Tityrus 9. 23-5 it is a sort of translation (in every sense) of Theocr. *Id.* 3.1-5. Also, if we think of Menalcas and Tityrus as both potential names for Virgil, we have something like a scale model of Virgil performing bucolic in which he appears himself under a bucolic name.

8. On the ownership of voice in this passage see Breed (2006b), 21-2.

9. One might think of *Ecl.* 7.70, *ex illo Corydon, Corydon est tempore nobis* ('Since then it has been "Corydon, Corydon" for us'), as playing on the equivocal status of Corydon or Corydons.

10. See Rumpf (2008), 78-7.

11. Lipka (2001), 173.

12. Virgil's bucolic inhabitants are able to allude to Hellenistic poets. For example, Moeris in the ninth Eclogue alludes to Callimachus' epigram in memory of Heraclitus (V. *Ecl.* 9.51-2, cf. *Anth. Pal.* 7.80.1-3). Cf. Breed (2006b), 12.

13. Cf. also the possible allusion to Macer at *Ecl.* 3.100 noted by Lipka 2001: 172 n. 9), and the possibility that Silenus represents the Greek, but approximately contemporary, poet Parthenius (Harrison 2007: 39-48).

14. Delia = Diana at *Ecl.* 7.29.

15. The name Phyllis is also used at *Ecl.* 3.76, 78, 107; 7.14, 59; 10.37, Alcon nowhere else in the *Eclogues*, and Codrus as a presumably Arcadian poet whose poetry's quality is disputed by Corydon and Thyrsis (7.22, 26).

16. Meliboeus ('he has care of the cattle'; Servius); Phyllis ('foliage'); Alphesiboeus ('producing a good yield of oxen'; note also Alphesiboea at Theocr. *Id.* 3.45).

17. Galatea is used (not as a sea nymph) in an erotic epigram by Paulus Silentarius (*Anth. Pal.* 5.256). See also Hor. *Odes* 3.27.14 with Nisbett-Rudd.

18. Not in Lipka (2001).

19. Lipka (2001), 188.

20. Aegon at Theocr. *Id.* 4.2 (a significant goat-type name); also at V. *Ecl.* 5.72.

21. For Lycoris as Gallus' mistress see Prop. 2.34.91-2, Ov. *Am.* 1.15.30; for Cytheris as the subject of his four books of elegies see Servius at V. *Ecl.* 10.1.

22. Not in Lipka (2001).

23. Cf. Henderson (1998), 221-2.

24. The corresponding cup in Theocr. *Id.* 1.27ff. came from a sailor from Calydnos and has no named maker, but at *Id.* 5.104-5 Comatas says Praxiteles might have made his cypress pail.

25. Lipka (2001), 184.

26. Delia is used for the goddess Diana at *Ecl.* 7.29. It is found conspicuously, but later than the *Eclogues*, as the poet's mistress in Tibullus' *Elegies* 1.

27. We might also think of Horace's Ilia or Egeria (*Sat.* 1.2.125-6) made of ordinary women.

28. According to Servius in the context of Virgil's reference to Gallus' poem on the origin of the Grynean grove (at *Ecl.* 6.72) Euphorion made this Mopsus a topic.

29. For Daphnis see Theocr. *Id.* 1.64-145; 5.20; 6; 7.73-7; post-Theocritean *Id.* 8, 9, 27. 'Unlike other pastoral characters D belongs to earlier mythology' (Coleman 1977): see Parth. *Erot.* 29, Aelian *VH* 10.18; schol. Theocr; Ov. *AA* 1.732. In the *Eclogues* see 2.26; 3.12; 5.20ff.; 7.1; 8.68ff.; 9.46.

30. [Theocr.] *Id.* 8 and 9, in tales of unhappy love (cf. Athen. 14.619c, schol. ad Id. 9 argum.).

31. *Cicuta* (*Ecl.* 5.85) may point to 'Lucretian bucolic' (Lucr. *DRN* 5.1383); see Saunders (2008), 28.

32. Saunders (2008: 28) links this crook with the staff given to Simichidas by Lycidas in Theocr. *Id.* 7 and the laurel rod given to Hesiod by the Muses (*Theog.* 30-1).

33. Possibly at the corrupt [Bion] 2.32; otherwise, a Bithynian princess (Suet. Iul. 49), the birthplace of Dionysus (h. Hom. 1.8), and a nymph who nursed Dionysus there.

34. Damon and Nysa echo Polyphemus and Galatea, so the model is perhaps not fully pastoral as such.

35. *Coniugis* also occurs later (*Ecl.* 8.66) in Alphesiboeus' dramatisation of a lovelorn woman's resort to magic. In this case too Virgil takes his characters outside the usual range of experience of the bucolic world.

36. Servius believed that the three names represent mythological figures. Lipka (2001), 184-7 and 188-90 argues that the dismissal of Servius' proposition misses important connotations.

37. This remains true even Theocr. *Id.* 3, whose opening Virgil plays with in at the start of *Ecl.* 3, has links with urban poetry.

38. Any more than Horace does when he refers to Glycera as though she were a topic of Albius' (perhaps Tibullus) poetry (*Odes* 1.33), or Mystes of Valgius' (*Odes* 2.9).

39. Cf. see Lipka (2001), 186-7.

40. Lipka (2001: 190 n. 133) makes a very tentative case for the latter proposition, and for accepting Maas' conjecture Simichon in support.

41. Servius saw Chromis and Mnasyllus as Varus and Virgil (at *Ecl.* 6.13).

42. So Lipka (2001), 46. The female form, Mnasylla, is found in an epigram by Perses (*Anth. Pal.* 7.730.1); see Lipka (2001), 46.

43. Werewolves occur, famously, in an included story in Petr. *Sat.* 61-2 where the speaker is vulgar: werewolves do not belong in polite literature at all, especially the ultra-refined Latin bucolic.

44. It is perhaps worth remembering that the names of neither Damon nor Alphesiboeus, the singers in *Ecl.* 8, in which unbucolic extremes are explored, have Theocritean backgrounds, although the female form, Alphesiboea, does appear (*Id.* 3.45).

45. Moeris' terminal formula (*desine plura puer,* 'No more of that, boy'; 9.66) is the same as that used by Menalcas (Virgil) to stop the preambling and get on with the exchange at *Ecl.* 5.19.

46. There is, of course, the precedent of Brasilas' tomb in Theocritus (*Id.* 7.10-11) for Bianor's tomb here.

47. The proverbial wolves that explain Moeris' silence at *Ecl.* 9.54 may link with the wolf that the other Moeris reportedly becomes at 8.97, and Bianor's tomb (9.59-60) may refresh a memory of the tombs that other Moeris raises ghosts from (8.98).

48. See Lipka (2001), 174.

49. Lipka (2001), 174-5 for discussion and details. With regard to the Homeric passage (*Iliad* 11.86-92), Tracy (1982) draws attention to the simile of the woodsman resting after labour among the pines that precedes Bienor's death and makes a connection with the farmers stripping the leaves in Virgil's lines immediately after the reference to Bianor's tomb (9.60-1).

50. Lipka (2001), 174 on historical characters of this name in many parts of Greece.

51. The MSS have *Hylas*; see Lipka (2001), 187.

52. Urban household guard-dogs appear conspicuously in the town house in the tale of the town and country mouse in Hor. *Sat.* 2.6.79-117.

53. See Pliny *NH* 8.148 for mongrels bred from wolves and dogs, known according to Servius (at 3.17) as *lycisci* ('wolflings'). Hylax is derived from Greek *hylaktein* 'to bark'.

54. Lipka (2001), 187, n. 107.

55. Menalcas: *Ecl.* 3; 5; 9.10, 16, 18ff.; 10.20. Tityrus: *Ecl.* 1.1, 4, 18, 38; 3.20, 96; 5.12; 6.4; 8.55; 9.23, 24.

56. Already so read by Quintilian (8.6.46-7).

57. In this reading it is particularly appropriate that the lines (*Ecl. 9*.23-5) are drawn from Theocritus (*Id.* 3.3-5).

58. Cf. Hahn (1944), 223.

59. In the bucolic world, the poetry listener is usually also a poet-in-waiting. Meliboeus himself acquires a Virgilian colouring retrospectively when his words are echoed later in the book: *ite ... ite capellae* ('go, go, little goats', 1.74) reappears in the last line of the collection (10.77), more or less explicitly as Virgil's farewell, and *insere ... piros* ('graft pears', 1.73) reappears in one of the fragments of bucolic song in the ninth *Eclogue* (9.50), fragments probably attributable to Menalcas who in some degree stands for Virgil. One might note also that Meliboeus introduces the substance of *Ecl.* 7 in a manner analogous to the Virgilian introductions to the even-numbered poems. There the rather Virgilian introducer turns out to be Meliboeus at line 9 in a manner not unlike that in which Virgil could be said to turn out to be 'Tityrus' in the fourth line of *Ecl.* 6. On the question of Meliboeus' identification with Virgil, see Hahn (1944), 223.

60. One should note also the programmatic etymologising of Tityrus as *calamus*; see Cairns (1999), 289-93; see also Lipka (2001), 155, 182-3.

61. Berg (1974; 147) takes Tityrus' relinquishing of Galatea (*Ecl.* 1.31) as a programmatic sign in which Galatea stands for the erotic element in Theocritean pastoral and the earlier poems (chronologically speaking) in the Eclogue-book. Galatea does so in her capacity of recalling the pairing of Polyphemus and Galatea, for which cf. below.

62. One might note here that Servius (at *Ecl.* 6.13) took Chromis and Mnasyllus in *Ecl.* 6 to represent Varus and Virgil.

63. Other mythological figures also appear in Theocritus' *Idylls*: Hercules and Hylas (13), the graces, Helen, the Dioscuri, Hercules (24), the Bacchantes (26)

64. Polyphemus' inability to swim is the source of the wit at Theocr. *Id.* 11.54; cf. 625ff.

65. Polyphemus derives his role ultimately from the Homeric Polyphemus (albeit a one-eyed monster) lives in a cave and tends sheep. Polyphemus appears as a quasi-bucolic figure a number of times in Roman art: a third style panel at the Casa del Sacerdos Amandus (Pompeii), at the House of Livia (Rome, Palatine, soon after 30 BC, and at the Boscotrecase Villa, soon after 11 BC. On the Galatea at *Ecl.* 1.31 cf. n. 61 above, citing Berg (1974), 147.

66. Pollio appears in the capacity of consul in the extra-bucolic frame of *Eclogue* 4 (11-12), and as both public figure and tragedian in the extra-bucolic frame of *Eclogue* 8 (6-13). In the latter case he appears anonymously.

67. As regards the outside world, *nova* might point towards Pollio's tragedies, or to neoteric-style poems (Pliny *Ep.* 5.3.5). Courtney (1993) argues that the 'notoriously harsh and old-fashioned' Pollio would not have written poetry in this mode, but he was certainly on good terms with, and the addressee of, three generations of modernising poets. He was the recipient of the lost, but then famous, neoteric *Propemptikon* by Cinna, and is (arguably) presented as the one who 'ordered' (*iussis*) the composition of the *Eclogues* (*Ecl.* 8. 11-12). He also regarded Gallus as a *familiaris* (Cic. *Ad Fam.* 10.31.6; 32.5) and was written of as a friend by Horace (*Sat.* 1.10.85; he is the addressee of Hor. *Odes* 2.1).

68. According to Servius on *Georg.* 1.210, Bavius and Mevius attacked Virgil for using the plural of a singular collective noun, *hordea* (also used at *Ecl.* 5.36).

69. The Verona scholiast bears witness to various ancient identifications of Codrus (Virgil himself, Cornificius, Cinna) and preserves the fragment of Valgius. See Clausen at 7.21-2.

70. At *Ecl.* 3.60-1, Damoetas' opening plays on an indefinite number of pre-Hellenistic, Hellenistic, and post-Hellenistic models (see Clausen and Coleman 1977), and both Damoetas and his partner in the song exchange, Menalcas, show a personal awareness of Latin literary figures and poetry.

71. Since love elegy after the *Eclogues* is so political (cf. Jones 2007) – and on the surface at least in varying degrees politically subversive, perhaps this was somehow relevant here too.

72. On the relevance of the mime for such role-playing in Roman poetry, cf. Jones (2007), 120.

73. Herrmann (1930) sees charade figures throughout the *Eclogues*; later commentators are more circumspect. Cf. Eahn (1944); Starr (1995). The feature is characteristic of Virgil rather than Theocritus.

74. Cf. also p. 170 n. 59 above.

75. See also Korenjak (2003). One can see some sort of analogy with Spenser's *Shepheardes Calender*, despite differences in Spenser's world, his place in society, and the social functions of his poetry. In his transformation of Virgilian bucolic he inserts real-world people into the poetic texture under pastoral names, and there is a strong element of provisionality about the reader's identifications.

76. Henderson (1998), 213. On Pollio and *recitationes* see p. 173 n. 24 below.

77. In the beer garden of a Liverpool pub, a customer inscribed in marker pen on one of the wooden tables 'ET ARCADIA EGO' (2008). This has since been erased.

78. Hartswick (2004), 14 takes *garrulus* as meaning the bird 'jay', but this sense is not attested in classical Latin (Watson 2002: 381). In proximity with *aves* ('birds'), *garrulus* suggests birdsong, which tempts us to imagine Maecenas singing rather than writing and correcting lines of verse. *Mollis* ('soft'; here applied to the gardens in which Maecenas cultivates the Muses) often connotes the smaller genres like elegy and lyric (Hor. *Odes* 2.9.17; Prop. 1.7.19; Ov. *Tr.* 2.307), and need not exclude bucolic if the context calls it to mind. We know that Maecenas composed verse (although the surviving fragments tend to suggest Catullan modes and not bucolic), but although we know nothing of the circumstances of his versifying, we are entitled to speculate that he may have fostered the image of himself as resembling a bucolic native. Shady trees often elsewhere provide a congenial setting for conversation (e.g. Cic. *De Or.* 3.5.18; *De Leg.* 1.4.14).

79. This element is much weaker in Theocritus; cf. *Id.* 4.29-30 and especially 5.36-9 where the handing on of song from the older to the younger is asserted by the older, but denied by the younger.

80. Death is more recognised in Theocritus than in the *Eclogues*, which draws attention to Damoetas and the inheritance motif. For death in Theocritus see *Id.* 2.70, 4.39-40, and the tombs at 1.125 and 7.10, and the grave at 5.121.

81. On inheritance cf. Alpers (1983), 284-7. The poet inherits the gift of song at *Lament for Bion* 95-7. Cf. Ovid's account of his place in the elegiac succession: *his ego successi* ('I was their successor', *Tr.* 4.10.63).

82. For the debate on Calpurnius' dating see Champlin (1978), 95-110; Townend (1980) 166-75; Mayer (1980) 175-6; Wiseman (1982) 57-67; Horsfall (1997).

171

8. Containing Reality; Realisms and Realities

1. On the naming profiles of non-epic genres see Jones (2006; 2007).

2. Cf. Jones (1991); Coleman (2005).

3. Jones (2007), 34-8, 71-2.

4. On the concept of dominant genres see Jones (2007), 71-3, 131-2.

5. Recorded by Donatus (*Vit. Virg.* 171ff.); *dic mihi, Damoeta; 'quoium pecus' anne Latinum? / non, verum Aegonis nostri; sic rure loquuntur*; 'Tell me, Damoetas; 'whose flock' – is that Latin? No, it's our Aego's; that's how they talk in the country.' Punctuating after *nostri* will give: 'No, it's Aego's; that's how our [bucolic types] talk in the country.' Kraggerud (2006) suggests reading *Aegones* (with no punctuation), giving, 'No, but that is how our Aegos talk in the country.'

6. On verisimilitude, *enargeia* etc. see Jones (1991).

7. Ryunosuke Akutagawa (1892-1927) in his short story 'Hell Screen' (*Jigokuhen*, 1918) tells, through a near contemporary mouthpiece, of a medieval Japanese artist whose horrifying depiction of infernal torment required living models enduring actual torments. The naivety of the mouthpiece focalises the astonishing impact of the sense of reality of the work.

8. Hacking (1983) offers the position that representation has primacy over reality. 'The first peculiarly human invention is representation. Once there is a practice of representing, a second-order concept follows in train. This is the concept of reality which has content only when there are first-order representations.' Conceptualising reality, or the world 'as reality is secondary. First there is this human thing, the making of representations. Then there was the judging of representations as real or unreal, true or false, faithful or unfaithful. Finally comes the world, not first but second, third or fourth ... The world ... was found by conceptualising the real as an attribute of representation' (136).

9. See Coleman (1990).

10. In *Hoogste Tijd* ('Last Call', 1985), the novel by Harry Mulisch, the matter is treated extensively as a major theme.

11. E.g. Catullus *Carm.* 64; V. *Ecl.* 6; Prop. 1.20; Ov. *Met.*; Petr. *Sat.*

12. On recursion in literature see Dällenbach (1989) and Deremetz (1995). The effect is sometimes also referred to – after a brand of Dutch coffee – as the 'Droste effect', due to the brand image of a lady bearing a packet of coffee upon which a lady bears a packet of coffee, upon which ... .

13. Ovid, for example, repeatedly plays with narration within narration in the *Metamorphoses*, and the figure of the craftsman/maker/singer is a recurrent programmatic character (e.g. Daedalus, Arachne, Pygmalion, Marsyas, Orpheus). Recursiveness is a frequent characteristic of Petronius' *Satyrica*, with (for example) Trimalchio acting as a scaled down and transformed version of the author. For the *Eclogues* cf. Saunders (2008), 6, 125-7.

14. Note here Harrison's (2007: 47-8) suggestion that Silenus in *Eclogue* 6 is Parthenius; and my tentative hint that Stimichon in *Eclogue* 5 (5.55) can be read as Pollio (see above).

15. For this term see Barthes (1968).

16. *Trompe l'oeil* is an important feature in the work of numbers of canonic masters, including Vermeer.

17. Angel Interiors (UK) Ltd accepts commissions and offers training; Hare and Humphreys offer bespoke murals and *trompe l'oeil*; Hampstead Decorative Arts offer training courses in *trompe l'oeil* and decorative painting. There are many others.

18. See Hollmann and Tesch (2004) for a convenient selection of renaissance to modern examples.

19. Ling (1991), 20-1, with illustration of a late second / early first century BC house in Herculaneum; 23-36 for the period including that of the *Eclogues*.

20. On linear perspective in architectural illusionism see Ling (1991), 25; on regard for shadows, see Ling (1991), 21, 24, 51; on still-lifes and illusionism, cf. Leach (2004), 80-2 (but see also p. 124 for the citation of doubts about the illusionistic intent).

21. On the viewer's point of view see Corlàita (1974-76).

22. Hollmann and Teach (2004), 10.

23. The anamorphic painting is part of the St Peter's Riverside Sculpture Project, which runs for approximately a kilometre along the banks of the River Wear.

24. Poetry reached its audience especially through its performance by the author. For poetry readings, Hor. *Sat.* 1.4.73; *Epp.* 2.2.67-8; 2.2.90-105; *Ars Poetica* 428-33, 453-76). The Elder Seneca tells us (*Controversiae* 4 *praef.* 2) that Asinius Pollio (the dedicatee of *Eclogues* 4 and 8) instituted the practice of reciting 'what he had written' (*scripta sua*) to invited audiences (*advocatis hominibus*). Although this reference comes in the context of the performance of declamation, the writtenness of the *scripta* suggests that Seneca is here talking about poetry recitations. For later evidence see Pliny *Ep.* 5.12.1; 7.17.5 (on speeches); 5.3 (on his own verse); 6.21 (on comedy); 7.17 (on history tragedy, and lyric; cf. Sen. *Contr.* 10 *praef.* 8 for history; Tac. *Dial.* 2.1 for tragedy); 1.13 (on a variety of unspecified poetry); Juv. 1.1ff. (on elegy, epic, etc.). For the problematic case of Horace's expressed distaste for recitation (Hor. *Sat.* 1.4.22ff.).

25. On performance see Jones (2007), 133-42. On the stage-performance of parts of the *Eclogues* soon after their publication see Morgan (2000), 81-2.

26. Seneca also records various comments on poets and poetic lines made in the context of declamations, but context and circumstances impose strong limits on the kind of literary criticism these involve; cf. *Contr.* 7.1.27; *Suas.* 1.12; 2.20; 3.4-5; 3.7; 4.4-5.

27. For such symbols in Roman maps, cf. Leach (1988), 89-9.

28. We do not know how close together the trees in Eclogue-land are, nor how many sheep typically make a flock, nor what clothes the herdsmen wear (contrast Theocritus, where we hear of cloaks and various other items of clothing (*Id.* 2.53; 5.15; 7.15ff.; 10.35), and elaborately and repeatedly in the urban mime of *Id.* 15); nevertheless, we do not feel these ignorances to be gaps in visualisation. For this essentially linguistic question, various language-processing and cognitive models have been suggested. For a review of some (overlapping) alternatives, see Brown and Yule (1983), 236-56; cf. also Leach (1988), 27-30.

29. On cognitive landscapes see Agnew and Duncan (1989); Barnes and Duncan (1992); Cosgrove and Daniels (1988); Craik (1975); Gould and White (1992); Kitchin (1994); Massey (2004); Porteous (1990); Tilley (1994); Tilley (2004); Tuan (1993). Adams (2007) deals with the specific case of the Eastern Desert of Egypt using the evidence of travellers' graffiti. On classical landscape generally see Spencer (forthcoming).

30. On this, see Leach (1974), 108-9. On descriptiveness in Latin and Greek poetry generally cf. Williams (1968), 634-81.

31. See Nicolet (1991). Cf. Brendel (1979: 25-47) on the scholarship of the

Roman development of spatial concepts. On the development of topographical systems in Roman landscape, see Leach (1988), 73-143. On maps, itineraries, and geographical knowledge see Miller (1916); Levi and Levi (1967); Weber (1976); Bosio (1983); Leach (1988), 89-94; Nicolet (1991) 5-10, 98-114; Brodersen (1995); Jacob (1999); Adams and Laurence (2001); Talbert (2004); Talbert and Brodersen (2004); Salway (2007); Talbert (2007); Talbert and Unger (2008). On topographical elements in literature, cf. Leach (1988), 109-143. For a brief indication of trends in landscape studies see Spencer (2010), 1-2 n. 5.

32. See Laurence (1994), 123, citing Pliny *NH* 2.182, 6.214; Vitruvius 9.8.

33. The emotional centrality of the house as the physical symbol of the family is reflected in Cicero's treatment of the separation of family from its home at *Philippics* 12.14.8-10. Ovid – relegated to the Black Sea – the foregrounds his now empty gardens as symbolising what he has lost (*Tr.* 4,8.25-8). On the gradiance of intimacy within the house itself see p. 181 n. 150 below.

34. This structure is reinforced by its similarity to that of the visual (or visuo-cognitive) field. Smith (1999); Clark (1996).

35. In any case Horace's jaunts are as likely to be urban as not (*Sat.* 1.6.111ff.; 1.9). Cf. Williams (1968), 634-81. For Horace's walk in Rome (*Sat.* 1.9), cf. Plautus *Curculio* 4.1.467-81.

36. Cf. Sall. *Cat.* 13.1; 20.11; Varro *RR* 3.17.9; Tib. 2.3.45; Hor. *Odes* 2.18.20-2 (with Nisbet and Hubbard's note; 3.1.33-6; Sen. *Ep.* 122.8.

37. One might make the point that Varro's *RR* is cast in the elite (and hence urban) form of didactic.

38. Cf. Cic. *De Republica* 2.4. On Horace's landscapes see Thomas (1982), 8-34; Spencer (2006).

39. Against qualms about comparative treatments of different art media see Leach (1988), 4-18. Skoie uses pastoral elements in Roman art to establish the cultural context of the Eclogues' audience (2006, esp. 311-22). Leach (1988: 198) withdraws somewhat from the position she occupied in (1974) seeing connections with contemporary wall-painting in elegy and lyric rather than in bucolic.

40. See d'Arms (2003).

41. Cf. Spencer (2010), 2, 137-9.

42. Cf. e.g. Hooke (2000).

43. Saunders is aware of problems with the post-classical associations of the term 'landscape', but accepts it nonetheless because of 'its ability to replicate and sustain' a pictorial quality, and because of its acceptance of the notion of 'frames and borders' (2008: 111; see further 102-27).

44. Cf. Nora (2001) on *lieux de mèmoire*, and Spencer (2010), 4-9, 33, 37 and (on the villa estate) 62-134.

45. Virgil, Roman garden designers, and Roman garden-painters all make contributions to the Roman conceptualisation of landscape. Likewise in the modern world, the installation art of Katrín Sigurdardóttir (1967-) embodies profound and sustained thought about landscape. Many of her landscape models, not unlike three dimensional compartmentalised relief-maps, composites of memory and imagination, are contained in hinged travelling boxes – complete with travel labels which preserve the memory of travel – which can be re-opened at a new destination; *Green Grass of Home* (1997), for example, has various parks near where she has lived; *Haul IV* (2004) and *Haul* (2005) are composite landscapes, *Odd Lots* (2005) a cityscape. *High Plane* (2001-2005) is a large horizontal Arctic landscape viewed by up to two people at a time through head-holes so that viewers become part of the 'landscape'. *Model* (1998-2000) is

like a relief model of a landscape in which only the fringes around a road are visible; *Untitled* (2008) a more extreme case, represents in the form of a fixed mobile a cluster of lit houses surrounded by the gallery space. Different again, *Circuit* (1999) is a landscape with roads, designed like a vastly enlarged computer-chip, thus encoding the way landscape and memory shape each other in the wiring of the brain. For landscape, language, and culture cf. Schama (1995), 61; Spirn (1998); Wylie (2007); Spencer (forthcoming), 4, 8-9.

46. See Ling (1991), 142-9. For a brief bibliographical survey of landscape scenes in Roman art see Spencer (2010), 21 n. 23.

47. In broad terms, mythological and historical themes are the most important subjects in Pompeian and contemporary wall-painting; Ling (1991), 101.

48. Wealthy collectors of original sculpture and the buying of copies of famous originals for home and garden ornament; cf. e.g. Cic. *Ad Att.* 1.6.2; 1.8.2; 1.9.2; 1.10.3; 1.4.31.1.5; *Ad Fam.* 7.23.1-3; Pliny *NH* 34.48; 35.130; Suet. *Iul.* 47. Public displays of art – Cic. *Verr.* 2.4.6; Pliny *NH* 36.33 (referring to Asinius Pollio), 7.34; Dio 54.29.

49. On the role of Greek art as an antecedent of Roman, see Ling (1991), 5-11.

50. On the *Porticus Pompeii* and other galleries, and the considerations behind the assemblages displayed, see Kuttner (1999); Leach (2004), 5, 123-55. L. Mummius gave the ornaments captured at Corinth to the state (Cic. *De Officiis* 2.21.75); see also Polybius 9.10.1-12; Livy 38.9.13. See Gruen (1993: 84-130) on the disposal of artistic spoils. On the public vs private distinction, see Leach (2004), 3-6. On domestic art see Gazda (1994).

51. Cf. Hartswick (2004), 16-18.

52. Ideas about art are varied in kind: technical material generated by artists, moralistic aesthetics, ideas of *mimesis*, the late Hellenistic view of certain artists such as Phidias as inspired visionaries akin to sages (a theory leaving traces in a variety of Roman and late Greek writers, including Cicero), informal/popular ideas centring on successful mimesis and illusion, and stylistic analogy with rhetoric and literature which incorporates some notion of history of style and personal styles (Cic. *Brut.* 70; Quint. 12.10.1-10). Cf. Leach (2004), 7-10. There is, on the other hand, virtually nothing comparable with, or analogous to, the Roman treatises on rhetoric; cf. Stewart (2008), 24.

53. On the social *milieu* of Augustan poets see White (2005).

54. Cf. Stewart (2008), 10-11. The status of artists is a complex issue (Stewart 2008: 18-21) involving artistic prestige, ethnicity, birth-status, organisation of workshops (or, perhaps better, 'decorators' teams'; see Allison and Sear: 2002, 80 n. 570) payment for services, and the nature of the painterly skills (which included plastering). See Ling (1991: 212-20) for the sociology of painting and painters, and 198-211 for the repertoire of skills. On the artists' names sometimes found on works of art see Stewart (2008), 14-18.

55. Cf. Cic. *De Officiis* 1.50 and *Tusc. Disp.* 1.2.4 on the low status of the skills of the practitioners of art. On connoisseurship see Stewart (2008), 19.

56. On the patron's role see Ling (1991), 212-20; Stewart (2008: 32-8, especially 35-6) on individuation, variation, and their relationship with the possible existence of pattern books, and (pp. 37-8) on the artist's desire to appeal to a clientele broader than the specific individual patron alone. On the indeterminate role of the workshop and apprenticeship in fostering artistic conservatism, see Stewart (2008), 28-32. There is much comment in Latin on the effects of patronage in the literary sphere (e.g. Juvenal 7).

57. Mural painting is found in temples, houses (even the smallest), tombs,

brothels, and *tavernae*, but in aristocratic and grand public contexts the materials and craftsmanship are different; cf. Ling (1991), 1-2. The evidence of Pompeian graffiti shows that as well as wall-painting (and the owning of small gardens or planted areas) knowledge of the *Eclogues* also percolated through the lower levels of society, probably by way of their staging (see Morgan 2000: 81-2). While there is a sense in which the owning of gardens and art, and metaphorical owning of literature are all markers of class division, and this is part of their function, the exclusivity is not complete.

58. Cf. Hölscher (2004: 1) on the importance of artistic style and imagery as social and collective cultural influences.

59. We probably cannot exclude the possibility of taking *mollius* with *spirantia aera* ('softly breathing bronzes') rather than *excudent*. In the sequence of permissions, *ducent, describent*, and *dicent* lack comparatives, while *orabunt* has *melius*. However, the contrast between the Romans and the unspecified 'others' is in any case comparative.

60. For the topographical elements of these paintings, see Leach (1988), 80. For the bird's-eye perspective (and analogues in Roman literature), see Leach (1988), 83-9.

61. Of painting on wooden panels, none survives (though we do have portraits painted on wood and set in mummy-cases; Ling 1991: 1). According to Pliny (*NH* 35.118), the mural paintings represent the desire of the commissioners to show off their wealth rather than evidencing artistic taste (hence, says Pliny, in a version of the literary decline motif, its inferiority). It may, however, be that panel-painting declined in importance from the first century BC; see Ling (1991), 1.

62. For these see Leach (1988), 361-408.

63. On architectural landscapes in Roman art, see Leach (1988), 261-306.

64. Cf. Leach (2004), 7; Kellum (1994); Hölscher (2004), 7.

65. For the sense of appropriateness of certain subjects for particular rooms or locations see Ling (1991), 135-40; Wallace-Hadrill (1994), 28; Bergmann (1998); Stewart (2004), 100-2; Leach (2004), 18-54. On mosaics see Stewart (2004), 94-5.

66. On the public-private polarity, see Leach (1988), 199-200. On the analogous issues of generic division in art and literature in the Augustan period, cf. Leach (1988), 209-10; Elsner (in Hölscher 2004). Zanker (1998), 282, connects a new simplicity in art-aesthetics with Augustus' (however politically motivated) moral reforms; cf. Leach (2004), 152-5.

67. See Ling (1991: 101-41) on mythological painting.

68. See Ling (1991), 37-8 and 113 with fig. 113, 142-3

69. See Ling (1991), 114-15. Hylas, who appears in Theocritus, Apollonius, and the *Eclogues* (6), and whose frequent poetic appearances are mocked by Juvenal, is also an art-subject (see Fowler 1989: 33).

70. Stewart (2004), 82-5; Leach (2004), 14-17. Ling (1991, 3, 12-100) is basically favourable to the four-style analysis.

71. Cf. Wallace-Hadrill (1994), 26.

72. Ling (1991), 25-31.

73. Stewart (2004), 85.

74. See Purcell (1995); Leach (2004), 56-8.

75. Stewart (2004), 85.

76. As in the concert hall in St George's Hall, Liverpool, where a large mirror creates a highly effective architectural *trompe l'oeil*.

77. Wallace-Hadrill (1994), 25; cf. also Zanker (1998), 199-200; Stewart (2008), 49 is more subtle in this point.

78. Cf. Elsner (1995), 74-85. For different views on the function of this sort of illusionism see Leach (2004), 85. In the context of the application of illusionistic skill in painting, we can see Roman Callimacheanism's aesthetic principle of poetic craftsmanship in a broader cultural background.

79. Theatrical scene-painting long preceded this: Pliny (*NH* 35.23) refers to 99 BC. On theatrical elements (without painted figures) in domestic decoration see Leach (2004), 93-122.

80. On theatricality as an element in Roman life as well as literature, see Jones (2007), 133-6. There may be subtle connections between the growth of behavioural theatricality and the increasing dominance of mural painting over panel painting (for which see Ling 1991: 1). On the influence of stage painting on domestic decoration see Ling (1991), 30.

81. For a *catalogue raisonnée* of garden paintings at Pompeii and Herculaneum see Jashemski (1979), appendix 2. For a discursive account see Jashemski (1979), 55-87. See also von Stackelberg (2009), 30-5, 55.

82. See further Gabriel (1955); Jashemski (1979), 79-80; Conan (1986); Bergmann (1992); Leach (2004), 124-7; Giesecke (2007), 123-5; Zarmakoupi (2008). On garden rooms see Kuttner (1999); Leach (2004), 124-32; Spencer (2010), 155-61. Kellum's (1994) account of the garden room in Livia's villa considers the significance also of the tensions between 'ordered' and 'natural' and 'real' and 'fictive', the specifically Augustan and Livian resonances of a significant number of the trees depicted, the connections of a group with the constituents of triumphal crowns, and the connections between various of the trees and the metamorphic myths of Graeco-Roman poetry. Clarke (2005) is more guarded about the 'Augustanism' of interior decoration. On garden painting in general see Jashemski (1979), 55-87; Ling (1991), 149-52. Garden paintings should perhaps be kept distinct from *paradeisos* paintings (e.g. the garden of the House of Lucretius Fronto; the *viridarium* of the House of the Ceii) which represent wild-animal parks.

83. Garden paintings are typically 'fourth-style' (Ling 1991: 152), beginning *c.* 40s AD. For the position of Livia's garden room in the tradition, see Ling (1991), 150; for the murals in which architectural openings show trees, gardens, and buildings (as at Boscoreale), Ling (1991), 29, 143.

84. Ling takes the irregular fringe at the top of the painting as belonging to a grotto (see Ling, 1991; 150), but it is difficult to visualise a grotto open on four sides. On the other hand one could easily conceive of internal pillars supporting a thatched roof.

85. Kellum (1994: 221) goes on to draw an analogy with the fruits of all seasons woven into the garlands of the interior altar enclosure wall of the slightly later *Ara Pacis Augustae* in Rome.

86. The element of transcending the natural seasons is also to be seen in real as well as painted gardens.

87. See Coleman (1990); Apuleius *Met.* 10.31.

88. Cf. Chapter 7, under 'Bucolic charades'.

89. See the epic reading among Fronto's plane trees, statues and columns at Juv. 1.9-13.

90. Cf. the passage from the anonymous *Elegiae in Maecenatem* (1.33-6) which gives the impression of being a picture of Maecenas composing verse while sitting under an oak tree in his Esquiline garden (see pp. 111, 140 above).

91. The Hall of Isis, Palatine (*c.* 25-20 BC) presents mythological and

non-mythological landscapes (Ling 1991: 39); the Villa Farnesina, close to the Tiber below the Janiculum (*c.* 19 BC), presents various landscapes with buildings and figures (Ling 1991: 41-2).

92. Cf. Stewart (2004: 79) on the 'Mysteries Room' in the Villa of the Mysteries.

93. See Leach (1988), 197-260.

94. On possible Augustan overtones in the sacral-idyllic corpus, see Leach (1988), 212-13.

95. Cf. Leach (1974).

96. Berg (1974: 133-4) sees the sacral-idyllic landscapes as part of the cultural background to the *Eclogues*, and is not worried by the slight lateness of known examples (cf. Skoie 2006: 311).

97. The goats, rocks, trees, and the pillar dominating the scene in this painting give it much in common with the sacral-idyllic scenes.

98. As we do in Hubbard's (1974) account of Propertius. See Leach (1988), 409-66. See further on poetry and art Barchiesi (2005); Spencer (2010), 43.

99. Cf. Breed (2006b), 22.

100. Cf. Spencer (2010), 4-15, 19-22.

101. So Pavlovskis (1971). Pavlovskis argues, however, that the *Eclogues* are conspicuous in their repeated manifestations of the pathetic fallacy, in the way in which animals understand human behaviour (cf. *Ecl.* 3.8-9) and have feelings of their own (cf. *Ecl.* 1.14-15), and that cumulatively this suggests a harmony between Nature and Man.

102. The distinction is effectively between the *urbs* and the agricultural hinterland (*ager*).

103. Antecedents are naturally various, but include intensification of agricultural production, the disposition of trees for shade or cultic significance in Greek sanctuaries, and the Persian *paradeisos*. Aesthetic and practical considerations mingle, and with the domestication of the latter in the fourth century BC – and especially in the Hellenistic and Roman periods – an aesthetic garden-tradition begins to develop. Cf. Spencer (2010), 139-41.

104. References to inns and taverns in poetry characterise them as disreputable and dirty (cf. Hor. *Sat.* 1.1.29; 1.5.4; 2.4.62; *Epp.* 1.14.21; cf. Cicero *In Pisonem* 6.13) and very frequently aristocratic travellers would have sojourned instead in their own villas or been guests at those of their friends, but according to the example of Pompeii (where most evidence comes from) there were also more refined restaurants and inns for merchants. See Jashemski (1979), 167-81; von Stackelberg (2009), 152, n. 28. For gardens at baths see Jashemski (1979), 163-5.

105. See Purcell (1987); (2001), 549; Hartswick (2004), 16; Beard (1998). For some idea of the variety of garden type and amount of space see Jashemski (1979), 24; (2002), 6-28; Carroll (2003: 34-5). On tomb gardens see Jashemski (1979), 141-53; Bodel (1986); Carroll (2003), 76-9; Pagán (2006), 51-2; on temple groves see Jashemski (1979), 155-60; Carroll (2003), 69-71. For roof gardens, see Cicero's dialogue of 45 BC, the *Hortensius*, frag. 78 ap. Nonius 216.14; see also Sen. *Contr.* 5.5; Sen. *Ep.* 122.8; *De Ira* 1.21.1; *Thyestes* 464. On Roman gardens generally, see also Jashemski (1979; 2002); Bowe (2004); Farrar (1998); Pagán (2006), 6-12. For a brief list of recent archaeological work in the Roman world see von Stackelberg (2009), 2. On the issue of definition in such a range of phenomena, cf. von Stackelberg (2009), 6; for her the key concepts are seclusion, social function, and symbolic value.

106. Carroll (2003, 9) cites Martial (11.18) for an elaborate humorous

comparison between a suburban farm (*rus sub urbe*, 1) and a window box (*rus in fenestra*, 2) in which a rue plant serves as a grove (*nemus*) of Diana. See further, Spencer (2010), 142.

107. See further, von Stackelberg, 2009: 2, 23. For the element of imagination and translation in the context of gardens cf. also Seneca *Controversiae* 5.5.24.

108. Kellum (1994: 217-8) draws attention to the significance of order and pattern in both gardens and paintings of gardens (citing Varro *RR* 1.7.2; Cic. *De Sen.* 17.59; V. *Georg.* 2.274-8) and to the interaction of order and natural disorder; see also Bergmann (2002); Pagán (2006), 1. Roman courtyard gardens were not always formal and ornamental, but these characteristics indicated that the owner was socially elevated and wealthy (Carroll, 2003: 32). On the importance of the garden as an enclosed space see Pagán (2006), 1, 5, 6, 10-11.

109. See Hartswick (2004), 16; von Stackelberg (2009), 9-10, and, on other Latin words, 16-21.

110. See Henderson (2004); Pagán (2006), 19-36.

111. Farrar (1998), 16; Pagán (2006), 7-8.

112. Laurence (1994) 64-8; Berry (2007), 216-18.

113. Cf. Hunt (1991) and Pagán (2006) on gardens as cultural objects. Von Stackelberg (2009: 11, citing Cicero *pro Caelio* 36, 38, 49, *Verr.* 2.87, 4.121) observes the subjective element in perceiving the display of taste as embodied in the garden: 'Once acquired, it becomes the locus for appropriate displays of educated taste and learning among a close circle of friends, unless it belongs to a political opponent, in which case it is the site of dissipation and luxury.'

114. See further von Stackelberg (2009), 83-5.

115. Pliny connects luxury gardens within the city (Rome) with the garden of Epicurus, who is called the instigator of the practice (*NH* 19.50-1). Cf. Hartswick (2004), 16. On the garden of Epicurus see Clay (2009). On the complex relation between the real and the imaginary garden cf. Hunt (1997); Pagán (2006), 1-2.

116. See further at Carroll (2003), 52-4. Atticus had a statue of Aristotle in his gardens; Cic. *Ad Att.* 4.10.1, Hartswick (2004), 18.

117. In addition, the garden – private and public alike – is a source of health-giving fresh air (cf. Vitruvius 5.9.5; Sen. *Ep.* 104.6). Given the prominence of love in the bucolic experience, one might also mention the use of the garden or garden features as erotic background (see von Stackelberg, 2009: 97-9).

118. Pliny *NH* 12.3 lists a number of such assignations.

119. The temple where the *spolia opima*, the spoils won in single combat with an enemy chief, were held – a subject of political controversy under Augustus (Livy 4.20.5ff.).

120. See Kellum (1994: 211-13, 218, 222); von Stackelberg (2009), 89-93.

121. Kellum (1994: 211-13).

122. Hartswick (2004), 14 with p. 157 n. 148. Perhaps this compensated for the apparent general absence of street names.

123. There are several brief descriptions of luxury gardens at Carroll (2003), 35-8; 58-9.

124. As well as those already referred to; cf. Juv.7.79-80 for Lucan's, and 10.16-17 for Seneca's. See also Juv.1.75-6 for gardens as a typifying feature of the property of the rich.

125. On art and galleries in this context, see Hartswick (2004), 16-17; Leach (2004).

126. See further Pliny *NH* 12.22; 16.76; 16.140: Pliny *Ep.* 5.6.35-6; Hartswick (2004), 15.

127. See on the range of flowers, von Stackelberg (2009), 46-7. The baskets of flowers for Alexis at *Ecl.* 2.46 parallel Corydon's bucolic singing (2.23) and piping (36ff.). The poetry he has wasted on Alexis is like the flowers he has left to the wind and the (Callimachean) springs to the boars (2.58-9).

128. In connection with the growth of public gardens, Favro (1996: 178) draws attention to Augustus' expansion and overhaul of the city's aquaduct system in the 30s BC.

129. See further, MacDonald and Pinto (1995); von Stackelberg (2009), 85-6, 95; Spencer (2010), 172-83.

130. On the probable function of the *topiarius*, see von Stackelberg (2009), 16-18; the concept seems to be Roman and have little or no Greek background.

131. Gardens figure also in the moralising tradition as a subsection of the architectural luxury motif (cf. Sen. *Ep.* 122.8); see Leach (2004), 153-4.

132. See von Stackelberg (2009), 23; Zarmakoupi (forthcoming).

133. Cf. Carroll (2003), 55-8.

134. See Hartswick (2004); Spencer (2010), 161-7. The shape and lay-out of large (and often very long-lasting) gardens is dynamic.

135. Gleason (1994: 13) calls Pompey's public park a 'strategic display of political as well as military power'. Kuttner (1999) connects Pompey's park with the iconography of world conquest (on which see also Nicolet (1991), 1-56), and sketches how it figures in contemporary and later poetry. See further Spencer (2010), 167-71. On the element of political display from late republic into the Augustan period, see von Stackelberg (2009), 74-80. 'Lucullus, Pompey, and Caesar all used their gardens to further their own political agenda, either as a symbol of personal power, evidence of military success, or a vehicle of communication. In this they laid the groundwork for Octavian Augustus' use of garden space to create a new political stability' (von Stackelberg, 2009: 78).

136. Technically the *Horti Sallustiani* were outside the city boundary (i.e. they were part of the *ager*) until about the third century AD; see Hartswick (2004), 5. See generally, Purcell (1987).

137. For the *Horti Luculliani*, see Kaster (1974).

138. Cf. also Favro (1996), 176-80, especially 178-9: 'Augustus and his adherents reconceptualised urban landscaping as a public amenity in line with eastern examples. ... Thus, the perception evolved that a great city needed great public gardens. Again, as in other developments, Caesar led the way. In his will he left the Horti Caesaris to the Roman People, making the sprawling park accessible to all residents of Rome (Suet. *Caes.* 83). Augustus followed suit ....'

139. The area of the Esquiline gardens – outside the *Porta Esquilina* – had earlier been a proletarian burial place with communal graves (Hor. *Sat.* 1.8.10); Fraenkel (1957), 123; Pagán (2006), 42. Cp. Hor. *Epod* 5.99; *Sat.* 2.6.33. See further Bodel (2000).

140. The *Campus Martius* – also occupied with large amounts of stonework of various kinds (see Coarelli 2007: 261-304) – was later to contain Augustus' tomb (28 BC).

141. Cf. Hartswick (2004), 19; Spencer (2010), 64. See also von Stackelberg (2009: 25): 'Cicero's search to buy Horti in Rome was motivated by his desire to erect a shrine to his daughter Tullia (Cic. *Att.* 12.12, 12.18, 12.19).'

142. Horace can stroll along a stretch of the old city wall which had become part of a terraced orchard for Maecenas' public garden (*Sat.* 1.8.14-15) and

Vitellius' troops resisted Vespasian's from the top of the walls of the *Horti Sallustiani* (Tac. *Hist.* 3.82); cf. also Juv. 8.43. Standing inside a public garden and looking at buttressed walls one might easily think of the steep rock formations of a Polyphemus and Galatea painting.

143. See Jones (2007), 139-40.

144. This is not a phenomenon associated with Athens (Jashemski 1979: 17-18); Giesecke 2007: xii, 75, 100). Carroll (2003: 10-11) points out the relevance of urban piped water to the distinctiveness of Roman culture in this regard (cf. Jashemski, 1979, 53). In the course of the second and first centuries BC, the 'kitchen garden' element of the Roman courtyard garden diminished, and was sometimes abandoned, and sometimes separated off into an extra garden (Carroll, 2003: 32). The *atrium* in an urban house might also have garden features, with plant boxes around the central pool (Carroll, 2003: 34). On the courtyard garden especially in and around Pompeii, see Leach (2004), 34-40; cf. also Zarmakoupi (forthcoming). On the development of the courtyard garden and the distinction between atrium houses and peristyle houses, see von Stackelberg (2009), 21-2.

145. Jashemski (1979), 5, 15-16, 25. For a random sample of garden spaces, showing variation in degree and kind of access to the rest of the house and to the outside in Pompeian urban gardens, see von Stackelberg (2009), 61; for further discussion of permeability, see 67-72.

146. Jashemski (2002), 16.

147. Jashemski (1979), 89-97.

148. For the garden as a seat of various leisure and social activities, see Dickmann (1997); Pagán (2006) 8-9; for poetry recitation, cf. Juv. 1.9-13. For music see Jashemski (1979), 97-101.

149. For the garden as a location for the reception of privileged guests see George (1997), 310.

150. Cf. Leach (2004), 18-54, esp. 53-4. On morning visitors cf. Cic. *Ad Att.* 1.18; *Ad Brut.* 2.4.1; Sen. *De Ben.* 6.34.1-5. On the *imagines* (ancestral portraits) see Leach (2004), 26. On the garden as a domestic 'room' see Purcell (1996). On houses see Wallace-Hadrill (1994, 1997). The rather alien sociological functions and combinations of function of some ancient rooms may lead to difficulties of identification (cf. Leach, 2004, 40, 49, 50-3). On different levels of art in rooms of different social functions see Allison (1992). On the gradient of intimacy within the Roman house see Clarke (2003), 222.

151. On garden sculpture see von Stackelberg (2009), 27-30.

152. Hartswick (2004: 13) observes that the under life-size scale of many garden statues, herm-form used for portraits of famous men, and the fact that garden statues are stone amidst the living material of trees and plants clearly distinguished them from reality (statues were painted, so we should not think of an emphatic contrast between stone on the one hand and flesh and clothing on the other), but it might be better to talk of different realities.

153. Cf. Hor. *Odes* 3.4.9-24; Tacitus *Dialogus* 9.6; 12.1; Pliny *Ep.* 9.10.2; Juv. 7.58-9; cf. also Hor. *Epp.* 2.2.77; Ov. *Tr.* 1.1.41; *Eleg. in Maec.* 1.33-6.

154. The first-century BC Pompeian House of the Golden Bracelet (otherwise known as the House of the Wedding of Alexander) had in its garden a marble fountain, an apsed mosaic fountain, and a pool with 28 jets; Berry (2007: 183), citing Jashemski (1979); (1993). On functionality see Pagán (2006) 8.

155. Jashemski (1979), 115; von Stackelberg (2009), 86-8.

156. The semiotics of the garden overlap with those of the house which

contains it. For the house, cf. Wallace-Hadrill (1994). For qualifications on the innerness of the garden, see von Stackelberg (2009), 67-72.

157. See Dickmann (1997); cf. Pagán (2006), 9. One can indeed apply the inside-outside and *otium-negotium* polarities with more finesse, as Dickmann does, by considering the garden as the centre of the house as regards *otium*, and the more formal *atrium* and *tablinum* as the sites of *negotium* and the closer contact between external and internal. On the division of public and private functions see further George (1997). For smaller houses cf. also George (1998).

158. Cf. Pagán (2006), 5-12 on boundaries, exclusion, and inclusion as core features of what a garden is.

159. The Esquiline Gardens of Maecenas used terraces because of the sloping of the ground upon which they were laid, but this in turn provided 'panoramic views of the city and towards Tivoli and Frascati (Hor. *Carm.* 3.29.6-10)' (von Stackelberg, 2009: 37), thus allowing the prospect from the peaceful inside of the bustle of the everyday, just as the Lucretius of the opening of Book 2 of the *DRN* might have enjoyed. On the permeability of architectural boundaries and the inter-relation of physical and social space, see von Stackelberg (2009), 55-9.

160. See von Stackelberg (2009), 72; for public gardens cf. 78.

161. Rooms in Roman houses were to some extent multi-purpose (Nevett 1997: 290-2). A given space could be a dining room by day and a bedroom by night, and the dining room can also be a reading room. Nevertheless, if we regard the space as defined by the social function it serves at any given time, the hierarchies of inner- and outerness are not infringed. On the issues of looking at Roman rooms see Nevett (1997); Allison (1997). On perceptions of the various symbolisms of different rooms see Nevett (1997), 289-90; on the gradiance of privateness see Grahame (1997).

162. As well as concentric boundaries, one should also be aware of clusters of bounded areas both inside and outside the house. Thus, the rooms in the house can be construed as forming into sets, and the city itself is made up of districts. On the regions and wards (*regiones, vici*) of Rome (reformed by Augustus from 7 BC), see Nicolet (1991), 194-204; Lott (2004). On edges and centres, see Romm (1992).

163. There is much educational secondary literature on 'learning styles' (see, e.g., Dunn and Dunn (1978); Honey and Mumford (1982); Gardner (1983); Kolb (1984); Curry (1990); Sprenger (2003); Pashler et al. (2009)). Classroom applications are strongly disputed (see e.g. Hall (2004) and Coffield et al. (2004)), and although the DfES endorses Learning Style based approaches (cf. www.standards.dfes.gov.uk/thinkingskills/resources), there is a lack of theoretical agreement about the how many learning styles there are, what they are, and their typology. However, it remains clear that a confluence of multisensory impressions has a profound effect on cognitive perception and development. We should picture the Roman child in the garden as the arena for a complex mix of simultaneous bodily and mental experiences which create a holistic and typologically dense experiential model, packed with meanings.

164. On mental or cognitive mapping see Gould and White (1992); Kitchin (1994); p. 173 n. 29 above. The idea that human organisation of space stems from the biological impulse to appropriate personalised territory (see von Stackelberg, 2009: 50) is not wholly incompatible with the account of space as a cognitive pattern based on the physiological growth and development of perception from infancy, though I believe the latter to have a more primary

importance, and von Stackelberg has other reasons too for finding the territorial approach limiting. Elsewhere, von Stackelberg makes a connection between the walled garden of the house divided by paths and the divisions of the sky in Roman augury (2009: 86), but it could also embody a figuration of the urban context, divided by streets. See Hillier (2003) for the relationship between urban space and social and intellectual structure.

165. Cicero uses the more general term *loci* ('places') in his discussion at *De Oratore* 2.350-60. On the relationship between architecture, landscape murals, self-projection, and ideology, see Spencer (2010), 145-55 and O'Sullivan (2006).

166. Von Stackelberg (2009: 132-4) uses the term *mise en abyme* with specific regard to one of Pliny's letters about a garden (*Ep.* 5.6), drawing attention to the passage in which Pliny describes topiary letters (5.6.35), but its use can be taken much further, and applied to the garden itself, and gardens generally.

167. See Giesecke (2007), 104-12. Like courtyard gardens, the pleasure gardens of villas are a Roman rather than a Greek phenomenon (Carroll, 2003: 30-1). For the combination of ornament and productivity, see Carroll (2003), 35. See further Jashemski (1979), 289-335.

168. Cf. Spencer (2010), 114-34 on Pliny's garden letters.

169. See further Hartswick (2004), 17.

170. Stoics saw usefulness as a major desideratum in poetry (see de Lacy (1948)); for the different position of the Epicureans cf. de Lacy (1939).

171. Zanker (1998), 142ff. Cf. also Purcell (1987) on the intermingling of town and country.

172. See Leach (1974) 263-4; cf. Leach (1988), 104-5. Cf. also von Stackelberg (2009: 1) on a fresco usually identified as Flora at the Villa Arianna in Campania. It has as well as the female figure 'a tall flowering plant and the suggestion of a lawn' and is set in a room with a view on to the peristyle garden. Von Stackelberg writes, 'The vegetative detail of the Flora panel connects the imaginative space within the painting to the physical space outside. It was a touchpaper to the Roman imagination, triggering associations between the gardens of myth and literature, and the gardens of personal and public experience.'

173. See Conan (1986) on the relationship between landscape painting and gardens. On garden painting generally see Michel (1980); Giesecke (2007), 123-5.

174. Jashemski (1979), 178-9.

175. See Chapter 2 above; cf. Jashemski (1979), 80-2. There is a much broader range of animals in the paintings than in the *Eclogues*. On the *locus amoenus* and the garden, cf. von Stackelberg (2009), 20-1.

176. Cf. Kellum (1994: 224) on the importance of the interplay of real and fictive as an aesthetic principle (citing Pliny *Ep.* 5.6.13, 22). On Petronius and mythological role-play, see Jones (1991); on execution charades see Coleman (1990). On Hortensius and his game preserve see Spencer (2010), 82-3.

177. Hartswick (2004: 12), citing Clarke (1996) and Purcell (1996). Hartswick (p. 7) also cites a garden wall 'decorated with a limestone encrustation of twigs and stones to create a "rustic" effect'.

178. Cf. Giesecke (2007), 114-16.

179. According to Pliny the Elder (*NH* 18.32), apricots, peaches, and cherries were brought to Rome by Lucullus in 73 BC. See further von Stackelberg (2009), 43, and (on the *Porticus Pompeiana*, for which cf. Prop. 2.32.11-12) 81-2, citing Pliny *NH* 12.111.

180. Cf. the production of winter roses, castigated as contrary to nature by Seneca (*Ep.* 122.7); for late and winter roses, see Nisbet and Hubbard at Hor. *Odes* 1.38.4. We should perhaps also remember Virgil's perhaps imaginary twice-blooming roses in the gardens of Paestum (*Georgics* 4.119) and the ever blooming trees in Alcinous' garden at Hom. *Od.* 7.117-21.

181. See von Stackelberg for dining arrangements in gardens (2009: 25-6).

182. The garden-State analogy was important in the Middle Ages and Renaissance, and a feature of (for example) Shakespeare's *King Richard II* (surviving in Hal Ashby's 1979 film with Peter Sellars, *Being There* and Fernando Meirelles' 2005 film, *The Constant Gardener*). It derives in part from Medieval preachers' use of the parable of the labourers in the vineyard (Matthew 20), and the occasional Classical motif of the lopping of tall plants symbolising the suppression of ambitious men (Herodotus 5.92; Arist. *Pol.*; Livy 1.54; Ov. *Fasti* 2.701-10). However, the parallelism does not figure largely in Classical literature. The Garden of Eden also provides a substrate for significance in garden representations, as for example in its venereal transformation in Chaucer's *Merchant's Tale*. Later, we find that informal part of the garden, the 'wilderness', suggesting the unruly aspects of human emotions in, say, Jane Austen's *Mansfield Park*.

183. See Hartswick (2004), 16-20.

184. Cf. also the Muses that Cicero chose (rather than a set of Bacchants) for a garden pavilion (Cic. *Ad Fam.* 7.23).

185. For overviews of alternative structural readings cf. Berg (1974), 107-13; Rudd (1976), 119-44; Van Sickle (1978), 17-37; Volk (2008), 9-10.

186. Cf. Harrison (2007), 34; Volk (2008), 8-9, citing earlier scholarship.

187. The principle of alternation and the division into two halves, 1-5 and 6-10, are both enhanced by the alternation of longer and shorter poems in each half.

188. Moreover, there are different categories of complexity, which are inevitably mixed in different degrees, e.g. lateral (melodic, rhythmic), vertical (harmonic – though this is not purely vertical), and of timbre.

189. For other applications of Complexity Theory, which originated in Mathematics and Computional theoretics, and has branched out widely into science, the cognitive and social Sciences, Management Science, Art History, and Musicology, see Kauffman (1993), Bar-Yam (1997), Byrne (1998). The *First International Conference on Complex Sciences: Theory and Applications* (COMPLEX'2009; http://www.complex-sys.org/) was held in Shanghai, on 23-25 February 2009; after the final day a one day workshop on the 'Complexity Theory of Art and Music'. Wiley periodicals publish a journal, *Complexity*, now in its fourteenth volume, and there are now various other journals in the field.

Bibliography

Adams, C., 'Travel and the perception of space in the Eastern Desert of Egypt', in Rathmann, M. (ed.), *Wahrnehmung und Erfassung geographischer Räume in der Antike* (Mainz, 2007), 211-20.

Adams, C. and Laurence, R. (eds), *Travel and Geography in the Roman Empire* (London, 2001).

Agnew, J.A. and Duncan, J.S. (eds), *The Power of Place* (Cambridge, 1989).

Allison, P., 'The relationship between wall-decoration and room-type in Pompeian houses', *JRA* 5 (1992), 234-49.

Allison, P., 'Artefact distribution and spatial function in Pompeian houses', in Rawson, B. and Weaver, P. (eds), *The Roman Family in Italy: Status, Sentiment, Space* (Oxford, 1997), 321-54.

Allison, P.M. and Sear, F.B., *Casa della Caccia antica (VII 4, 48). Häuser in Pompeji*, ed. Strocka, V.M., vol. 11 (Munich, 2002).

Alpers, P., *The Singer of the* Eclogues: *A Study of Virgilian Pastoral* (Berkeley, CA, 1979).

Alpers, P., 'What is pastoral?', *Critical Enquiry* 8 (1982), 437-60.

Alpers, P., 'Convening and convention in pastoral poetry', *New Literary History* 14 (1983), 277-304.

Alpers, P., *What is Pastoral?* (Chicago, 1996).

Anderson, W.S., '*Pastor Aeneas*: on pastoral themes in the Aeneid', *TAPhA* 99 (1968), 1-17.

Barchiesi, A., 'Learned eyes: poets, viewers, image makers', in Galinsky, K. (ed.), *The Cambridge Companion to the Age of Augustus* (Cambridge, 2005), 281-305.

Barnes, T. and Duncan, J. (eds), *Writing Worlds: Discourse, Text and Metaphor in the Representation of Landscape* (London, 1992).

Barthes, R., 'L'effet de réel', *Communications* 11 (1968), 84-9.

Barthes, R., *Image, Music, Text* (London, 1977), originally *La Mort de l'auteur* (1968).

Bar-Yam, Y., *Dynamics of Complex Systems* (Reading, MA, 1997).

Bate, J., *The Song of the Earth* (London, 2000).

Beacham, R., 'The emperor as impresario: producing the pageantry of power', in Galinsky, K. (ed.), *The Cambridge Companion to the Age of Augustus* (Cambridge, 2005), 151-74.

Beard, M., 'Imaginary *horti*: or up the garden path', in Cima, M. and La Rocca, E. (eds), *Horti Romani. Atti del Convegno Internazionale, Roma, 4-6 maggio 1995* (*BullCom*, Supplement 6, Rome 1998), 23-32.

Berg, W., *Early Virgil* (London, 1974).

Bergman, M., *All that is Solid Melts into Air: The Experience of Modernity* (London, 1983).

Bergmann, B., 'Exploring the grove: pastoral space on Roman walls', in Hunt, J.D. (ed.), *The Pastoral Landscape.* Studies in the History of Art 36 (College Park, 1992), 20-46.

Bergmann, B., 'Rhythms of recognition: mythical encounters in the Roman landscape', in de Angelis, F. and Muth, S. (eds), *Im Spiegel des Mythos. Bilderwelt und Lebenswelt* (Wiesbaden, 1998), 81-107.

Bergmann, B., 'Art and nature in the Villa at Oplontis', in McGinn, T.A. (ed.), *Pompeian Brothels, Pompeii's Ancient History, Mirrors and Mysteries* (JRA, Supplement 47, 2002), 87-120.

Bernsdorff, H., 'The idea of bucolic in the imitators of Theocritus, 3rd-1st century BC', in Fantuzzi, M. and Papanghelis, T (eds), *Brill's Companion to Greek and Latin Pastoral* (Leiden, 2006), 167-208.

Bing, P., *The Well-read Muse: Present and Past in Callimachus and the Hellenistic Poets* (Göttingen, 1988).

Bodel, J., 'Graveyards and groves: a study of the *lex Lucerina*', *American Journal of Ancient History* 11 (1986), 1-333.

Bodel, J., 'Dealing with the dead: undertakers, executioners, and potter's fields in Ancient Rome', in Marshall, E. and Hope, V. (eds), *Death and Disease in the Ancient City* (London, 2000), 128-51.

Bosio, L., *La Tabula Peutingeriana. A Description of the Ancient World* (Rimini, 1983).

Bowe, P., *Gardens of the Roman World* (Los Angeles, 2004).

Bowie, E., 'Theocritus' Seventh *Idyll*, Philetas and Longus', *CQ* 35 (1985), 67-91.

Boyle, A.J., *The Chaonian Dove: Studies in the Eclogues, Georgics, and Aeneid of Virgil* (Leiden, 1986).

Braund, S.H., 'City and country in Roman satire', in Braund, S.H. (ed.), *Satire and Society in Ancient Rome* (Exeter, 1989), 23-48.

Breed, B., 'Time and textuality in the book of the Eclogues', in Fantuzzi, M. and Papanghelis, T. (eds), *Brill's Companion to Greek and Latin Pastoral* (Leiden, 2006a), 333-68.

Breed, B.W., *Pastoral Inscriptions: Reading and Writing Virgil's Eclogues* (London, 2006b).

Brendel, O.J., *Prolegomena to the Study of Roman Art* (New Haven, 1979).

Brenk, F.J., 'The Tomb of Bianor', *AJPh* 102 (1981), 427-30.

Brodersen, K., *Terra Cognita* (Hildesheim/Zürich/New York, 1995).

Brown, G. and Yule, G., *Discourse Analysis* (Cambridge, 1983).

Byrne, D., *Complexity Theory and the Social Sciences: An Introduction* (London, 1998).

Cairns, F., *Virgil's Augustan Epic* (Cambridge, 1989).

Cairns, F., 'Virgil *Eclogue* 1.1-2: a literary programme?', *HSCPh* 99 (1999), 289-93.

Carroll, M., *Earthly Paradises: Ancient Gardens in History and Archaeology* (London, 2003).

Champlin, E., 'The life and times of Calpurnius Siculus', *JRS* 68 (1978), 95-110.

Cima, M. and La Rocca, E. (eds), *Horti Romani. Atti del Convegno Internazionale, Roma, 4-6 maggio 1995* (*BullCom*, Supplement 6, Rome 1998).

Clark, A., 'Three varieties of visual field', *Philosophical Psychology* 9 (1996), 477-95.

Clarke, J.R., *The Houses of Roman Italy 100 BC-AD 230: Ritual, Space and Decoration* (Los Angeles, 1991).

Clarke, J.R., *Art in the Lives of Ordinary Romans: Visual Representation and Non-Elite Viewers in Italy, 100 BC-AD 315* (California, 2003).

Clarke, J.R., 'Augustan domestic interiors: propaganda or fashion?', in Galinsky, K., *The Cambridge Companion to the Age of Augustus* (Cambridge, 2005), 264-78.

Bibliography

Clausen, W.V., 'On the date of the First *Eclogue*', *HSCPh* 76 (1972), 201-5.

Clausen, W.V., 'Theocritus and Virgil', in Kenney, E.J. and Clausen, W.V. (eds), *The Cambridge History of Classical Literature* (1982), 301-19.

Clausen, W., *A Commentary on Virgil Eclogues* (Oxford, 1994).

Clay, D., 'The Garden of Epicurus', in Warren, J. (ed.), *The Cambridge Companion to Epicureanism* (Cambridge, 2009), 9-28.

Coarelli, F., 'I luci del Lazio: la documentazione archeologica', in Le Cazanove, O. and Scheid, J. (eds), *Les Bois Sacrés. Actes du Colloque International organisé par le Centre Jean Bérard et l'École Pratique des Hautes Etudes (Ve section), Naples, Novembre 1989* (Naples, 1993), 45-52.

Coarelli, F., *Rome and Environs: An Archaeological Guide* (Berkeley, 2007).

Coffield, F., Mosely, D., Hall, E. and Ecclestone, K., *Should we be Using Learning Styles? What Research Has to Say to Practice* (London, 2004).

Coleman, K.M., 'Fatal charades: Roman executions staged as mythological enactments', *JRS* 80 (1990), 44-73.

Coleman, K.M., ' "Truth severe, by fairy Fiction drest": reality and the Roman imagination', in Tomlin, R.S.O. (ed.), *History and Fiction. Six Essays Celebrating the Centenary of Sir Ronald Syme* (London, 2005), 40-70.

Coleman, R., *Vergil Eclogues* (Cambridge, 1977).

Conan, M., 'Nature into art: gardens and landscape in the everyday life of Ancient Rome', *Journal of Garden History* 6 (1986), 348-56.

Conte, G.B., *The Rhetoric of Imitation: Genre and Poetic Memory in Virgil and Other Latin Poets* (Ithaca, 1986).

Corlàita, D. Scagliarini, 'Spazio e decorazione nella pittura pompeiana', *Palladio* 23-5 (1974-76), 3-44.

Cornell, T.J., 'The City of Rome in the Middle Republic (400-100 BC)', in Coulston, J. and Dodge, H. (eds), *Ancient Rome: The Archaeology of the Eternal City* (Oxford, 2000), 42-56.

Cosgrove, D. and Daniels, S., *The Iconography of Landscape* (Cambridge, 1988).

Courtney, E., *The Fragmentary Latin Poets* (Oxford, 1993).

Craik, K.H., 'Individual variations in landscape description', in Zube, E.H., Brush, R.O. and Fabos, J. (eds), *Landscape Assessment: Values, Perceptions and Resources* (Stroudsburg, PA, 1975), 130-50.

Curry, L., 'One critique of the research on learning styles', *Educational Leadership* 48 (1990), 50-6.

Dällenbach, L., *The Mirror in the Text* (Cambridge, 1989).

D'Arms, J., *Romans on the Bay of Naples*, ed. Zevi, F. (Bari, 2003^2).

D'Herouville, P., *À la Campagne avec Virgile* (Paris, 1930).

de Lacy, P., 'The Epicurean analysis of language', *AJPh* 60 (1939), 85-92.

de Lacy, P., 'Stoic views of poetry', *AJPh* 69 (1948), 241-71.

Deremetz, A., *Le Miroir des Muses: poétiques de la réflexivité à Rome* (Lille, 1995).

Dickmann, J.-A., 'The peristyle and the transformation of domestic space in Hellenistic Pompeii', in Laurence, R. and Wallace-Hadrill, A., *Domestic Space in the Roman World* (JRA, Supplementary series 22, 1997), 121-36.

Dix, T.K., 'Virgil in the Grynean Grove: two riddles in the third Eclogue', *CPh* 90 (1995), 256-62.

Dunn, R. and Dunn, K., *Teaching Students through their Individual Learning Styles: A Practical Approach* (Reston, VA, 1978).

DuQuesnay, I.M., 'From Polyphemus to Corydon: Virgil, *Eclogue* 2 and the *Idylls* of Theocritus', in Woodman, A.J. and West, D.A. (eds), *Creative Imitation and Latin Literature* (1979), 35-69.

187

Bibliography

Eck, W., *The Age of Augustus*; tr. Schneider, D.L. with new material by Takács, S.A. (Oxford, 2003).

Edwards, C. and Woolf, G. (eds), *Rome the Cosmopolis* (Cambridge, 2003).

Elsner, J., *Art and the Roman Viewer* (Cambridge, 1995).

Fantuzzi, M., 'Theocritus' constructive interpreters, and the creation of a bucolic reader', in Fantuzzi, M. and Papanghelis, T. (eds), *Brill's Companion to Greek and Latin Pastoral* (Leiden, 2006), 235-62.

Farrar, L., *Ancient Roman Gardens* (Stroud, 1998).

Favro, D., *The Urban Image of Augustan Rome* (Cambridge, 1996).

Favro, D., 'Making Rome a world city', in Galinsky, K. (ed.), *The Cambridge Companion to the Age of Augustus* (Cambridge, 2005), 234-63.

Ferguson, P.P., *Paris as Revolution: Writing the 19th-Century City* (Berkeley, 1994).

Fowler, B.H., *The Hellenistic Aesthetic* (Bristol, 1989).

Fowler, D., 'Narrate and describe: the problem of *ekphrasis*', *JRS* (1991), 25-35.

Frayn, J., *Subsistence Farming in Roman Italy* (New York, 1979).

Frayn, J., *Sheep-rearing and the Wool Trade in Italy during the Roman Period* (ARCA 15, Liverpool 1984).

Gabriel, M.M., *Livia's Garden Room at Prima Porta* (New York, 1955).

Galinksy, K., *Augustan Culture: An Interpretive Introduction* (Princeton, 1996).

Gardner, H., *Frames of Mind: The Theory of Multiple Intelligences* (New York, 1983).

Garson, R.W., 'Theocritean elements in Virgil's *Eclogues*', *CQ* 21 (1971), 188-203.

Gazda, E.K. (ed.), *Roman Art in the Private Sphere: New Perspectives on the Architecture and Decor of the Domus, Villa and Insula* (Ann Arbor, 1994).

Genette, G., *Palimpsests* (New York, 1987).

George, M., 'Repopulating the Roman house' in Rawson, B. and Weaver, P. (eds), *The Roman Family in Italy: Status, Sentiment, Space* (Clarendon Press, Oxford, 1997), 299-319.

George, M., 'Peristyle decoration in Campanian *atria*', *JRA* 11 (1998), 1-15.

Giesecke, A.L., *The Epic City: Urbanism, Utopia, and the Garden in Ancient Greece and Rome* (Centre for Hellenic Studies, Washington, 2007).

Gleason, K.L., '*Porticus Pompeiana*: a new perspective on the first public park of Ancient Rome', *Journal of Garden History* 14 (1994), 13-27.

Gould, P. and White, R., *Mental Maps* (London, 1992).

Grahame, M., 'Public and private in the Roman house: the *Casa del Fauno*', in Laurence, R. and Wallace-Hadrill, A. (eds), *Domestic Space in the Roman World* (JRA, Supplementary series 22, 1997), 137-64.

Griffin, J., *Virgil* (Oxford, 1986).

Griffin, K., 'Augustan poetry and Augustanism', in Galinsky, K. (ed.), *The Cambridge Companion to the Age of Augustus* (Cambridge, 2005), 306-20.

Grimal, P., *Les jardins romains a la fin de la république et aux deux premiers siècles de l'empire: essai sur le naturalisme romain* (Paris, 1943).

Gruen, E., *Culture and National Identity in Republican Rome* (Ithaca, NY, 1993).

Haber, J., *Pastoral and the Poetics of Self-contradiction* (Cambridge, 1994).

Hacking, I., *Representing and Intervening: Introductory Topics in the Philosophy of Natural Science* (Cambridge, 1983).

Hahn, E.A., 'The characters in the *Eclogues*', *TAPhA* 75 (1944), 196-241.

Hales, S.J., *The Roman House and Social Identity* (Cambridge, 2003).

Bibliography

Hall, E., 'Researching learning styles', *Teaching Thinking* (Spring 2004), 28-35.

Halperin, D.M., *Before Pastoral: Theocritus and the Ancient Tradition of Bucolic Poetry* (1983).

Hardie, P., *Virgil*, Greece and Rome New Surveys in the Classics No. 28 (Oxford, 1998).

Hardie, P., 'Cultural and historical narratives in Virgil's *Eclogues* and Lucretius', in Fantuzzi, M. and Papanghelis, T (eds), *Brill's Companion to Greek and Latin Pastoral* (Leiden, 2006), 275-300.

Harrison, S., *Generic Enrichment in Vergil and Horace* (OUP, 2007).

Hartswick, K.J., *The Gardens of Sallust: A Changing Landscape* (Oxford, 2007).

Harvey, D., *Paris: Capital of Modernity* (New York, 2003).

Helck, H., '*Incondita iactare*: ein Betrag zur Erklärung der 2. Ekloge Vergils', *PhW* 52 (1932), 963-72.

Henderson, J., 'Virgil's Third *Eclogue*: how to keep an idiot in suspense', *CQ* 48 (1998), 213-28.

Henderson, J., *Writing down Rome: Satire, Comedy and Other Offences in Latin Poetry* (Oxford, 1999).

Henderson, J., *The Roman Book of Gardening* (London, 2004).

Herrmann, L., *Les masques et les visages dans les Bucoliques de Vergile* (Brussels, 1930).

Hillier, B., 'The architectures of seeing and going: or, are cities shaped by bodies or minds? And is there a syntax of spatial cognition?', *Proceedings of the 4th International Space Syntax Symposium, London*, 2003. http://www.spacesyntax.net/SSS4.htm

Hinds, S., 'Essential epic: genre and gender from Macer to Statius', in Depew, M. and Obbink, D. (eds), *Matrices of Genre: Authors, Canons, and Society* (Harvard, 2000), 221-44.

Holleran, C., 'Commerce and the Roman street', in Newsome, D. and Laurence, R. (eds), *Movement in the Roman City: Infrastructure and Experience* (Oxford, forthcoming).

Hollmann, E. and Teach, J., *A Trick of the Eye: Trompe l'Oeil Masterpieces* (Munich, 2004).

Hölscher, T., *The Language of Images in Roman Art*, tr. Snodgrass, A. and Künz-Snodgrass, A., with a foreword by Elsner, J. (Cambridge, 2004).

Honey, P. and Mumford, A., *The Manual of Learning Styles* (Maidenhead, UK, 1982).

Hooke, D. (ed.), *Landscape: The Richest Historical Record*, Society for Landscape Studies, supplementary series 1, 2000.

Horsfall, N., 'Criteria for the dating of Calpurnius Siculus', *Rivista di Filologia e di Istruzione Classica* 125 (1997), 166-96.

Horsfall, N. (ed.), *A Companion to the Study of Virgil* (Leiden, 1995).

Hubbard, M., *Propertius* (London, 1974).

Hubbard, T.K., 'Allusive artistry and Vergil's revisionary program: *Eclogues* 1-3', *MD* 34 (1995), 37-67.

Hubbard, T.K., 'Intertextual hermeneutics in Vergil's fourth and fifth *Eclogues*', *CJ* 91.1 (1995), 11-23.

Hubbard, T.K., *The Pipes of Pan: Intertextuality and Literary Filiation in the Pastoral Tradition from Theocritus to Milton* (Ann Arbor, 1998).

Hunt, J.D., 'The garden as cultural object', in Wrede, S. and Adams, W.H. (eds), *Denatured Visions: Landscape and Culture in the Twentieth Century* (New York, 1991), 19-32.

Bibliography

Hunt, J.D., 'The garden as virtual reality', in Kohler, M. (ed.), *Das künstliche Paradies* (Worms am Rhein, 1997), 5-14.

Hutchinson, G.O., 'The publication and individuality of Horace's *Odes* Books 1-3', *CQ* 52 (2002), 517-37.

Jacob, C., 'Mapping in the mind: the earth from ancient Alexandria', in Cosgrove, D. (ed.), *Mappings* (London, 1999), 24-49.

Jashemski, W.F., *The Gardens of Pompeii* (1979 and 1994).

Jashemski, W.F., 'The Vesuvian sites before AD 79: the archaeological, literary, and epigraphical evidence', in Jashemski, W.F. and Meyer, F.G. (eds), *The Natural History of Pompeii* (Cambridge, 2002), 6-28.

Jashemski, W.F. and Meyer, F.G. (eds), *The Natural History of Pompeii* (Cambridge, 2002).

Jashemski, W.F., Meyer, F.G. and Ricciardi, M., 'Plants: evidence from wall paintings, mosaics, sculpture, plant remains, graffiti, inscriptions, and ancient authors', in Jashemski, W.F. and Meyer, F.G. (eds), *The Natural History of Pompeii* (Cambridge, 2002), 80-180.

Jenkyns, R.H.A., 'Virgil and Arcadia', *JRS* (1989), 26-39.

Jenkyns, R.H.A., *Virgil's Experience. Nature and History: Times, Names and Places* (Oxford, 1999).

Johnston, P., *Vergil's Agricultural Golden Age* (Leiden, 1980).

Jones, F., 'Realism in Petronius', in Hofmann, H. (ed.), *Groningen Colloquia on the Novel* IV (Groningen, 1991), 105-20.

Jones, F., 'Naming in "soft" Poetry', *Studies in Latin Literature and Roman History XIII* (Latomus, 2006), 5-31.

Jones, F., *Juvenal and the Satiric Genre* (London, 2007).

Kaster, G., *Die Gärten des Lucullus: Entwicklung und Bedeutung der Bebauung des Pincio-Hügels in Rom* (Munich, 1974).

Kauffman, S.A., *The Origins of Order: Self-organization and Selection in Evolution* (Oxford, 1993).

Kellum, B.A., 'The construction of landscape in Augustan Rome: the Garden Room at the Villa *ad Gallinas*', *The Art Bulletin* 76 (1994), 211-24.

Kennedy, D., '*Arcades ambo*: Virgil, Gallus and Arcadia', *Hermathena* 143 (1987) 47-59.

Kenney, E.J., 'Virgil and the elegiac sensibility', *ICS* 8 (1983), 44-59.

Keppie, L.J.F., *Colonisation and Settlement in Italy, 47-14 BC* (London, 1983).

Kidd, D.A., 'Imitation in the Tenth *Eclogue*', *BICS* 11 (1964), 54-64.

Kitchin, R.M., 'Cognitive maps: what are they and why study them?', *Journal of Environmental Psychology* 14 (1994), 1-19.

Kolb, D., *Experiential Learning: Experience as the Source of Learning and Development* (Englewood Cliffs, NJ, 1984).

Korenjak, M., 'Tityri sub persona: Der antiki Biographismus und die bukolische Tradition', *A&A* 49 (2003), 58-79.

Kraggerud, E., 'Numitorius' parody of Vergil, *Ecl.* 3.1-2', *Symbolae Osloenses* 81 (2006), 85-7.

Kuttner, A., 'Culture and history at Pompey's museum', *TAPhA* 129 (1999), 343-73.

Laurence, R., *Roman Pompeii: Space and Society* (London, 1994).

Laurence, R., 'Space and text', in Laurence, R. and Wallace-Hadrill, A. (eds), *Domestic Space in the Roman World* (JRA, Supplementary series 22, 1997), 7-14.

Bibliography

Laurence, R. and Wallace-Hadrill, A. (eds), *Domestic Space in the Roman World* (JRA, Supplementary series 22, 1997).

Lavagne, H., *Operosa Antra: recherches sur la grotte à Rome de Sylla à Hadrien* (Rome, École française de Rome, 1988).

Leach, E.A., *Virgil's Eclogues: Landscapes of Experience* (Ithaca, NY, 1974).

Leach, E.A., *The Rhetoric of Space: Literary and Artistic Representations of Landscape in Republican and Augustan Rome* (Princeton, 1988).

Leach, E.W., *The Social Life of Painting in Ancient Rome and on the Bay of Naples* (Cambridge, 2004).

Lee, M.O., *Death and Rebirth in Virgil's Arcadia* (Albany, NY, 1989).

Levi, A. and Levi, M., *Itineraria Picta. Contributo allo studio della tabula Poitingeriana* (Rome, 1967).

Ling, R., 'Studius and the beginnings of Roman landscape painting', *JRS* 67 (1977), 1-16.

Ling, R., *Roman Painting* (Cambridge, 1991).

Lipka, M., *Language in Virgil's Eclogues* (Berlin, 2001).

Lipka, M., 'Notes on *fagus* in Vergil's *Eclogues*', *Philologus* 146 (2002), 133-8.

Little, A.M.G., *Roman Perspective Painting and the Ancient Stage* (Maine, 1971).

Lott, J.B., *The Neighborhoods of Augustan Rome* (Cambridge, 2004).

Loughrey, B., *The Pastoral Mode: A Casebook* (London, 1984).

MacDonald, W.L. and Pinto, J.A., *Hadrian's Villa and its Legacy* (New Haven, CT, 1995).

MacDougall, E. (ed.), *Ancient Roman Gardens* (Washington DC, 1981).

MacDougall, E. (ed.), *Ancient Roman Villa Gardens* (Washington DC, 1987).

Maggiulli, G., *Incipiant silvae cum primum surgere: Mondo vegetale e nomenclatura della flora di Vergilio* (Bibliotheca Athena, N.S. 5) (Rome, 1995).

Martindale, C.A. (ed.), *Virgil and his Influence* (Bristol, 1984).

Martindale, C.A. (ed.), *The Cambridge Companion to Virgil* (Cambridge, 1997).

Massey, D., 'Landscape as a provocation', *Journal of Material Culture* 11 (2004), 33-48.

Mayer, R., 'Calpurnius Siculus: technique and date', *JRS* 70 (1980), 175-6.

Mayer, R., 'Missing persons in the *Eclogues*', *BICS* 30 (1983), 17-30.

Meiggs, R., *Trees and Timber in the Ancient Mediterranean World* (Oxford, 1982).

Michel, D., 'Pompejanische Gartenmalereien', in Cahn, H.A. and Simon, E. (eds), *Tainia: Roland Hampe zum 70. geburtstag am 2. Dezember 1978* (Mainz am Rhein, 1980), 373-404.

Miller, K., *Itineraria Romana: Römische Reisewege an der hand der Tabula peutingeriana* (Stuttgart, 1916).

Morgan, Ll., 'Creativity out of chaos: poetry between the death of Caesar and the death of Vergil', in Taplin, O. (ed.), *Literature in the Roman World* (Oxford, 2000), 75-118.

Nevett, L., 'Perceptions of domestic space in Roman Italy', in Rawson, B. and Weaver, P. (eds), *The Roman Family in Italy: Status, Sentiment, Space* (Oxford, 1997), 281-98.

Nicolet, C., *Space, Geography, and Politics in the Early Roman Empire*, tr. Leclerc, H. (Ann Arbor, 1991).

Nisbet, R.G.M., 'Virgil's Fourth *Eclogue*: Easterners and Westerners', in Volk, K. (ed.), *Vergil's Eclogues* (Oxford, 2008), 155-88 (= *BICS* 25 (1978), 47-65).

Bibliography

Nora, P. (ed.), *Rethinking France. Les Lieux de Mémoire, Vol. I. The State*; tr. Trouille, M. (Chicago, 2010).

O'Hara, J.J., *True Names: Vergil and the Alexandrian Tradition of Etymological Wordplay* (Ann Arbor, 1996).

O'Sullivan, T.M., 'The mind in motion: walking and metaphorical travel in the Roman villa', *CPh* 101 (2006), 133-52.

Opacki, I., 'Royal genres', in Duff, D. (ed.), *Modern Genre Theory* (London, 2000), 118-26.

Pagán, V.E., *Rome and the Literature of Gardens* (London, 2006).

Paschalis, M., '*Semina ignis*: the interplay of science and myth in the song of Silenus', *AJPh* 122 (2001), 201-22.

Pashler, H., McDaniel, M., Rohrer, D. and Bjork, R., 'Learning styles: concepts and evidence', *Psychological Science in the Public Interest* 9 (2009), 105-19.

Pavlovskis, Z., 'Man in a poetic landscape: humanization of nature in Virgil's *Eclogues*', *CPh* 66 (1971), 151-68.

Porteous, J.D., *Landscapes of the Mind: Worlds of Sense and Metaphor* (Toronto, 1990).

Posch, S., *Beobachtungen zur Theokritnachwirkung bei Vergil* (Innsbruck, 1969).

Purcell, N., 'Town in country and country in town', in E.B. MacDougall (ed.), *Ancient Roman Villa Gardens* (Washington DC, 1987).

Purcell, N., 'The Roman villa and the landscape of production', in Cornell, T. and Lomas, L. (eds), *Urban Society in Roman Italy* (New York, 1995), 151-79.

Purcell, N., 'The Roman garden as a domestic building', in Barton, I. (ed.), *Roman Domestic Buildings* (Exeter, 1996), 121-51.

Purcell, N., 'Dialectical gardening', *JRA* 14 (2001), 546-56.

Putnam, M.C.J., *Virgil's Pastoral Art: Studies in the Eclogues* (Princeton, 1970).

Reed, J.D., 'Continuity and change in Greek bucolic between Theocritus and Virgil', in Fantuzzi, M. and Papanghelis, T. (eds), *Brill's Companion to Greek and Latin Pastoral* (Leiden, 2006), 209-34.

Romm, J., *The Edges of the Earth in Ancient Thought* (Princeton, 1992).

Rosen, R.M. and Sluiter, I. (eds), *City, Countryside, and the Spatial Organisation of Value in Classical Antiquity* (Leiden, 2006).

Rosenmeyer, T.G., *The Green Cabinet: Theocritus and the European Pastoral Lyric* (Berkeley, 1969).

Ross, D.O., *Backgrounds to Augustan Poetry: Gallus, Elegy and Rome* (Cambridge, 1975).

Rudd, N., *Lines of Enquiry* (Cambridge, 1976).

Rumpf, L., 'Bucolic *nomina* in Virgil and Theocritus: on the poetic technique of Virgil's Eclogues'. in Volk, K. (ed.), *Vergil's Eclogues* (Oxford, 2008), 64-78 (= 'Bukolische Nomina bei Vergil und Theokrit: Zur poetischen Technik des Eklogenbuchs', *RhM* 142 (1999), 157-75).

Salway, B., 'The perception and description of space in Roman itineraries', in Rathmann, M. (ed.), *Wahrnehmung und Erfassung geographischer Räume in der Antike* (Mainz, 2007), 181-210.

Sargeaunt, J., *The Trees, Shrubs and Plants of Virgil* (Oxford, 1920).

Saunders, T., *Bucolic Eulogy: Virgil's Eclogues and the Environmental Literary Tradition* (London, 2008).

Schama, S., *Landscape and Memory* (London, 1995).

Scheid, J., '*Lucus, nemus*. Qu'est-ce qu'un bois sacré?', in Le Cazanove, O.,and Scheid, J. (eds), *Les Bois Sacrés. Actes du Colloque International organisé*

Bibliography

par le Centre Jean Bérard et l'École Pratique des Hautes Etudes (Ve section), Naples, Novembre 1989 (Naples, 1993), 13-20.

Schmidt, E.A., 'Arcadia: modern Occident and Classical Antiquity', in Volk, K. (ed.), Vergil's Eclogues (Oxford, 2008), 16-47.

Scott, S., 'The power of images in the late Roman house,' in Laurence, R. and Wallace-Hadrill, A. (eds), Houses and Society in Pompeii and Herculaneum (Princeton, 1994).

Segal, C.P., Poetry and Myth in Ancient Pastoral: Essays on Theocritus and Virgil (Princeton, 1981).

Sens, A., 'Epigram at the margins of pastoral', in Fantuzzi, M. and Papanghelis, T. (eds), Brill's Companion to Greek and Latin Pastoral (Leiden, 2006), 147-66.

Skoie, M., 'City and countryside in Vergil's Eclogues', in Rosen, R.M. and Sluiter, I. (eds), City, Countryside, and the Spatial Organisation of Value in Classical Antiquity (Leiden, 2006), 297-326.

Smith, B., 'Truth and the visual field', in Petitot, J., Varela, F.J., Pachoud, B. and Roy, J.-M. (eds), Naturalizing Phenomenology: Issues in Contemporary Phenomenology and Cognitive Science (Stanford: Stanford University Press, 1999), 317-29.

Smith, P.L., 'Lentus in Umbra: a symbolic pattern in Virgil's Eclogues', Phoenix 19 (1965), 298-304.

Smith, P.L., 'Vergil's Avena and the pipes of pastoral poetry', TAPhA 101 (1970), 497-510.

Spencer, D., 'Horace's garden thoughts: rural retreats and the urban imagination', in Rosen, R.M. and Sluiter, I. (eds), City, Countryside, and the Spatial Organisation of Value in Classical Antiquity (Leiden, 2006), 239-74.

Spencer, D., Landscape and Identity in Roman Culture, Greece and Rome New Surveys in the Classics 39 (Cambridge, 2010).

Spirn, A.W., The Language of Landscape (New Haven, CT, 1998).

Sprenger, M., Differentiation through Learning Styles and Memory (Thousand Oaks, CA, 2003).

Starr, R.J., 'Vergil's Seventh Eclogue and its readers: biographical allegory as an interpretive strategy in antiquity and late antiquity', CPh 90 (1995), 129-38.

Stewart, P., Roman Art, Greece and Rome New Surveys in the Classics 34 (Oxford, 2004).

Stewart, P., The Social History of Roman Art (Cambridge, 2008).

Talbert, R.J.A., 'Small-town sources of geographic information in the world of Imperial Rome', CB 80 (2004), 15-25.

Talbert, R.J.A., 'Peutinger's Roman map: the physical landscape framework', in Rathmann, M. (ed.), Wahrnehmung und Erfassung geographischer Räume in der Antike (Mainz, 2007), 221-30.

Talbert, R.J.A., and Brodersen, K. (eds), Space in the Roman World: its Perception and Presentation (LIT, Münster, 2004).

Talbert, R.J.A., and Unger, R. (eds), Cartography in Antiquity and the Middle Ages: Fresh Perspectives, New Methods (Brill, 2008).

Thomas, R.F., Lands and Peoples in Roman Poetry: The Ethnographical Tradition (Cambridge, 1982).

Thomas, R.F., Virgil and the Augustan Reception (Cambridge, 2001).

Tilley, C., A Phenomenology of Landscape: Places, Paths and Monuments (Oxford, 1994).

193

Bibliography

Tilley, C., 'Introduction: identity, place, landscape and heritage', *Journal of Material Culture* 11 (2004) 7-31.

Townend, G.B., 'Calpurnius Siculus and the *Munus Neronis*', *JRS* 70 (1980), 166-74.

Tracy, S.V., '*Sepulcrum Bianoris*: Virgil *Eclogues* 9.59-61', *CPh* 77 (1982), 328-30.

Tuan, Yi-Fu, *Passing Strange and Wonderful: Aesthetics, Nature and Culture* (Washington DC, 1993).

Van Sickle, J., *The Design of Virgil's Bucolics* (Rome, 1978).

Volk, K. (ed.), *Vergil's Eclogues* (Oxford, 2008).

Von Stackelberg, K.T., *The Roman Garden: Space, Sense, and Society* (Routledge, 2009).

Wallace-Hadrill, A., 'The Golden Age and sin in Augustan ideology', *Past and Present* 95 (1982), 19-36.

Wallace-Hadrill, A., *Houses and Society in Pompeii and Herculaneum* (Princeton, 1994).

Wallace-Hadrill, A., *Domestic Space in the Roman World* (JRA, Supplementary series 22, 1997).

Watson, G.E., 'Birds: evidence from wall paintings, mosaics, sculpture, skeletal remains, and ancient authors' in Jashemski, W.F. and Meyer, F.G. (eds), *The Natural History of Pompeii* (Cambridge 2002), 357-400.

Weber, E., *Tabula Peutingeriana. Codex Vindobonensis 324* (Graz 1976).

Whitaker, R., 'Did Gallus write "pastoral" elegies?', *CQ* 38 (1988), 454-8.

White, K.D., *Agricultural Implements of the Roman World* (Cambridge, 1967).

White, K.D., *Roman Farming* (London, 1970).

White, P., 'Poets in the new milieu: realigning', in Galinsky, K. (ed.), *The Cambridge Companion to the Age of Augustus* (Cambridge, 2005), 321-39.

Williams, G., *Tradition and Originality in Roman Poetry* (Oxford, 1968).

Wimmel, W, '*Hirtenkrieg' und arkadisches Rom: Reduktionsmedien in Vergils 'Aeneis'* (Munich, 1973).

Wiseman, T.P., 'Roman Republican road-building', *Papers of the British School at Rome*, 38 (1970), 122-52.

Wiseman, T.P., 'Calpurnius Siculus and the Claudian civil war', *JRS* 72 (1982), 57-67.

Witek, F., *Vergils Landschaften: Versuch einer Typologie literarischer Landschaft* (Hildesheim, 2006).

Wray, D., 'What poets do: Tibullus on "easy" hands', *CPh* 98 (2003), 217-50.

Wylie, J., *Landscape* (Abingdon, 2007).

Zanker, P., *Pompeii: Public and Social Life*; tr. Schneider, D.L. (Harvard, 1998).

Zarmakoupi, M., 'The Roman villa and its cultural landscape from the late Republic to the early Empire', in Brauer, A., Mattusch, C. and Donohue, A. (eds), *Common Ground: Archaeology, Art, Science and Humanities: The Proceedings of the 16th International Congress of Classical Archaeology (Boston, 2003)* (Oxford, 2006), 245-8.

Zarmakoupi, M., 'Designing the landscapes of the Villa of Livia at Prima Porta', in Kurtz, D., Meyer, C., Saunders, D., Tsingarida, A. and Harris, N. (eds), *Essays in Classical Archaeology for Eleni Hatzivassiliou 1977-2007* (Oxford, Studies in Classical Archaeology, The Beazley Archive Series, 2008), 269-76.

Zarmakoupi, M., 'Porticus and cryptoporticus in Roman luxury villas: architectural design and cultural implications', in Cole, K., Poehler, E. and Flohr, M. (eds), *Pompeii: Cultural Standards, Practical Needs* (Oxford, forthcoming).

Bibliography

Zarmakoupi, M., 'The peristylium-garden in Roman luxury villas: an architectural and cultural history', in Ladstätter, S. and Scheibelreiter, V. (eds), *Städtisches Wohnen im östlichen Mittelmeerraum. 4. Jh. v. Chr.-1. Jh. n. Chr. Vienna: Verlag der Österreichischen Akademie der Wissenschaften* (forthcoming).

Index of Passages

References to the pages of this book are given in bold type.

Index